Lesbian Love Story.

A MEMOIR IN ARCHIVES

Amelia Possanza

CATAPULT NEW YORK

First Catapult edition: 2023
First paperback edition: 2024

Hardcover ISBN: 978-1-64622-105-9
Paperback ISBN: 978-1-64622-223-0

Library of Congress Control Number: 2022951359

Cover design by Dana Li
Cover art of swimmers © Sarah Butterfield / Bridgeman Images;
handwriting © whitemay
Book design by Laura Berry

Catapult
New York, NY
books.catapult.co

Printed in the United States of America

10 9 8 7 6 5 4 3 2 1

"In her audacious heartthrob of a memoir, Amelia Possanza revives seven queer romances from the past, hoping to better understand her own lesbian identity . . . A triumph, as romantic as it is perceptive."

—DAVE WHEELER, *Shelf Awareness* (starred review)

"*Lesbian Love Story* has all the vivid detail of a great novel and all the intelligence of a great study . . . I was continually fascinated, frequently moved, and completely in awe of Possanza's wit, intelligence, and empathy. I can't wait to reread this outstanding, unforgettable book."

—STEPHEN MCCAULEY, author of *My Ex-Life*

"Intimate and sexy, voraciously researched and vibrantly imagined, Amelia Possanza has given us the romantic history all lesbians deserve."

—NINA LACOUR, author of *Yerba Buena*

"*Lesbian Love Story* cracks open a vault of queer lives that were so meaningful to dig into—sporty girls, masc forebears, illicit loves. These juicy stories are filled with pathos and inspiration, and Amelia Possanza's thrill at excavating them is personal, palpable, and contagious."

—MICHELLE TEA, author of *Knocking Myself Up: A Memoir of My (In)Fertility*

"A creative, joyful approach to the queer past. *Lesbian Love Story* weaves together history, memoir, and theory in this refreshing work of historical imagination. A very smart love letter to lesbians across time."

—JEN MANION, author of *Female Husbands: A Trans History*

"Amelia Possanza's *Lesbian Love Story* is a tender and sensual swim through lesbian history—thoroughly researched and brought to dazzling life by Possanza's imaginative prose."

—HUGH RYAN, author of *When Brooklyn Was Queer*

*To all the queers, ordinary and extraordinary,
whose names have been destroyed by history,
and to the rosy-fingered custodians of the queer archive.*

Contents

Introduction.

Collecting Lesbians

You look like anyone else. Molly, don't be silly; you can't be a lesbian. You're joking. I'd know if you were such a thing.

—Rita Mae Brown, *Rubyfruit Jungle*

I HAVE BEEN LUCKY ENOUGH IN MY LIFE TO FALL IN LOVE three times: first with water, then with stories, and, finally, with lesbians. It was easy to share those first two loves. I come from a family of storytellers, and even my enemies on the swim team loved the water. That last love, though, left me lonely.

My middle school classmates claimed they would recognize a lesbian if they saw one. A lesbian would wear Dr. Martens and cargo pants and would walk out onto the street in broad daylight with a bare face and nails clipped short. If you asked a lesbian to look at those nails, you'd watch their hand curl into a claw, not stretch out, the way a real woman would admire her manicure. Under a full moon, you might find a lesbian awake at midnight, talking to cats and casting spells. If you got too close, you might be struck by a lesbian's hatred of men.

Had everyone learned all this when I was stuck at home with strep

throat? The only person I had ever seen who resembled this mythical lesbian was a woman in a photograph I had been shown during a first-grade psychology experiment. A visiting researcher had separated the girls, in matching plaid jumpers and Mary Janes, from the rest of the class. She spread a series of glossy photos across the craft table. "Which of these women is the most beautiful?" she asked. "There is no right answer." I only glanced at the woman in the ballgown. I skipped over another in strappy heels and a tulle skirt. Finally, I found her. When called on, I pointed at a black-and-white photo of a figure in a flannel and ripped jeans. Everyone, researcher included, looked at me with concern. I realized too late I had been the only one to choose her. I wondered if she was a drug addict, or something worse, and if this was proof I might become one too.

Mostly grown and living in New York City, I still rarely spotted other lesbians. I joined a queer swim team, but it was full of gay men who didn't recognize me. After a grueling ocean swim at Coney Island, a whiskered teammate asked if I wanted to have kids.

"No."

"Are you a lesbian or something?"

"I'm on a gay swim team!" I had a cat and Dr. Martens. I kept my nails short.

"I just don't think about women," he apologized. "I mean, I don't think about women like *that*. As having a sexuality."

I was furious. I had always found both solace and freedom in the water, like many queer people before me, and I was surprised he could not see how we shared this. How much could I blame him, though? If I had yet to find role models who could show me how to live, where would he have seen a lesbian? I craved more than simple stereotypes. I wanted stories and heroes that would explain to my teammate how to recognize us. More moments of private intimacy and public recognition. More reflections that rendered my own image visible. Simply put, I wanted more lesbians.

There on the sizzle of sand, I resolved to become a collector of lesbians. I took as my inspiration Herman Melville's Sub-Sub Librarian, who opens *Moby-Dick* not with the famous line "Call me Ishmael" but with a series of miscellaneous extracts about whales. This imaginary archivist *appears to have gone through the long Vaticans and street-stalls of the earth, picking up whatever random allusions to whales he could anyways find in any book . . . affording a glancing bird's eye view of what has been promiscuously said, thought, fancied, and sung of Leviathan.*

I vowed to follow in his footsteps, to scour libraries and archives and the *street-stalls* of the internet to put together a record of everything that has been *said, thought, fancied, and sung of* Lesbians. I was certain that if I uncovered enough lesbians in history, they would reveal a message or a lesson, a blueprint of how I might build my own life. Lesbians, I suspected, would have something to teach us all about love.

A dear friend once told me, "All it takes to be a lesbian is the desire. Do you want to be a lesbian? Then you're a lesbian!" History is filled with too many rooms—psych wards and factory floors—where it wasn't safe to be a lesbian for that simple definition to hold true. Still, it seemed a good place to start.

I followed the word. I began to search for it in first-person narratives that date as far back as the turn of the century. I found it in out-of-print memoirs, in forgotten books relegated to library storage rooms, in texts I was allowed to read only under the watchful eye of librarians and archivists. Lesbians were easiest to spot in pairs, inside the structure of a love story. These were not the objectified bodies of lesbian porn, but they were a bit like an obscenity: you know one when you see one.

I consulted the feminists who came before me on a clear definition of *lesbian*, one that could help me pin my specimens to cork, seal them behind glass, and place them in a museum. Their definitions centered around women: women who love women, women who build

their lives with women, women who touch and text other women. The lesbians I met, though, the ones I encountered in silent archive rooms, on research road trips, through digital libraries, the ones whose voices, captured on oral history tapes, I carried into bed with me on frozen winter nights, might not have chosen the word *woman* if the vocabulary available today were laid out before them. They might not have even chosen the word *lesbian* either. The word has, historically, been used to describe both a gender presentation and a sexuality, and it was only recently that we accepted the distinction between these often-overlapping categories. It is not my place to assign anyone a new word, but it became my obsession to trace its shifts, the way it expands and contracts over the decades. It is not a fixed identity but rather a word that marks my lineage, a flag raised to help me lift these ancestors out of obscurity.

Throughout history, before we became concerned with genitalia and chromosomes and biological sex, women have been defined by their status as people who can be exchanged. You can see it from the opening lines of the classic romance *Pride and Prejudice*: "It is a truth universally acknowledged, that a single man in possession of a good fortune, must be in want of a wife." A fortune can be exchanged for a wife, and a wife will bear sons who can inherit a father's fortune. Gayle Rubin, a lesbian feminist of the 1970s, coined a term for this oppressive social custom: the traffic in women.

Lesbians stand in defiance of these traditions. They are people who, in an effort to become subject rather than object, have resisted being traded. "It would be incorrect to say that lesbians associate, make love, live with women," writes Monique Wittig, another lesbian feminist thinker of the 1970s. "'Woman' has meaning only in heterosexual systems of thought and heterosexual economic systems. Lesbians are not women."

Lesbians, in my eyes, are defined as the ones who invent their own systems of love: Romantic love. Family love. Friend love. A love for

community, and for strangers too. They love when there is nothing to gain—no kingdom, no castle, no seat in the official record books of history—even when they are at risk of losing everything. It is an inventive and original kind of love, rarely the same story told twice. I use this love to identify the people I will include in my collection. They tell a story of lesbian lives ungoverned by the rule of men.

In the end, I found more lesbians than I could count. Among them, there were seven I wished I could have summoned to the beach that day and introduced, one by one, to my whiskered teammate.

First in line is Mary Casal, fresh from a night at the theater with her *best girl* in celebration of the anonymous publication of her life's story, which she is certain will show the world that no lesbian is alone. She wears a long wool skirt that might have been popular at the turn of the century but is too long and proper for this stifling heat. Mabel Hampton, a Black *stud* and dancer and activist who shared lesbian love with an entire community of people *in the life*, is still a bit grumpy over being asked to ride the train all the way down from the Harlem apartment where she lives with the woman who will be her *wifey* for forty years. Babe Didrikson marches up with a javelin still in hand, ready to brag about her three medals from the 1932 Olympics and the track meet she won as a one-woman team, but with a little coaxing I get her talking about the path she paved for all lady athletes.

Sappho interrupts, lest she be forgotten. "You wouldn't even have the word *lesbian* if it weren't for me," she shouts. It's hard to hear her over the waves, and I worry that my teammate will find her words enigmatic, fragmented by the roar of the wind.

Then there's Rusty Brown, who wants to hurry things along so she's not late to perform her male impersonation act, a line of work that will give birth to a generation of drag kings, just as her work in the navy during World War II, alongside countless other anonymous lesbians, helped give birth to a burgeoning culture and community. Gloria Anzaldúa, short, shock of white hair hennaed brown, in the

throes *of isolation and frustration in Brooklyn*, insists that lesbian is a political identity and, for her, one that is inextricable from her life as a Chicana and a feminist. Amy Hoffman brings up the rear, and my teammate and I can both sense the empty space where her friend Mike, *such an asshole*, once stood, before his body, the body she cleaned and carried, was consumed by AIDS. Our stories, she reminds us, depend on one another.

These lesbian love stories span decades, from the turn of the century to the 1980s, and crisscross the country, though every single one makes a stop in New York City. Most of them would have recognized the spot on Coney Island where I stood with my whiskered teammate. I chose them because their stories are singular, each a match struck against the grain of their eras until their lives burned bright, and yet they also represent the broader history of lesbians at each moment in time. Since these stories are, at heart, love stories, the dates given at the start of each chapter mark the birth and death of a central relationship in each lesbian's life.

All their stories are true, mostly. I feared that the facts alone, the facts demanded by real historians, would not amount to enough to teach my teammate how to spot a lesbian, or to satisfy the lonely girl I had been in middle school. Time has eroded these stories, softened and obscured their details, but more active and intentional forces have played a role in their destruction too. Lesbians faced pressure from intolerant eras to hide behind a pseudonym or to leave out key details in their stories. They often died without children and without public recognition of their contributions to history, leaving no one to preserve their documents, from birth certificates to photographs. To resurrect and uncover these characters the way a doting daughter might, I had to commit to an attentive, obsessive research process, but I also had to leave room for invention. Historical accuracy and rigor had only excluded us from the narrative.

My main focus was on libraries and archives, the public record

available to us all, the way each lesbian constructed the story of their own life for anyone to see. Where possible, I have used their own words, taken from memoirs and published interviews and oral history tapes, to give a sense of their voices. These direct quotes are noted in italics, and, on occasion, I have rearranged the words or applied them to a new context.

Just as these historical figures had to invent new blueprints for how they loved as lesbians, I have invented entire scenes, moments that are absent and inaccessible, the very ones I crave. Until very recently, no one set out to preserve queer stories. Much of the historical record, such as prison records and newspaper articles about recent arrests, was shaped by institutions that wanted get rid of the very queerness they documented. Even when lesbians took up a pen or a microphone to set down their own story, they left out the romantic and erotic details that might bring further scrutiny. Sometimes they hid behind pseudonyms or thinly veiled fiction. It is unlikely that we will unearth new facts about their lives. Imagination and invention are often the only tools left to create something more than a dry story from the fragmented record, to breathe life into characters who must have loved and felt deeply.

My invented scenes are always marked by the present tense and were crafted only after careful study of both the individual lives and the social customs and forces at work during the eras in which they lived. I hope they contain traces of fidelity. To anyone who would argue that this is not how histories are made, I will say that the rules of history were invented by those who wanted to deny us a past, a present, and a future. In other words, by the very people who destroyed our history.

I became a character in this story, too, because I want to be clear about who has imagined these scenes and the biases I bring to my vision. I am an upper-middle-class, college-educated cis white woman. I am a swimmer and a reader and a cat person. I am a homeowner and

a daydreamer. I am also a character because I have never held an accurate archive of my own life as a lesbian. It was a story I hid, even from myself. When had it begun? At the moment when I asked my high school best friend out on a date? At Girl Scout camp, when I wrote my tentmates letters long after the summer session ended? Or even earlier, when I buried my Ken doll in a shoebox in the backyard in an effort to put men behind me?

As I grew, so too did the rights available to and the media representations of queer people. I witnessed firsthand the ripple effects of these material changes and the cultural shifts they caused, as well as their failure to protect the most vulnerable or to bring dignity and respect to all queers. I witnessed the irony of begging to be admitted to an institution we had worked so hard and for so long to reinvent. Growing up alongside these historic changes, and documenting a few of them here, has only deepened my resolve to collect lesbians, to chart the paths they paved before there was a map and the lives they built in an effort to escape the trap of marriage. We never needed permission to love.

I grew up loving stories. Here, let me tell you one.

Extracts | WORDS AND NAMES FOR LESBIANS

Bulldiker / Bulldyker /
Bulldagger / BD

Butch

Carpet Muncher

Companion Lovers

Cuntlapper

Daddy

Dyke

Diesel Dyke

Female Invert

In the Life

Jockey

Lady Lover

Lavender

Lesbian

Lesbo

Lezbitch

Lezzie

Marimacha

Manatee

Pearl Diver

Poppa

Queer Bird

Sapphic

Sil

Spook

Stud

Top Sergeant

Trapeze Artist

Tribad

Virago

Women Lovers

1.

The Names for Love:
Mary Casal and Juno

(1892–1928)

IN THE HIGH HEAT OF JULY 1892, A WOMAN TRAVELING alone on business ducks into New York City's YWCA hotel on Sixteenth Street between Fifth and Sixth Avenues. Her attire is unusual for a woman, a skirt paired with a man's shirt, a tie, and a dark fedora to top it all off. For the better part of a year, she has traveled the country this way, in a circle of towns whose radius expands ever outward from her home in New England, selling a small children's toy of her own invention, made out of paper on which businesses could buy advertisements. Now she had come to the great city to take a meeting with a big department store in the hopes of securing her largest contract yet, to the tune of one hundred thousand toys.

The lobby of the little hotel is stuffy and overfull with the three women stationed there: the matronly one behind the desk, the respectable Christian already waiting in line for a room, and, tucked away in a corner, a young woman perched on a stool, bent over like a wilted lily. She is weeping. The newcomer is struck not by the girl's

11

crying but by her hands, poised as if to catch her tears. *The most beautiful hands*, as she would later describe them in her memoir, she has ever seen.

"What are your wishes?" I imagine a voice from behind the desk that interrupts the newcomer's reverie.

"Excuse me?" she might reply. She wishes to kiss those hands.

"How can I help you?"

Please comfort that girl, she wants to say. "I'd like a room," is all I imagine she can muster.

The proprietor—*fat, forty,* and *unfair*, Mary remembered—looks her potential customer up and down. "Name?"

"Casal. Mary Casal."

"You can only engage a room for one night at a time." Mary never recorded the proprietor's exact words, but I can almost hear her stern tone. "We'll see how I like you. No smoking. No drinking. No cursing. No bringing men around. Curfew's at ten. We'll lock up, and if you aren't inside, well, you better ask forgiveness from the Lord and find somewhere else to sleep."

Mary meets the proprietor's standards and is led up to her room. She sits on the bed and places the hat down beside her. It is too warm, and the walls are covered with admonishments from Christ himself, *expensively printed* and *framed*. But Mary is kept awake that night by something else entirely. The memory of those exquisite hands. "What had brought the girl to tears?" Mary wonders. "Was the matron of this stifling hotel too mean to even comfort a crying girl at her bosom?"

Mary passes an uncomfortable night. She wakes from fitful gasps of sleep with the certainty that she needs to stay in this stuffy hotel. She marches down to the front desk. Seated behind it is the woman with the shining eyes, a kind face, and the most exquisite hands she had ever seen. Something tells Mary that here is the girl of her dreams. Mary hadn't been looking; the girl *just came into* her *life, and* she *knew.*

I hadn't been looking for Mary, either. She just came into my life.

~~~~

I first stumbled on Mary's name in a history book. New York City was preparing to celebrate the fiftieth anniversary of the 1969 Stonewall Riots, a moment in queer history that is often studied as an inflection point in the fight for gay liberation. I picked up a book on the subject to join in the festivities. Before I could make it through the first chapter, though, this woman stopped me in my tracks: "Among the rare early American books to depict lesbian love is the autobiography of 'Mary Casal,' *The Stone Wall*, published in 1930."

If I wanted to build a collection of lesbians, then surely I needed to include one of the first to write down her love story for publication. Mary's life, I would come to learn, straddled the turn of the century, an era when new doors to economic independence were opened to women, from the opportunity to attend recently formed women's colleges to the creation of secretary jobs that allowed women to use the skills they had learned at school to earn their own income. Women formed relationships far from the watchful eyes of their fathers and future suitors. Still, few could afford to set down the intimate emotional and physical details of their relationships outside the confines of personal letters and private diaries. Through the act of writing, Mary showed herself and others that *lesbian* meant something more than a private sexual perversion. It was a way of life, a kind of love that could connect her to an entire community.

The only other detail that I could find about Mary in that first book was the suggestion that the title of her autobiography served as the inspiration for the name of the bar where the riots ignited, originally called Bonnie's Stone Wall. If Mary's story gave us the name for the place where it all happened—where Marsha P. Johnson, a Black trans woman, supposedly threw the first brick, and Stormé DeLarverie, a Black male impersonator, threw the first punch—why had I never heard of it? I ditched Stonewall. I needed to track down Mary.

I searched *the long Vaticans and street-stalls of the* internet for her.

The Brooklyn Public Library didn't have her book, and the New York Public Library would let me read their copy only onsite at the Rose Reading Room. The copies on Amazon, a company that promised to deliver any product imaginable within two days, were all over forty dollars, a price I refused to pay unless there were illustrations. When I finally found and ordered a copy from another online seller, I checked the mail for days, as if expecting a letter from a lover at sea. When it arrived, I tore through the envelope, through the bubble wrap that protected the cover's crisp corners, and through the shrink wrap that bound the pages shut. The edition had no frills, save for a frayed yellow ribbon that gave the book the appearance of a stranger's diary. Faint line drawings crisscrossed the dust jacket to frame a set of cursive words: "Yankee Doodle beat the drum." Those couldn't possibly be from Mary's book.

I tried to track down the publisher. The back jacket listed a price in rupees and an address in New Delhi. I followed the trail back to an online shop, Isha Life, stocked with natural lotions, yoga mats, and meditation books. The profits funded mobile health clinics for rural communities. How had Mary ended up here? What was the connection between the spiritualism of Isha Books and Mary's life story? There wasn't one. The book had entered the public domain and could be published by anyone or, just as easily, forgotten.

I cracked the spine. A firm click told me it had never been opened before.

*Does one often have the courage to tell the whole truth about himself or herself?* Mary writes in the opening pages. *I am going to do it, come what may. Do we all have two lives to lead? I have led two distinct lives all my life.*

Mary admits early on that she is a *Gemini*, but her twinned nature runs deeper than her astrological sign. She is a woman in a skirt and also a man in a tie. She is Mary, a character protected by a pseudonym and free to share the fullness of her experience, and she is also a

historical figure, a person who lived and died under a different name and left behind clues that I will never fully piece together. She is a proper business owner in public, one who can gain admittance to a Christian hotel in New York City, and she is also a lesbian in private, one who freely pursues her sexual and romantic desires. All these parts, though, saw eye to eye on one thing: Juno.

After she spied Juno across the lobby of that hotel, Mary began a *rapturous period of wooing*. She brought Juno *a bunch of lovely violets* disguised as a thank-you for Juno's efforts to put her in a nice, airy room for her second night at the YWCA. Mary stayed a third night. And a fourth. Soon, Juno ran into Mary wherever she turned, on the stairs and in the halls, and never suspected that these little *chance meetings* had been engineered by Mary.

One afternoon, Mary dared mention that she had two theater tickets for that very evening, but no one to go with her. Could Juno take pity and come along? After a moment of initial hesitation, Juno accepted.

The two women headed out into the night, arm in arm. I try to picture them there: Juno stood a head taller than Mary with a *magnificently proportioned figure*. She wore *a charming, simple little gown which just suited her*, while Mary wore *a handsome black tailored suit with a black hat and white silk shirt*, once again adopting the popular Victorian fashion of wearing a skirt paired with a structured jacket. *My personal appearance?* she writes, an echo of the question already on my mind. *If someone else were writing about that I believe they would say: She had a wonderful complexion and smooth skin, soft brown hair which curled in little ringlets about the forehead and neck (it is now snowy white, wavy in front and cut in a "boyish bob"), which were white and with correct lines; not too fat (as I am now), artistic hands, also pronounced as capable ones; a figure true to form, of about "size forty" at that time; graceful in all movements; a voice soft and well-modulated.*

Mary was distracted all evening. *I remember little of the play. By*

*this time, I was madly in love with Juno and longed to put my arms about her and tell her of it.* But Mary held back. She wanted to be certain that Juno felt the same.

Afterward, they dined together at a little *hotel, where it was permissible and wholly respectable for two ladies to have supper without a male escort.* Juno spoke of her past, and Mary leaned across the table to drink up every word. An orphan, Juno and her siblings had been raised by a rich relative, but she had since been cut off, *without a penny,* from the family fortune over an engagement gone wrong. She had been *deeply in love with the man,* but in the end, they could not marry, and she was left with little except the resolve *that she would never marry* and would instead *find solace in hard work,* which, at the moment, meant a job at the Christian hotel. They linger—they must—long after the other diners have left, heads bent close over a guttering flame. Mary fights the impulse to reach across the expanse of table for Juno's hand. At the end of the night, Juno told Mary that *she had enjoyed* [it] *more than anything she had done since she had left her home.* There was hope.

Mary was well-versed in the art of wooing. The pair went out for long walks, visited art galleries, and returned to the theater. Juno began to unfurl. She revealed to Mary the reason for her tears that very first afternoon when she had burst into the lobby. Juno had been crying over a tip. A woman had left her a measly twenty-five cents, and those coins threw into sharp relief how drastically her life had changed. *She had heard my voice when I was going through the awful questioning and longed to look up, even through her tears, but she did not dare to with those eyes so red.* But after Mary had gone up to her room, Juno admitted, she had wiped away her tears and marched straight up to the front desk to search the register for the name of the newcomer. So Juno had seen something in her too. Mary dreamed of bringing Juno the happiness of a shared life, a dream that just might be possible, as the woman had already decided never to marry. Her feelings

ran deeper than physical attraction. *My heart was calling for her as a mate.* Mary was just *patiently waiting for the right time to declare my love—until a beautiful foundation of sympathy and companionship should be firmly established.*

The hotel staff warned Juno against spending so much time with this handsome stranger. Accepting invitations from guests was against the hotel's custom, and besides, they relied on Juno and couldn't bear the thought of anyone taking her away from her job. Their words went unheeded. Juno began to visit Mary at night, on her way up to her own room. Mary would leave the door ajar while she read in bed as an invitation to Juno to come in and give her *very proper little kisses* goodnight. One night, something about Juno's enthusiasm and the time the two women had spent together made Mary certain *that she not only loved me but was also "in love" with me (but did not realize it),* and the moment to find out whether the yearning she felt could ever be reciprocated had arrived. Mary spoke her love aloud in words that have been lost to history and sealed her speech with a kiss *more intense than ever before, and her lips willingly yielded to mine.*

<center>~~~~~</center>

That night might have been Juno's first passionate kiss with a woman, but it was not Mary's. She had plucked queer joy like a shell from the sand on the seashore at the age of twelve. That eye-opening, preteen summer, she went to stay with her sister and her sister's new husband by the shore. She swam. She rowed. She met a girl. They spent every moment they could together. The girl's family owned a boat, and Mary would row while the special lady, I imagine, would sit on the prow twirling a parasol in her white-gloved hands. When they were together, Mary felt *a great thrill right at the end of my breast bone. I could feel my heart beating faster, but there was no desire for anything more than that sweet response to my love.*

I longed to know the details of their first kiss. I rode the ferry out

to Rockaway Beach and parked myself on the shore, empty in the early season, to read. Sand blew across my back and into the book. It burrowed into the valleys between the pages and made the whole thing fatter, as if new pages had been added.

Mary wrote nothing of their lips meeting. If this was a moment I wanted, it would be one I had to invent. I am certain it happened on the water. The two have taken the boat out in an effort to escape the hot, still day and everyone's foul mood. Mary can finally feel perspiration evaporate from her temples. The girl laughs at some joke and shifts her body closer to Mary. Mary shifts too. She has to move slowly to keep the boat from tipping. A curl has come loose from the girl's pins and sticks to the dried sweat on her neck. Mary lifts it and looks up into the girl's face, freckled from the sun. She sees an openness there, the possibility that the girl also felt the cool spark of their touch. She leans in. The oars knock against the boat. Their lips meet. The girl pulls away only to giggle before she comes back for more.

Perhaps I am guilty of borrowing details from my own first kiss with a woman. It happened at a college Christmas party. I sat with my swim teammates in someone's off-campus apartment and passed around a bottle of whiskey to the steam engine chug of "Wagon Wheel." I would call it a drinking game, except that it was really all drinking and no game. The song changed, and, in silent agreement, we got up to dance, our elbows and hips set in motion while our feet remained firmly planted. Everyone's feet, that is, except one girl who shuffled toward me. She was a freshman who I knew only by her purple plastic glasses, her shoulder injury, and her strained but enthusiastic cheers on the pool deck.

I recognized this shuffle. It was a familiar move at swim team parties, an inevitable advance that happened when you brought together athletic men and women who already knew the lines of each other's naked bodies. At the library, when my teammates and I grew bored of studying, someone would always wheel out a chalkboard and draw

a chart of who had kissed who over the years. The archive stretched so far back it featured people I had come to know only as hubs in this tangled web.

A friend crossed the living room to check in on me. She circled her fingers around my wrist. "Do you want to come dance with us?" she asked. Her eyes met mine with concern, and she gestured back at our little group of friends. The freshman's approach had felt familiar to me, but now I realized that to everyone else it looked different. Two girls. Did I need to be rescued? I shook my head, no. My friend walked away, and I grabbed the hand of this newcomer.

I led her to the bathroom. *Somewhere,* my thoughts sloshed through whiskey, *where no one can see.* We lay down in the bathtub, adrift in our own little boat, sweaty, even in winter, from dancing in the overfull apartment. We pressed our lips together and fumbled for each other's clothes. I found a tattoo across the top of her ribcage, something that had escaped my notice in the locker room. In spite of the booze on our breath and the clumsy knock of our glasses, in spite of the fear that our teammates would barge in at any moment, this was better than anything I had known before, better than the boys who were just a pale imitation, the boys who had been, I now saw, my practice.

"Why didn't you tell me sooner?" my roommate asked a few weeks later, when I finally mustered up the courage to tell her. We sat in a secluded section of the dining hall for our weekly roommate lunch. The soda machine wheezed at our backs. This table was where we had spent many depleted afternoons playing One, Two, Three, a game she had learned from watching *Gilmore Girls* on repeat during sleepy Connecticut summers. To play, you simply had to sit. Each time a man passed the table, you had to decide whether you wanted to marry him or wait for someone better to come along. You could only count the men who came from behind you. One. Two. Three. If you passed on the first two, you had to take the third one, no matter what. We

had spent three semesters hoping that our crushes—boys with new whiskers as soft as their vintage sweaters, boys we were too tongue-tied to approach, boys who might someday soon become men—would pass at just the right moment.

"I'm hurt you didn't say anything," she said. There was no way I could distract her with a game today. "You know I would have been accepting. My best friend from high school is a lesbian."

"You never told me! You're always on the phone talking about that terrible guy she's dating."

"You know," she continued, on the defensive, "I always wanted to be a lesbian." Here it was! She was about to confess her own attraction to women, I thought, or the details of one joyful, drunken night. "It just seems so much easier. I hate shaving my legs. I love hanging out with my girl friends."

I seethed in my seat, but I didn't dare say a word. She wanted to be a lesbian because she thought it would be a way to opt out of a life spent with men, to escape their unattainable beauty standards, their catcalls, and their hopes of trading women. I couldn't bear to tell her everything I had learned long before my night of drunken kisses. I would always have to deal with men, their leering eyes and stifling expectations. Couldn't she reject shaving without rejecting men? Wasn't there a way for her to resist heterosexual systems without stealing my word?

I had kissed a woman only once, but I suddenly considered myself the expert. Being a lesbian wasn't just about the rejection of razors and men. I had loved my old boyfriends and might again someday, and I still shaved my legs before every swim race. It wasn't even about sex either, no matter how much I itched to bring up the subject as a provocation. It was about desire, the desire to forge something new.

*We spent many nights together,* Mary writes of her shore girl, *always in a loving embrace, repeating all the little love sayings, and sleeping in each other's arms, perfectly happy.* She never names their *love sayings*

or the mechanics of their *loving embrace*. Still, there is desire there. I recognize it.

~~~~~

Until the second half of the nineteenth century, all that could be imagined for a woman was a life spent in the houses and embraces of men—first with her father, and then, after he traded her, with her husband. The marriage plot took center stage in the novels Mary might have read growing up, classics like *Pride and Prejudice* and Louisa May Alcott's *Little Women*. Perhaps Mary even recognized something of herself in Austen's Elizabeth, one of the five Bennet sisters in possession of little fortune and very much in want of a husband. I saw something of myself in her, at least. Fiery, stubborn, and quick-witted, Elizabeth had the gall to turn down a decent marriage proposal. Each time I sank into our striped blue couch to watch a new adaptation of the story with my mother, I held out hope that this time, the movie would give Elizabeth a future as independent as her spirit. Every time, she ended up married, and I felt a fresh disappointment. The story taught me—and maybe Mary too—that if a woman must marry to receive financial support, if she must be traded, then her only chance at having a say in the direction of her life is to fall in love, to choose the man who can transform obligation into a passionate happily ever after.

If Mary had turned instead to Alcott's *Little Women*, the fate of the March sisters wouldn't have offered a better moral. When their father left home to fight for the Union in the Civil War, the girls were free to build a utopia without men, but they had little money to spend on it. Everything they invented, from games to dresses, was made from scraps. My favorite of the bunch, Jo, earned her own money when she sold her stories. Could she have been Mary's inspiration to start writing too? Jo's literary aspirations were larger than anything women of the day were taught to hope for and suggested she was,

perhaps, a fictionalized version of her creator, Alcott. Everything about Jo, from her boyish nickname, short for Josephine, to her cold rejection of a marriage proposal from best friend and verbal sparring partner Laurie, gave me something to look up to, a role model for how a woman could set the terms of her own life.

That is, until she finds her own man to marry, the mysterious Professor Bhaer who arrives in deus ex machina fashion. Some scholars believe that the professor was added to the story only at the behest of Alcott's publishers, as marriage was the only suitable ending for the heroine of a story for young ladies. In fact, all the March sisters end up married, save Beth. Death, it seems, was the only true escape from the marriage plot in fiction.

In real life, though, Alcott found her escape. "I am more than half-persuaded that I am a man's soul put by some freak of nature into a woman's body," she said in an interview about her romantic life. "I have fallen in love with so many pretty girls and never once the least bit with any man." Like Mary, she *lived two distinct lives*. Man and woman. Author and character. Conformist and rebel. Louisa May Alcott, author of the story nearly every little girl is told, the rubric by which we define ourselves as an independent Jo or a beautiful Meg or a practical Amy or a kind but tragic Beth, was, in fact, a lesbian. Her attempt at an autobiographical novel was papered over until readers like me and Mary can see only the edges of the truth poke out, but still, I will count Louisa as one of us.

Mary was born in New England in June 1864 to a family of poor farmers with nine children, and she arrived into a world that was just beginning to offer more possibilities for women than these heroines could've ever hoped for. Mount Holyoke Female Seminary opened its doors in South Hadley, Massachusetts in 1837 to offer further Christian education for young women, joining the ranks of female seminaries that had opened in the first half of the nineteenth century. After receiving a collegiate charter in 1888, the school became Mount

Holyoke Seminary and College, now the oldest remaining women's college. Even writing on the edge of seventy, *the last one of all that large family left*, Mary leaves the town where she grew up unnamed. Still, she could not have been far from this new school.

Vassar and Wellesley followed suit, modeling themselves after Mount Holyoke. Before the turn of the century, Smith and Bryn Mawr joined the ranks of women's colleges. (I was born at Bryn Mawr. A lesbian from the start.) The schools gave young upper-middle-class white women the opportunity to live independently from their families, receive an education, and potentially earn their own income after graduation, all without becoming attached to a man. They also created just the right circumstances for women to fall in love with each other.

The schools held all-women dances, and the students coined funny new words to describe the relationships that blossomed there: Crushes. Smashes. Spoons. An 1837 article in the Yale student newspaper noted: "When a Vassar girl takes a shine to another, she straightaway enters upon a regular course of bouquet sendings, interspersed with tinted notes, mysterious packages of 'Ridley's Mixed Candies,' locks of hair perhaps, and many other tender tokens, until at last the object of her attentions is captured, the two women become inseparable, and the aggressor is considered by her circle of acquaintances as— *smashed*." Sometimes teachers smashed on students, as with eventual Mount Holyoke president Mary Woolley and her student Jeanette Marks, who remained her partner for forty-eight years. Women continued these relationships off campus, too, where they became known as Boston marriages, a term referring to two unmarried women living together in New England. No matter what they were called or who they took hold of, these "romantic friendships" between women were encouraged. They were seen as a stepping stone, a practice run for the romances with men that would surely come later in life.

I am inured to a history of homophobia, of dangerous consequences

for visible same-sex couples and others who defied gender norms, so I am surprised that these women and their relationships were met with acceptance. It was an acceptance, I learned, that stemmed from the fact that few saw these relationships as sexual. Historians have dismissed romantic friendships as nothing more than platonic for over a century, characterizing the women who enjoyed them as the kind of woman my own college roommate longed to one day become: politically minded, on a brief hiatus from men, and enjoying the depth of female friendship without ever crossing the line into physical intimacy. They insist that without an explicit historical record of their sexual encounters—diagrams, detailed descriptions of their conquests—to serve as undeniable proof, there's no need to invent a queer history for them. Perhaps they had watched the same episode of *Sex and the City* that I had—"If you're not going to eat pussy, you're not a dyke"—to come up with their standard for being labeled a lesbian. But who can be blamed for respecting the privacy of a lover? And exactly what kind of physical intimacy needs to be shared to legitimize a relationship?

I wanted to decide for myself, to become, for a moment, the arbiter of queerness. I don't have a history degree, but I do have lived experience, and that should make me just as qualified as the scholars who have come before me. I read snippets from letters between women of the era, collected by the incredible lesbian historian Lillian Faderman, to see for myself how the authors measured up.

My Ever Dear . . . I miss you dreadfully and am yours 'til death.

You must know, dear, how I long for you all the time, and especially during the last three weeks. There is reason in the habit of married folks keeping together.

These aren't the kinds of lines I would write to my female friends, not even the two I've known since high school, who have seen me

through more breakups than I can count on one hand, and who I'm certain will be with me longer than any romantic partner.

These words were written by philanthropist Jane Addams, who history best remembers as the founder of Hull House settlement, an institution founded to uplift immigrants and other factory workers through education, an effort that would help her win the 1931 Nobel Peace Prize, though in later years her view of educational charity was seen as a cover for racist attitudes toward Black women. No one remembers Hull House's cofounder Ellen Starr, whom Jane met at Rockford Female Seminary on September 11, a date the two would celebrate as their anniversary for all the years they were together. No one remembers Mary Rozet Smith either. She arrived at Hull House just as Jane's passion for Ellen began to cool and became both Jane's partner and travel companion for the next forty years. Jane, often out on lecture tours, would send home letters filled with a longing that bordered on lust. And when Mary joined her on the road, Jane would call ahead to the hotel to ensure there would be a double bed for the couple. No one batted an eye. There was no need to hide—no one would think to scrutinize a deep friendship between women.

I found another letter, loving words shared between another pair:

Ah, my Cleopatra is a very dangerous Queen, but I will look her straight in those wide open eyes that look so imperious and will crush those Antony-seeking lips, until her arms close over (alas, for my hair with all those armlets), and she becomes my prisoner because I am her Captain . . . How much kissing can Cleopatra stand?

This one was written by Rose Elizabeth Cleveland, sister of U.S. president Grover Cleveland, who took on some of the duties of First Lady on behalf of her unmarried brother. Her doting letters, complete with epistolary role play, were sent to Evangeline, a woman who could be nothing short of her lover.

And this, from M. Carey Thomas:

A word or a photo does all, and the pulses beat and heart longs in the same old way.

M. Carey first fell for a woman (and another and another) at her Quaker boarding school, where she kept a diary of all the smashing that took place. She refused to get married, as her father wanted her to, and went to college instead. Determined to continue her studies even after Johns Hopkins refused to take her on as a PhD student, she went to study at the University of Zurich. She was so committed to women's education that she became president of Bryn Mawr College in 1894. She lived with her lover, Mary, the woman who inspired those *pulse beats*, right on campus, where all—faculty, students, fellow administrators—could see. Still haunted by Johns Hopkins's rejection, Thomas used her wealth to found a medical school at the university, on the condition that they admit women and treat them as equals to men.

M. Carey Thomas, advocate for women's education.

Rose Elizabeth Cleveland, de facto First Lady.

Jane Addams, Nobel laureate.

I hereby claim these figures as lesbians. I refuse to join the historians who deny the legitimacy of their relationships because they failed to leave a map of where they touched one another. It's undeniable that these pairs shared passion, for their work and for each other, and they were able to invent lives for themselves far outside the confines of a traditional marriage. So why have they remained as invisible as I was that day on Coney Island, unseen by my whiskered teammate?

~~~

*The side of my nature which called for a female mate worried me, as I thought I was the only girl with such a nature.* Mary Casal saw herself as

the only lesbian alive. Or rather, the only woman who loved women; the word *lesbian* doesn't appear once in the narrative. Without a word to name her identity and without representations of others like her out in the world to understand what her future might look like, Mary had no way of knowing that there were women with *such a nature* nearby in New England and that they lived happy, fulfilled lives. Still, she dreamed of a life shared with a woman, and she risked everything to make that dream come true.

After Mary declared her love, Juno *was mystified . . . She was truly worried. She said she loved me madly, but not as she had ever supposed she could love a woman—even more than she had loved the man whom she was engaged to marry. She wondered whether I really were a woman.*

The time came for Mary, *having at last concluded the deal upon which I had been working,* to leave the Christian hotel and New York City for a town half a day's journey away by train, where she would continue her business. Before her departure, she had one more question to ask of Juno: Will you marry me? There was a certain logic to her proposal. *Why not?* She argued. *A union between two women could be of a higher type, and creative of a more secure happiness and good than any other.*

Juno gave no answers before Mary boarded the train. They promised to write often, and Mary *arranged* in advance *for flowers and fruits to be sent to her regularly during my absence.* After arriving in that distant, unnamed town, Mary sat down and wrote a letter to her beloved.

What I wouldn't give to read that letter, to have my own role model, to know something beyond the fumbling postcards and emails and texts I have sent to my beloveds over the years.

The answer came the next afternoon, by telegram: *Come, every bit of me wants you.*

Mary canceled all her business engagements and boarded the night boat bound for New York City.

Mary's life was marked by dramatic journeys, a drama she seemed to take for granted.

Her memories rub up against each other, clamoring for some elbow room and yanking at my attention, asking me to put the pieces together. She interrupts one story from her first few months of college with a simple memory from her childhood: galloping bareback on the farm one afternoon to the point of orgasm. She inserts disruptive lectures into the narrative that cover everything from the need for frank sex education so that children may know and defend themselves to the need for further study of homosexuality. She leaves herself little room to reflect, to notice the strange convergences that turn her life into a soap opera.

Mary's many lives collided one day on a train headed west, more than a decade before she met Juno, on the return trip to the unnamed coed college out in the Midwest where she was earning her degree. Her family had not questioned whether she would continue her education. The only limiting factor was their finances, so in the fall of 1880, Mary set out for the school where her sister's husband, Peter, taught. On the journey back for her third year—perhaps dozing, wary of her vulnerability, a single suitcase stowed above her head—I like to think she filled the hours with the memories of everyone who had stopped by her New England home to visit that summer.

First, it had been the new professor, fresh off his first year of teaching at the college, and the professor's wife, Flo. The couple had also moved out from the East Coast, and perhaps this accident of geography alone had been enough to bring them all—Mary, her sister, her sister's husband Peter, and the newcomers—together. In the autumn evenings, the light falling fast, Mary would head over to the couple's house after finishing her schoolwork, staying on until dinner and lingering late into the evening. I scour the book for snatches of their conversations, something of the passionate debates had by young people

learning how to wield their burgeoning knowledge, or a whiff of the food they ate, but Mary has left me nothing. Her attention was elsewhere. It was on the professor's wife.

Mary's *affections were turning Flo-ward very rapidly,* and she made her feelings known through small gestures: sending flowers and doing other kind deeds, known as "making love" in the nineteenth century. The very things she would later do for Juno, that she must have invented on her own, with no one else around to teach her how one woman should woo another. Flo softened. Mary began to stay on, sleeping at the couple's house after their Thursday night dinners. There's another scene missing, one I must write for myself.

One night, not so different from the rest, Flo gets up from where she was sleeping with her husband and tiptoes over to the guest bedroom. Her knock is timid, so as not to disturb the candle burning at half-mast in her other hand. Flo wears a nightgown that touches the floor, stained brown in places with use, little frills around the neck and cuffs.

Mary blinks her eyes open and comes to the door. "What are you doing here?" she asks, hoping she already knows the answer.

"I wanted to make sure you could sleep all right." She pauses, peers past Mary, into the guest bedroom. "I know I couldn't."

Mary feels bold in these moments when slumber still lingers. "Would you like to come in?"

They kiss at the threshold, tentative, gentle, before the door is shut. Visible, for a moment, in the candlelight.

Flo's Thursday night visits to Mary's bedroom became routine. The two shared *little kisses and big kisses.* When Flo got up to return to her marriage bed, *I would be left with a longing for her that I could hardly bear.*

That summer vacation, when Flo and her husband showed up on Mary's doorstep back east, Mary could not contain her excitement. After so many weeks apart, the pair yearned for a moment alone. They

snuck off together for long walks and drives, risking suspicion just for the pleasure of one another's company. Mary's mother began to notice the absences. She pulled her daughter aside to chastise her. The accusation? That her daughter was spending too much time with a married man. Mary *protested*, and confessed the truth: It was Flo who held her affections. I dug my nails into my forearm to slow my racing heart. From my twenty-first century vantage point, this seems a riskier proposition than pleading guilty to the charges of adultery.

Mary's mother didn't believe a word of it, though. She took to her bed, feigning illness so that the couple would have to leave and remove the temptation, whoever it was, from the premises. When Mary explained why the visit was cut short, Flo agreed it would be best if she left with her husband. Back in her own home, Flo took it upon herself to write a letter to Mary's mother explaining the truth, that the *attachment* was between the two women. *Whatever mother thought I never knew, for she was a woman of few words. The matter was then dropped.* Mary escaped a confession of queer desire unscathed. Perhaps, beneath her silence, Mary's mother saw the relationship as just another romantic friendship, one she hoped her daughter would soon outgrow.

Mary's next visitor that summer would confirm her mother's dreams were coming true. Flo and her husband were soon replaced by Mary's young lover, who went *through the family inspection as a candidate for my heart and hand. He was approved and the engagement was announced, with the usual festivities. This fellow was good looking, a wonderful dancer, and did give the "sweetest kisses" . . . I was becoming more and more worried because I was not like other girls, so I felt that I had better get married as soon as my school days were over, and become normal.* This young gentleman, sketched with few words and no name, was Mary's second fiancé. At the age of fourteen, she had accepted an older boy, one who matched her high marks in school, first as her beau, then as her fiancé. That one disappeared, a narrative thread dropped, without a word from Mary about how the relationship ended.

An engagement secured, the second fiancé boarded the westbound train with a smile on his face. Mary followed a few weeks later to return for the fall semester, carried by a drumbeat of pistons and steam through the forests of Pennsylvania and Ohio, toward her unnamed fiancé, and once again *Flo-ward*. *I felt that I was quite "in love" and had the proper feelings for this swain, yet deep in my heart it was the feeling that I was to be again with Flo that made me happy to go back.*

Mary's young fiancé walked out of her thoughts and into the train car. He had traveled a day and a night to meet her, bringing flowers, candy, and company for her final day of the journey. I am amazed that he arranged such a surprise without a cell phone. His gesture was not purely selfless, though: he *begged* her to get off the train and *be married then and there and have it all over*. Mary refused. She had to finish school first and couldn't let down her family. Undeterred by the refusal, her fiancé snuck into her berth that night, parting the curtains and hopping into the narrow bed that likely shook and rumbled with the motion of the train. He wanted to consummate a marriage that had yet to happen. To him, he argued, putting his college education to use, they were already *married in the sight of God*. Mary obliged, hoping that this time her feelings for a man, her pleasure, might be different than all the times before with other men. But the engagement had changed nothing. *I knew then that I could never bring myself to the point of really marrying him.*

There was yet another surprise waiting for Mary when she stumbled down to the dining car the next morning: her sister's husband, Peter. His face fell when he saw that his sister-in-law was joined by her new fiancé, as *Peter probably thought he would be able to have a little seance of his own*. The man who made her education affordable also made it unbearable. *The two of them sitting there, hating each other, and I hating them both.* He had begun sexually abusing her from her very first semester.

Peter ran the university library and enlisted Mary to help with the

work. *All the new books had to be catalogued, leaves cut, and so forth, before they were ready for the shelves . . . This work was done in a private room which was always kept locked . . . One day while we were working he grabbed my hands and told me how he had grown to love me. I was going to leave the room, but it was locked, and he had the key. I found he was determined to make love to me, as he called it, and I was equally determined that he should not.*

In spite of everything in Mary's nature that screamed against the contact, she *yielded,* if only *to keep the peace in the family,* and felt like nothing more than *an unwilling piece of furniture. How I wished that I could experience some pleasure in that awful contact which I seemed fated to endure. The first of my first year in college! How I hated myself by this time. I felt that I was nothing but a low animal, and might well have been a prostitute. I just didn't care much what happened.*

*Fated to endure.* This was not the first time Mary had been the victim of sexual abuse.

Growing up on the farm, Mary's family had treated her like their other little girls, teaching her to sew and knit and gifting her dolls at Christmas. But Mary found *all the conventional things that a New England girl was supposed to do* to be *a nightmare.* She preferred to play outside with the neighborhood *boys—one brother and three cousins who lived just across the road*—or whittle a stick beneath an elm tree, and, when it came time for chores, she would rather pull weeds from the yard or chop firewood. She even insisted on covering her girl's body in boy's clothes, and her mother let her. *To be a called a "Tom Boy" never grieved me; in fact, I think I was rather proud of the epithet.*

One day, while inventing *great and glorious games in the big barns* or perhaps reenacting the slaughter of the indigenous peoples who once lived on the land, Mary had to run back to the house to pee. When she returned, the boys asked her where she had been.

"You don't have to go back to the house," they explain. "You can just pull it out and pee through the hole in the front of your trousers."

I imagine the boys as rude and crass, but Mary explains that they had a little childhood euphemism for the act: *bo-bo*. The next time she felt that call of nature, the boys showed her to a corner of the barn and left her to do her business. She found the hole in the front of the boys' trousers her mother permitted her to wear, but she couldn't figure out what to do next. What was she meant to pull out? She protested to the boys, and one by one, they came to inspect what she was lacking. They *pulled and hauled* at the bud of flesh, one she decided might someday grow into something large enough to pull out of her trousers and relieve herself. They soon discovered not all children are *alike*.

Mary—I can only call her to mind by her first name at the age of four, at this moment of deep vulnerability—ran back to the house crying, *crushed and broken*, to use the bathroom. Through her tears, she told her mother all that had happened. Her mother spanked her. She gave Mary a pile of sewing to keep her in the house for several days. There was no explanation of what had gone wrong. Without the words to describe the thing that had happened, the thing that brought her to tears, the biological differences between the genitalia and how they could be used, Mary grew frustrated with her mother's efforts to keep her indoors and out of trousers, ashamed that she was not an equal to the boys in all things.

With no one around to educate Mary about her own body, the abuse continued. When she was finally allowed to rejoin the boys outdoors, a new ritual was added to their games. Before her brother and her cousin would allow her to join in the fun, they forced her to submit to inspections of what she came to know as her *private parts*. At first, they said they were looking for growth, and Mary felt disgust at her delayed development, at the inferiority and inconvenience of her own parts. As the boys grew, though, they began to learn about sex from their older classmates and the men who came to work on the farm, and they discovered that their penises could lift and harden. While they kept the former knowledge from Mary, they

were eager to share the latter. They forced themselves upon her in a game they called *playing hen and rooster* in mimicry of the farm animals they saw climb atop one another with the same attention they paid to scratching or pecking. Mary never describes the mechanics of what happened to her, whether they took her clothes off to play hen or whether they tried to penetrate her. The propriety of the time kept her mouth shut and her descriptions vague, but now we can name it for what it was: abuse.

It continued throughout her adolescence, often at the hands of men close to her family.

At the age of eight or nine, a hired hand on the farm thrust his hand beneath her skirt.

A man who lived next door and had gifted young Mary with a love of music led her to the barn one day and threatened to whip her until she pleasured him. For years, he forced her to have painful intercourse with him in dim hallways and dark corners.

Her cousin, eleven years old at the time, took her for a sleigh ride along a frozen river. When the sleigh stopped at the narrowest part of the river, he threatened not to drive her back unless she had sex with him.

An old gentleman who lived with his wife in the other half of the duplex where Mary lived invited her over to play cards, then shoved his hand up her dress on the stairs.

I wanted to pick up the book and throw it across the room.

Writing more than eighty years before Tarana Burke's phrase *me too* went viral on social media, leading more women than ever before to publicly share their experiences with sexual assault, Mary (my Mary!) was ahead of her time when it came to speaking out against abuse. I want to claim her not just as my own but also as an early feminist who gave voice to her traumas in an era when the subject was still taboo. She reports the physical and emotional details of the abuse frankly, acknowledging the memories like clouds rolling past her

window, weather patterns that can't be changed or stopped. *During the earlier sessions he was apparently very careful not to hurt me, using his finger "to make the place big," as he said.* It's a frankness I imagine would have caused a stir when first published. Sometimes she dips her toe into the well of feelings stirred up by these memories—*I was terrified* or *I was filled with disgust*—but these assertions are always followed by an immediate insistence on her happiness, the narrative that is truly her own. *I was not wholly cast down, however, but like all normal children I was able to forget between times.* She uses her own experiences as *an argument for the enlightenment of youth on questions of life and sex!* And as hateful as these experiences with men were, she is still certain that her love of women was not born out of trauma but rather was a part of her very nature, from the very start. *The dislike for men as males was inherent.*

After she left school, Mary tried to deny her nature and become a normal woman. Flo and her professor husband had a baby boy who consumed all her old lover's attention. *As our lives fell far apart, the flame just naturally flickered out, though we always remained friends.* Mary wanted to start a family too. She moved back home to New England, far from her tormentors, and took up teaching at a nearby school. The fiancé who had met her on the train disappeared from the narrative, as if he were simply forgotten rather than dumped, but in her early twenties, Mary replaced him with a third nameless fiancé, a family friend twelve years her senior. *I felt that I could never love any man, and as I had to marry one in order to have the desired children, it might as well be one who would perhaps prove a clean and good father.* That sentence is the closest thing I can find to a description of the man Mary would soon marry, a man as hollow as Alcott's Professor Bhaer. Together they moved to a *large rambling house . . . on a lovely spot on a large farm, with the Connecticut River flowing through it, and a little lake near the house. In the summer, it was open to boarders from the cities.*

*Friend husband,* as she would come to call him, had his own plans

for their shared life. He did not want a child. *Much to my horror, he took great care lest any accidents should happen.*

Still, by some untold subterfuge, Mary did become pregnant, filled with *pure delight* and unquenchable sexual desire and a new life. *At night I would sing or pat it to sleep with the same tenderness as a mother with her baby in her arms.* Her goal achieved, she could now refuse to have sex with her husband because if sex was divorced from producing children, then *pleasures . . . could be bought and sold on the open mart*, and *the thought of being a legitimized prostitute the rest of my life did not appeal to me.* No longer just *an unwilling piece of furniture*, she channeled the energy of her pregnancy into a new teaching post the next town over, one that required her to ride a sleigh and a train on those dark, cold January mornings.

Whatever energy was left over after the journey and a hard day's work she put into a new affair. I am struck by, and perhaps a bit jealous of, how often Mary finds romance, how quickly she slips into intimacy with other women in spite of their marriages and the Victorian taboos around sex. This time, she seduces (*I did not care to be wooed, still preferring to be the one to do the capturing*) her husband's cousin, whom she calls Gladys. As her due date drew nearer, Mary was no longer able to help out on the farm, so she went to stay with her mother, where Gladys would visit her often. *I was happy mentally, but physically always hungry for that something which was lacking, and of which I knew nothing from personal experience . . . that longing for sexual relief could not be relieved.* One morning, after Gladys *made strenuous efforts* all night to give Mary that relief, the labor pains began, and with them, the end of her happiness.

After several days of labor, a child came, cold and stillborn, and the doctors laid *that little body* beside Mary for a *short minute.* Mary wondered if it was punishment for failing to commit fully to the role of wife and mother, for her long morning journeys to the school, for the feverish nights she spent with Gladys, but she brushed those thoughts

away. It was a long summer of recovery for both Mary's body and her spirits. She was *anxious to become pregnant* again, a new baby to mend her broken heart, but her husband remained even more determined now that he knew how much medical care for his wife could cost.

Peter returned. His wife had died shortly after Mary's wedding, perhaps, Mary suspected, of a heart broken by his many infidelities, though the sisters had never discussed them openly. (How I wish it was Peter who had died!) He visited Mary often and tried to resume their abusive relationship. *In no gentle manner did I let him see how I despised him for the role to which he had subjected me.* Thwarted, he turned his attentions to the next nearest target, Gladys. *She promptly fell in love with him, as so many poor females had before.*

This was not the first time Peter had seduced one of Mary's girlfriends—he had done it at least once before, at the college—but this time around Mary presents herself as unbothered by a pursuit I can only imagine to be motivated by a desire to torment her further. If anything, she took pity on Gladys for falling prey to Peter. Perhaps Mary hid her true disappointment from the page, or perhaps she was truly ready to let the girl go because her eyes had already alit on yet another woman: one of the boarders who came from New York City to stay for the summer at the big house by the Connecticut River, a society lady with three children, a love of music and the theater, and beautiful eyes. Mrs. Barr-Jones, as she is called. Together, they *began planning a play, to be given in the great barn for some special occasion*, with Mrs. Barr-Jones taking the female lead and, at her insistence, Mary taking the male. She seduced the boarder both onstage and off.

That *mad summer* filled with *grief* waned to winter. The house emptied of boarders, the sun slid quickly down the slope of the sky, and a little bit of lightness crept back into Mary. She got *consent* from her husband to visit her new society smash in New York City. Mary writes little of her time there with Mrs. Barr-Jones, denying me yet again the thing I crave most. Instead, she focuses on a journey to

Brooklyn to dine with two old friends, Flo and her husband, and their baby boy. Mary spent the meal wondering whether there was still some spark between her and Flo and lamenting the loss of her own baby. There was to be no comfort found in the house of old friends. When dinner ended, the professor took Mary back to Manhattan.

*Both the Professor and I were in a dangerous mood . . . It was suggested that we stop on the way home at a remote little hotel, which the professor seemed to know quite well as being one where no questions would be asked. I think I rather demurred, but then it flashed across my mind that I would throw discretion to the winds and endure the moment in the hope that perhaps there might be a chance of becoming pregnant. We stopped, and my whole hope for the future lay in the next hours.*

Mary meets this soap opera–worthy moment with her signature frankness. *These disclosures are to show what lengths one will go in the desire for a child, and to have a lasting excuse for marriage.* She frames the decision, yet another plot twist in an astounding life, as nothing more than a practical consideration, something she could finally choose for herself.

The gamble paid off, at first. She went back home and discovered that she was, in fact, expecting. But it was to be another long labor, and another stillborn child. The doctors told her it was too dangerous for her health to ever try for a child again. She could not carry on with her husband. *I simply refused to stay with the man who should have bought his pleasures and hired a housekeeper.* She left for New York to live with Mrs. Barr-Jones and her husband.

*Mrs. B.-J. and I enjoyed our life together, but I was still groping for the real soul mate who I always felt was waiting somewhere for me—some one with whom I could experience a oneness which had been my ideal.*

~~~

The love scene I've longed for.

After receiving Juno's telegram, Mary sent word back for Juno to

meet her the next morning at the little hotel where they had shared that first dinner. Too excited to sleep, she paced the rain-soaked deck of the night boat until morning came. *The boat docked*, and still the drops came in *torrents*, heavy and sensuous against her skin. Mary staggered into a cab, her legs perhaps still unsteady from the rocking of the sea or nerves or both, and directed the driver first to a wholesale florist, where she bought a *big bunch of violets*, and then on to the hotel. Her heart in her throat and her hands holding fast to those flower stems, she hardly took in the sights of the city as they swam past the window in the gray morning light.

Juno stood waiting in the parlor of the hotel, her face ablaze with an eager, loving anticipation. *We were shown to our room. When we were alone our arms were about each other and our lips met in the first kiss that was a pledge of a great and beautiful love.* Yet before things could go any further, they needed to attend to a more basic hunger. In the dining room, the one where they had shared their first meal, they planned their future together over a *delicious* breakfast. They decided on marriage, one that *could be made as holy and complete as the most conventional marriages, if not more so.* Returning to their room, they read the marriage ceremony aloud to one another. *We lingered and loved and rested, and felt there could be no end to the desires which arose.*

If Mary's life were a movie, perhaps this is where it would end. *(Oh, yes,* she writes, *there came a break, but our union lasted much longer than most marriages do nowadays.)* I want to trap them there, two lovers, united, falling into bed, the kind of lesbian happily-ever-after I so rarely get to see in history books. Sex isn't a qualification for being a lesbian and neither, certainly, is marriage, but isn't it nice to see every once in a while? I allow myself a few more pages of Mary's book, testing how long I can savor it. There is the couple moving in together in a furnished New York City apartment and adopting a cocker spaniel, Mary giving up her business to start another private schoolroom so she doesn't have to travel and can fully settle in with Juno. The death of Mary's father

brought them even closer together. Juno and Mary moved back to the farm where Mary grew up, where she was abused by the neighborhood boys. *Juno and Mother loved each other from the very first. To her death, my mother was always happy in our love and friendship for each other.* This is the kind of ending I would want for Alcott's Jo and perhaps, even, for myself. Yet I still had over sixty pages to go, and I could already tell that it was not to be a happy ending, for Mary or for love.

A life in love was still a double life for Mary. The newlyweds set up a joint bank account and invited over male friends so that it would look to the rest of the world as though they had male suitors. Friends looked upon their union with jealousy, seeing it as an *ideal friendship*, but *no one knew of the real union, of our bodies.* Mary often played the role of protector, once pushing a man into the mud so her Juno could get a seat on the streetcar. She arranged more date night outings to the theater, a place that had always been a refuge for her, one where the roles she had tried so hard to play in real life—woman, wife, mother—were finally made explicit and, once rendered visible, could be more easily transgressed. There are even moments when she wonders what kind of life she would have had if she had not spent so much time fighting her nature and concludes that it might have been the life of an artist, a painter or an actor or a musician.

Mary and Juno went several times to see an actress who was particularly skilled at impersonations. *When she appeared as a young man we were both fascinated. She took the part to perfection and was more than attractive to us.* These kinds of onstage gender swaps, both in the form of male and female impersonators, became popular at the tail end of the Victorian period, in part because audiences were eager to see the rigid gender roles of the era turned on their heads. Mary and Juno recognized themselves in this actress, Little Ben, or L.B. for short.

Finally, on what might have been their third or fourth or ninth time at the show, they worked up the courage to send her flowers, violets, perhaps, along with a little note asking to meet after the show. They

told L.B. where they would be sitting, so that she could look them over. After the now familiar performance, an usher guided them backstage, where the star sat smoking, an activity deemed unsuitable for women at the time, with her *best girl*. L.B. *insisted* her admirers stay on for dinner in her suite, and the young couple eagerly accepted. During the meal, they *were very careful not to betray by word or glance that our relationship was more than that of good friends*, yet, at the same time, they also couldn't help but wonder if L.B. shared something similar with her *best girl*. Mary was so convinced she was the only real, live lesbian that she could not see what was staring her right in the face.

~~~~

My encounter with L.B. was not the first time I had crossed paths with a woman from the era dressed in men's clothing. When I explained the archive I was building to a *New York Times* editor over lunch, she suggested I search the paper's archives for the phrase *male garb*. She followed up after the meal with a series of PDF attachments, scans of microfiche archives laden with heavily serifed font and four-part headlines, stories from across the Western Hemisphere—Wisconsin, North Dakota, West Virginia, Paris, London, Montreal—that spanned several decades, from the second half of the nineteenth century into the 1920s. I opened the first file.

### *Ella Wesner Lies in Man's Garb*

A story from New York. An obituary. Ella was a stage actress and "one of the first women to win recognition on the stage as a male impersonator." She easily could have been Mary's enchanting L.B. The nearly four decades Ella spent onstage, adopting characters like the "Swell," the "Dude," and the "Captain," opened a space where it was safe—and even profitable—to defy gender norms. But Ella didn't confine her "man's garb" to the stage. "It was said that throughout her

life Miss Wesner had preferred man's apparel." In fact, men's clothes were so much a part of her that not only did she carry out her daily life inside their seams, she also insisted she be buried in them.

Other women put on *male garb* for everyday use in order to access the jobs and spaces that were typically available only to the men of their day.

## GIRL IN MALE GARB TRIES TO SEE FIGHT

*Fans at the Moran-Palzer Contest Detect Her Curls as They Peep from Under Her Cap.*

### GETS HYSTERICAL IN CROWD

*Men Crush Her to See Her Confusion—She is Fiancee of Jack Britton, She Tells the Police.*

## DRESSED AS A MAN TO EARN HER LIVING

*Ten Years' Masquerade of 19-Year-Old Marion Hamilton-Grey Exposed by Her Arrest*

### MAGISTRATE SETS HER FREE

*No Evidence at Hand That She Professed to Be Heir to the Dukedom of Hamilton, as Detective Alleged*

The headlines alone read like items pulled from a police blotter or salacious true crime story. These two women were wanted for their crimes—entering a men's-only boxing match and posing as someone's heir—but it was their choice of outfit that made the news. Their stories reveal a nascent attitude toward queerness, a swift, dark current running counter to the accepted romantic friendships, one that sought to

locate it on the body, something that could be criminalized and then removed, as easily as a costume.

Margaret O'Connor, eighteen years old, put on a man's "raincoat and a cap of bright colors" to watch the Moran-Palzer prizefight at St. Nicholas Rink in New York City. A young boy spotted the long curls peeking out from under her cap and shouted, "It's a girl!" His revelation caused such a commotion that Detective Rose arrested her, and "hundreds in the throng deserted the fight to follow the young woman to the West Sixty-eighth Street Station." Outraged "not only to miss seeing the fight but to be humiliated," Margaret defended herself to the lieutenant. She had wanted to see her fiancé, "a well-known lightweight," fight in the ring, a simple wish that she had been granted out on the "Pacific Coast." "You have no respect for women here." Margaret was ultimately charged with "impersonating a person of the opposite sex" and dismissed with "a lecture on deportment." The record of Margaret's arrest, one constructed without her consultation, suggests that for her, men's clothes were a disguise inexpertly worn to serve a purpose, one that had little to do with her fiancé—who had perhaps even lent her the raincoat—her sexuality, or her gender identity.

The news story about Marion Hamilton-Grey, who "dressed as a man to earn her living," hints at more complex motives for wearing men's clothing. After receiving several tips about an impostor claiming to be the "heir to the Dukedom of Hamilton in Scotland" with a hotel debt to his name, Detectives McKenna and Cassassa tracked him down on Twenty-Fourth Street and Eighth Avenue. At the sound of her voice, Detective Cassassa realized Marion wasn't a man at all.

"I never said I wasn't," Marion responded. She went on to explain that she had adopted men's clothing at the advice of a friend, "as an easier means of making her living." The plan not only allowed her to earn a better income but also to purchase fifty acres and become a

landowner. Like Margaret, she was charged with "masquerading in men's clothing."

While there weren't any laws on the books in the nineteenth century that specifically targeted queer people—perhaps, in part, because there were few names for us at the time—police still found ways to use other laws to arrest vulnerable people who transgressed the gender and sexuality norms. When these people were brought to court, they were charged using a bastardization of New York state's Masquerade Law. "The statute was based on an older law that was enacted in 1845 as a way to prosecute upstate New York farmers who rioted and fought off tax collectors while dressed in faux–Native American garments." In spite of the specificity of its origins, the law was interpreted liberally to punish people whose gender presentation defied the era's rigid standards, regardless of whether they were committing another crime.

What then, exactly, was Marion's crime? Wearing men's clothing? Masquerading as a man to earn more money and acquire property? Perhaps it was a deeper threat to the social order that the law didn't yet know how to name. In his comprehensive study of queer life in Brooklyn before the Stonewall Riots, *When Brooklyn Was Queer*, historian Hugh Ryan encourages contemporary readers of cross-dressing arrest stories to look past the often-utilitarian reasons that were given for wearing *male garb*. "While they cross-dressed to gain employment," he writes, "they did so in part because their gender presentation was already so at odds with what was expected of them."

The blotter item goes on to mention that Marion "made a handsome youth in her boy's clothing." Perhaps Marion was someone I might have seen at a bar and fantasized about taking home with me, all the while feeling too shy to make my approach. Perhaps she was someone who loved outside the bounds of a traditional early twentieth-century marriage. "I wouldn't be surprised to learn that a wealthy widow of Newark was behind this," she told authorities in response to the accusation that she had been masquerading as an heir

to a dukedom. "She fell in love with me and never forgave me when I wouldn't marry her." Perhaps some part of Marion loved the wealthy widow back. Perhaps some part of her was lesbian.

"One of the most interesting things I've found," *The New York Times* editor had told me about her collection, "is a whole bunch of pieces about women living together at the turn of the century, and no one really made a big deal about it." *Romantic friendships*, I thought. "Sometimes the fact that two women were living together only came up in someone's obituary. It wasn't odd at all." Several of the articles she sent me from the paper's archives showcased these relationships.

## FEMALE HUSBANDS

### MURRAY HALL FOOLED MANY SHREWD MEN
#### How for Years She Masqueraded in Male Attire.

**HAD MARRIED TWO WOMEN**

*Was a Prominent Tammany Politician and Always Voted— Senator Martin Astonished*

### HER "HUSBAND" A WOMAN.

*Colorado Girl Says They Wished to Earn an Education*

Scholar Jen Manion makes a study of these figures in *Female Husbands: A Trans History*. "Though assigned female at birth, female husbands assumed a legal, social, and economic position reserved for men: that of husband." Manion examines these female husbands through the lens of trans identity, the way they *transed* and moved across the gender binary, regardless of what identity label—trans, nonbinary, lesbian, butch—they might have chosen if presented with the bouquet

of options we have today. Their partners, Manion points out, also upended the social order in choosing a female husband, rather than a male husband, as a partner. These female husbands made headlines when they were outed either by a scorned lover or a suspicious community member, and their stories made the perfect fodder for local daily newspapers, which were expanding rapidly both in circulation and influence.

Mary Casal's college education and position as a white woman firmly in the upper middle class allowed her to hide her relationships with women in plain sight under the guise of romantic friendship, an alibi so airtight that Mary's own mother didn't protest when Flo told her of their relationship, and also to evade the kind of public scrutiny and ensuing punishment that female husbands of lower classes faced.

Was Mary a female husband? Maybe. The popular newspaper term never turns up in the manuscript, but those headlines, and Manion's analysis of the genre, open an avenue for observing not just Mary's love of Juno but also her personal gender expression. The spark that had ignited when she played games outside with the boys as a child flickered within her as she grew into adulthood. *I looked at life through a man's eyes . . . The masculine role was the one which appealed to me far more than that of female, which I had been trying to play and with such little success.* She identified her *role* in her relationship with Juno as *that of the male.* It was a role she had played before, onstage opposite Mrs. Barr-Jones, to critical acclaim from *all the summer girls and the winter ones, too,* [who] *begged me to keep on my costume of the play.*

Of course Mary was drawn to L.B. She, too, had tried her hand at male impersonation and had suffered no consequences for her time in *male garb.*

~~~

After several weeks of chaste dinners with their new friend, weeks when neither Mary nor Juno dared broach the question of whether

L.B. and her *best girl* had a union of both body and spirit, their unspoken question still remained unanswered when L.B. had to leave for her next gig out west. The day of her departure, on a train bound for San Francisco, Mary and Juno went to see her off at Grand Central. L.B. left the young couple a parting gift. There, amid all the hustle and bustle, the comings and goings of the trains and their passengers, they found a *tearful* young lady. She was called Smith, and L.B. asked the two women to take care of her, at least for the night.

Smith's first request that evening was that the covert couple take her along to Brooklyn, to see another friend. Together they made the journey and, *upon arriving*, were greeted at the door by *a little woman with short, black hair tinged with gray, wearing heavy white silk pajamas, smoking and, very hospitable. Phil,* Mary called her host, *short for Philosopher. She looked us through, and I knew at once that she too knew! At last, and too late, did I find that I was not a creature apart as I had always felt.* Mary was not alone in the world. *We saw her frequently and we became warm friends.*

I long for a seat at these lesbian soirées, hosted in Brooklyn a century before I arrived. What was everyone drinking? Did they dance cheek to cheek? And, most importantly, who went home with whom? Yet again, Mary refuses to give me what I want. She has eyes only for Juno. Even after stumbling into this community of queer women, Mary still sees her relationship with Juno, *the purest and most ideal of any type of union known*, as setting her apart from her new friends. *She was my child, my sister, my sweetheart, my wife, my pal, my friend.* Where they are loyal, her new friends, including the famous actress L.B., are promiscuous. Even worse to Mary are the male "inverts," whom she sees as motivated only by sex.

One of the first scientific terms for queer people, *invert* was used to describe men who were attracted to other men and adopted any traditionally feminine habits, thus inverting their gender. Doctors of the era conflated gender and sexuality, capturing gay men, trans

women, and intersex people under one term. No matter the identity
of those caught in the diagnosis, it was always a derogatory label for
them. Mary is careful to align herself with the acceptability of roman-
tic friendship rather than this inversion, a subject doctors were just
beginning to study.

In spite of her insistence that her relationship with Juno was a
cut above, the pair was not immune to wandering eyes. Juno's affairs
could fill a novel all their own. My own love for Mary grows with
each of Juno's betrayals. First, there is the young woman they both
befriended at a summer boarding house, Mollie. Then Jack, a local
French teacher twelve years her junior, who eventually became her
fiancé. A young Irish woman, then a married man.

The final pages of Mary's autobiography rush by in a series of
fights and estrangements, fraught reconciliations, months spent living
together in resentment. The plot becomes so incredible that I would
not have been at all surprised had Peter made a sudden reappearance
to once again whisk away Mary's beloved. Truth, they say, is stranger
than fiction.

*Even now I can feel the physical pain in my heart as I heard those
words!* she writes. I feel suddenly protective of Mary. I cannot bear to
repeat it all, to put her through it once again.

Instead, this is the image of Mary I want to endure: Heartsick, she
once again goes on a solitary journey, this time boarding a boat bound
for England, where she plans to stay in a cottage with Phil and an-
other friend of hers, *an artist of note* whose *idea of curing broken hearts
was with alcohol.* Standing by the rail, the wind tugging at her hair
and her skirts, part of her must have already known that she would
never love anyone the same way again. *I will always look upon those
years with my beloved Juno as the most perfect that anyone could have,
and worth all the suffering they have brought into my life.*

*Courage failed me when I saw the big ocean with no land in sight, so
I held on to life.*

~~~

Somewhere along the way, I fell for Mary. Hard. Where she enjoys wooing, I love to be wooed. I prickle at every bunch of violets she buys for another woman. Her words of adoration bite at the back of my neck, nip at the pit of my stomach. I love her in an obsessive way that perhaps only astrology can explain. My Scorpio to her Gemini is one of the most toxic matches in the zodiac. I memorize every detail, catalogue her life, piece it together on the page until it becomes an archive. This is also how I love the living: to the point of possession.

There are pieces of Mary that still escape me: the patent for the toy that brought her to New York, likely filed under a male alias; an article about her teaching said to have run in the *Evening Sun*; a photo of her, any photo, perhaps tucked into the yearbook of the Massachusetts schoolhouse where she taught. I never could find a review of the book, or evidence that it had, in fact, been the namesake of the Stonewall Inn and the pivotal riots that happened there. Would a clear connection between the two have been enough to lift Mary out of obscurity, to secure her place in history as a lesbian hero?

I wanted more. I wanted all of her.

Grasping at leads, I reached out to Hugh Ryan, the chronicler of queer Brooklyn, who wrote not just about women who made headlines for dressing as men but also about the object of my affection, Mary Casal. In his book, he mentions a dissertation that came out of the drama department at Tufts University, unmasking Mary Casal and the other women in her orbit. I read Sherry A. Darling's dissertation, "A Critical Introduction to The Stone Wall: An Autobiography," at my parents' house, gasping every few pages at her revelations, as if it were a detective novel or a thriller, and brushing off their questions about what I was reading. Mary Casal was born Ruth White Fuller on June 17, 1864, and later took her husband's name, becoming Ruth Fuller Field. Her chosen pen name, Casal, "is a Portuguese word meaning 'a married couple; a pair, male and female.'" Mary (I

will always think of her that way, a persona, a character dreamed up for the printed page) once again highlights the duality in her life—the public self she wrote about and the private life she lived; the male and female traits she adopted with equal ease.

Ruth wrote Mary into being at the behest of Eyncourt Press, a private imprint in Chicago run by two men moonlighting as publishers: Douglas C. McMurtrie, who worked by day at a typography company and wrote frequently about homosexuality for medical periodicals, though he himself was not a doctor; and Samuel Putnam, who worked at a New York City publishing house and likely brought his business know-how to the partnership. As attitudes toward homosexuality shifted, a new market for books on the topic opened up, fueled by the free publicity generated by the Comstock laws, which banned the trade of such explicit materials. The end of Mary's life saw the days when society smiled politely on romantic friendships coming to a close. No longer was queerness seen as something worn on the body in the form of "male garb" or other transgressions in gender presentation but as a medical condition that perhaps had deeper roots in the physical body. Publishers, independent and professional alike, stepped in to satiate the curiosity of both a clinical and a general audience.

"The 'Lesbian' manuscript I told you about has come in," McMurtrie wrote to his business partner in 1929. I grinned to see the word that never once appeared in Mary's published narrative. Darling suspects that McMurtrie may have excised it from the book, as subsequent letters state that he had to edit out the more explicit parts of the manuscript, and Mary's original has yet to be found. "It is not a great manuscript all the way through," he continues in another letter, and I bristle with the urge to defend Mary, "but it includes the faithful description of female love affairs more convincing in detail than any I have ever [cross-out] read."

In an incredible feat of historical sleuthing, Darling used the

location of Mary's sister's home, the one where Mary had spent such joyful seasons smitten with her *summer girl*, described as *enjoined* to that of the *Governor of Massachusetts*, to uncover the real names of Mary's sister, Mary herself, and the women she loved through the use of property records. Other identities unfolded from there. The male impersonator L.B. was, in fact, a woman named Johnstone Bennett, and the Philosopher "Phil" was Vittoria Cremers, an Italian woman who was "the illegitimate daughter of a wealthy Englishman."

Mary's beloved, the character of Juno, was a woman named Emma Altman. Darling confirmed her ties to Mary through a family address book uncovered in Mary's hometown of Deerfield, Massachusetts. Darling had also searched for the couple at the New-York Historical Society, which houses the papers of Helen Gould, a philanthropist who employed both women. "While Ruth Fuller Field's name does not appear anywhere in the manuscript collection, there are several letters signed by a personal secretary named Elizabeth Altman from the period in which they were in Gould's service." There is no one left alive to tell us, me and Sherry both, whether Emma was simply a nickname for Elizabeth or if this Elizabeth was someone else altogether. There is so much we'll never know.

"How strange it is to retrace someone's life so intimately," Darling writes, "and still not know what she looks like."

~~~~~

My research appointment at the New-York Historical Society fell on a frigid January day. I insisted on riding my bike, dragging her onto the ferry to cross the dozen or so miles between my house and the archives. I arrived already tired, fingers numb. Three accordion boxes waited for me, a full day's work. Darling hadn't found anything here after tedious hours sifting through Helen Gould's correspondence, but perhaps I could, proving once and for all my love for Mary was made of stronger stuff.

I sat stiff in my chair and read letter after letter. Letters to Helen from female admirers, ledger sheets accounting how many children she had helped, a typewritten note about the status of her refrigerator shipment with the Pittsburgh, Cincinnati, and St. Louis Railroad. Many of them were written in a slanted, indecipherable cursive. I lifted the letters off the table to squint into the ink. When that didn't work, I dropped them down into my lap, as if the distance would bring me clarity. A watchful librarian came over and tapped the edge of my desk. "You must keep the letters on the desk," she chided. I snapped photos with my cell phone to enlist my father's help with the handwriting, one of his many areas of expertise after a Catholic boyhood. He drew my attention to the penciled instructions in the top margin on many of the letters. Instructions to the secretaries about how to respond. Did these letters—this one, a request for Helen's help with an entry about her father, Jay Gould, in a Texas history book—pass through Mary's hands?

Sometime after lunch, I found her. Not Mary, but Juno, or rather, this woman who might be Juno, Elizabeth Altman. She wrote a series of letters on behalf of Miss Gould to Father T. J. Earley of the Roman Catholic Church in Irvington, New York, dated Halloween 1903. The purple mimeographed copies reveal just one side of a dispute about whether children should be fed sandwiches and the decision to read scripture aloud at sewing school. "The children need not have taken the sandwiches if they did not approve of them, but there can be no choice about hearing the Bible." At such a remove, there is something comical about the precision of her language, the preservation of such a small, petty disagreement. I laughed, and then looked around the room. There was no one to share in it.

If I had been Helen, I would have written letters only about the lesbians in my employ: "I caught the secretaries kissing today." Perhaps those very words are hiding in the cursive I can't read. Sherry was right—nothing here beyond my imaginings.

In the fourth folder of the first box, I found a detailed report of Helen's comings and goings from the Kirkside School in Roxbury, New York. Determined, I read every cramped line. "August 7, 1902. Miss Gould was accompanied by Miss Elizabeth Altman and Mrs. Ruth Fuller Field." Their true names, linked in the record book. I wanted to stand in the library and shout. I wanted to take out my pencil and add the word *lesbians* next to their names for all to see. It would have created a more useful archive than this dry report. I still feared the librarians. I held back.

Fueled by my discovery, I kept going. In 1900, Miss Gould was to give an inspirational address to the soldiers on Christmas. On November 22 that year, she wrote a short note to Mrs. Field to telephone a Mr. Miller to get his feedback on a draft of the speech. My heart beat faster. I turned over the stout piece of cardstock. There. A note in stiff cursive I could actually read. Signed, R. F. Field. Not just her name but her handwriting, something akin to the intimacy of a photograph. Words she had created by her own hand. Tears pricked my eyes.

So much of what I knew about Mary, about the lesbians of her era, came filtered through lurid headlines and the editorial notes of crass publishers. Stories were passed down through subterfuge, fact obscured by fiction, a way to protect the author while still putting the words out into the world: Gertrude Stein's *Autobiography of Alice B. Toklas*, her life's story written from the perspective of her life partner; Radclyffe Hall, publishing many personal experiences as fiction in *The Well of Loneliness*; Louisa May Alcott, doing the same with *Little Women*; Mary Casal, publishing her autobiography under a pseudonym, with all the names changes.

But here she was, Mary, Ruth, R. F. Field, untouched by other hands. She led me here. To the New-York Historical Society. To Juno, and to the community of queer women the couple stumbled upon. To the male impersonator Johnstone Bennett and to Vittoria "Philosopher" Cremers, to the professor's wife Flo, and to that unnamed

Extracts | NEW YORK TIMES HEADLINES
FEATURING FEMALE HUSBANDS

"Female Husbands"

(November 4, 1883)

"Murray Hall Fooled Many Shrewd Men.

How for Years She Masqueraded in Male Attire.

Has Married Two Women.

Was a Prominent Tammany Politician and Always Voted"

(January 19, 1901)

"Her 'Husband' A Woman.

Colorado Girl Says They Wished to Earn an Education"

(September 21, 1913)

"Mother Says 'Jack' Really Is 'Lena.'

Girl Who Was to Wed Girl Always Wore
Boy's Clothes When She Could.

Fiancée Wouldn't Credit It.

Came to Home in Search of Betrothed and
Insisted on the Ceremony"

(August 11, 1921)

"Girl posed as Man 2 Years and Married"

(December 16, 1921)

"Woman Lived as Man, Wed to One of Her Sex.
'Peter Stratford,' Married to Beth Rowland, Reveals Secret
Before Death at Oakland, Cal."

(May 4, 1929)

2.

In the Life:
Mabel Hampton and Lillian Foster

(1932–1978)

I WENT LOOKING FOR MABEL HAMPTON ON A FRIDAY AF-
ternoon, not yet spring, dusk and a quiet snow falling all around me.
From the 1920s into the early 1930s, Mabel rented three rooms *on the
ground floor—a bedroom, a living room, and a big kitchen—for $10 a
week* at 120 West 122nd Street. The building has since been demol-
ished, but I went anyway, determined to find something, a shadow, a
spirit, some trace of the dancer, the activist, the Black *stud* who *never
felt ashamed of being a lesbian*, something physical to tie me to the
voice that had kept me company through the winter months.

The brownstones of East Harlem were lit up from within, cur-
tains pulled like a smile, warm interiors grinning back. Overburdened
bookcases. Stained glass windows set with jewel tones. Spindly lamps
that cast a soft glow over couches and armchairs, tables where families
began to gather for the evening meal.

I had a new lover in tow, our fingertips frozen white and stuffed
into the pocket of my parka, a lover I hoped to impress with my

knowledge of lesbians long gone. I wished for a blazer with elbow patches, a pocket square to wipe the flurries from my glasses, anything to give my lecture the illusion of belonging to the official record.

Too wrapped up in each other, we blew past the spot. A monument behind a set of brownstone gates caught my eye: a little iron statue of a woman holding a child. We stopped to study the placard. Funded by both Yoko Ono and Donald Trump, it was built in honor of another of the block's former residents. Not Mabel. We backtracked. I followed our glowing blue dot on the map until it led us to where 120 once stood. We looked up at the building that has since taken its place, the Hans Christian Andersen Complex, home to a public school. We paced the block arm in arm. I recited the facts I could remember about Mabel.

"She hated oral sex," I said. "It was too overwhelming. *If you don't be just so, it'll kill you.*" We found it too soft. Pleasant, but not enough.

At the end of the block, we spun around, too cold to let go of each other.

"This is where Mabel came to live after she got out of prison," I said. "This is where she brought her girlfriend, Lillian Foster, to live. Only four weeks after they met."

"The original U-Haulers," they joked. I laughed. I was looking for Mabel because I wanted to know how she did it, how she made it work with her partner, Lillian Foster, for over forty years, more years than I had been alive. I was looking because I knew I'd never live with my lover, because I knew that, like this season of snow, it couldn't last.

After more turns of the block than I could count, nose runny from the cold, we paused for one last look at the unremarkable spot where Mabel once lived. I closed my eyes against the streetlamps and the passing headlights and tried to imagine what it had been like during the Harlem Renaissance, to hear the rattle of the streetcars and the sound of her voice—the way she aspirated her *W*s, how her voice grew louder at the end of a sentence—filling the block. When I opened

them again, there was my lover's face, hands brushing the snow from my hair. They laid their frozen fingers against my cheek and leaned in to mark this spot with the only tools we had around. Lip to lip, we marked the spot with a kiss. And another. And another.

~~~~~

The life of Mabel Hampton, a Black working-class lesbian, spanned almost the entirety of the twentieth century. She bore witness to and participated in both world wars, the Great Depression, the civil rights movement, and the fight for gay liberation. Mabel is perhaps best remembered by history as a daughter of the Great Migration and a dancer during the Harlem Renaissance. Her *New York Times* obituary, little more than two column inches, celebrates her as a "Gay Rights Advocate" and the Grand Marshall of the Pride March in 1985.

I see a different side of her. Everywhere I find a trace of Mabel, she is always among women.

That's her in the black-and-white photo, rehearsing with a dance troupe on the Coney Island boardwalk. The four teenage girls wear matching dresses with skinny shoulder straps, white trim, and dark skirts that end just above the knees. It's Mabel's voice, her laugh, that fills up the apartments where the queer women of Harlem hosted rent parties with big buffets and pillows strewn across the floor, a charge at the door to help pay the landlord. That same voice echoes in the cavernous rooms of the white ladies' apartments she is paid to clean, one of the only options for her to earn a living as a Black woman without a husband. That's her slanted cursive on holiday cards, vacation postcards, and a series of letters she wrote to friends and family while in prison. So many of these notes were addressed to women. And there Mabel is next to Lillian, always Lillian.

Mabel extended her lesbian love beyond this traditional pairing, though, to a broad community of people living alongside her *in the life*, a phrase she uses time and again as a descriptor for other queer

people. Before mutual aid was a trend, it was something Mabel practiced without much thought, whether she was sharing money with her neighbors for their rent or exchanging care and support with the women she met in jail. This love for an entire community of lesbians became tangible when she helped found the Lesbian Herstory Archives, a place where lesbian stories live on, unfiltered by newspaper reporters or doctors, where they don't have to hide behind pseudonyms or subterfuge. It's where Mabel's story lives, just as she wanted to tell it. She was interviewed for a series of oral history tapes by her friend Joan Nestle, another founder of the Lesbian Herstory Archives, who introduces herself on the mic as a "white, working-class-born, Jewish-born lesbian." I listen in no particular order and let Mabel's story, just as she remembers it, wash over me.

There's Mabel in a *gray dress that buttons down the front, black stockings,* and *oxfords.* Summer, 1924. Greeted on her first day at the Bedford Hills Correctional Facility for Women in upstate New York by a group of strangers.

"*Oh, you're a kid. Come on in,*" said *a tall, good-looking, brown-skinned woman* of *about thirty years old. She hollered over her shoulder,* "*Look what we got here.*"

"*I hope you can stand the pressure,*" said another *one of the girls.*

"*Well if she can't, I'll take care of her.*"

"*God,*" thought Mabel, alarmed by the chorus of women in front of her. "*I'm in for it now, what am I going to do?*"

"*Now don't cry, cause nobody's gonna hurt ya.*"

"*No, not while you're here,*" said *one in the back of the room.*

It had begun on July 4, when Mabel traveled from her home in Jersey City to Manhattan to attend the cabaret with one of her girlfriends, Viola. At the show, a man who looked like a true gentleman approached the two women and invited them out to dinner. From the start, Viola was smitten with the stranger, and Mabel was smitten with Viola. They accepted his invitation. Mabel gave the address of

her employer, Virginia K. Howard, who considered her housekeeper of two years "an efficient servant, obliging, neat about her work and person and honest."

As promised, the gentleman came around again the very next night with a friend in tow to pick up Mabel and Viola for a double date. Mabel noticed that the newcomer *had a belt on and this belt, a watch was made into this belt . . . I never forgot it.*

When Mabel opened the door into the New York City night, though, she discovered *two great big men and a cop.*

*"What do you want?"* she asked.

"We're *raiding the houses*," he replied.

*"For what reason?"*

*"Prostitution . . . We'll have to take you down."* The gentleman at the cabaret and the promise of a double date had been nothing more than a setup.

In the early 1920s, New York City was caught in the grip of two opposing forces. Bohemians were eager to cast off the shackles of decency and morality they had inherited from the Victorian era and walk through the door flung open by Freud to explore their sexuality. Alongside this rise in shared pleasure came an equal but opposite force that sought to enforce law and order, both on the streets and in the privacy of the home. For those who chose to stand on the side of law and order, there was money to be had.

A woman on the street without a man was an easy target for a *stool pigeon* to set up as a prostitute. What reason did she have to be on the street alone, and what man would turn up to defend her honor? Black women were an even easier target. "Every black woman was a prostitute in the eyes of the law," writes Saidiya Hartman in her choral history of the lives and communities Black women built around the turn of the century, *Wayward Lives, Beautiful Experiments: Intimate Histories of Social Upheaval*. In the wake of the failed promises of both emancipation and the Great Migration, Black women had

few options for employment. Many of them became domestic work-ers. "Who didn't hate domestic work? No colored woman would ever forget that it carried the taint of slavery." Some turned to prostitution, which had its own violent consonance with the slave trade. For Black bodies, the legacy of the traffic in women meant their literal sale, not into marriage but into slavery, to be used however the white man chose. Hartman's portrait brings to light how for many Black women, regardless of occupation, forces beyond their control—poverty, abuse, infidelity—denied them the opportunity to build traditional families. Under the law, anything other than man and wife could easily be made to look like prostitution.

Mabel spent the night in jail, and in the morning she appeared before Judge Jean Norris, a *very striking white woman*. Like the *stool pigeons* who ensnared Mabel, Judge Norris had made a living off the promise of bringing decency and morality to the streets of New York City. In trying to make good on that promise, she had gone crooked. *It's a damn shame that she's a judge.* Despite serving as the first female magistrate in the city, "she prided herself on the number of women she found guilty on vice charges," reported *The New York Times*. Norris was disbarred in 1931 for altering records. But not before she found Mabel guilty and sentenced her to three years at Bedford Hills.

Mabel quickly settled into the rhythms of prison life. *It's early, you have to get up and wash up and get dressed.* She was surprised to find Bedford mornings *beautiful*, the way the sun shone in through the windows, the *front yard* with *chairs sitting around. It was beautiful out there.* After *breakfast—they had good food, always did—we would go back and make our beds and sit around and talk.*

Even after *two or three days*, Mabel's fellow inmates continued to *whisper* about the newcomer.

"*Don't pay those girls any mind*," one girl encouraged her. "*Those dykes don't mean anything.*"

*What the hell does she mean by dykes?* Mabel wondered, but *didn't*

*say nothing.* Even if Mabel had never heard the word before, she already knew a thing or two about women. *I had messed around with a couple girls in Jersey City.* A woman at the Christian aid society working to set up Mabel's parole, Amy M. Prevost, wrote to the prison superintendent, Dr. Amos T. Baker, that back in New York City, Mabel had been "very much infatuated with a middle aged colored woman."

One of the inmates, perhaps able to sense this history, invited Mabel out for a walk around the *beautiful* yard.

"*Any of the girls up here you like?*" she asked. *She took my hand and guided me along.* "*You don't know me," she says, "my name is Ruth. I know yours. You're Mabel.*"

Slowly, Ruth worked to make her own intentions known. She *put her arm around me and says, "I like you.*"

"*Yeah, all right," I said. "I like you too.*"

"*You wanna come sleep in my bed tonight?*"

"*I don't know.*"

"*You'll come and sleep in my bed.*"

They carried on like this, all words, until one summer day when they shared an ice cream in the yard.

"*I don't know whether you like me the way I like you,*" Ruth said.

"*No, I guess not.*"

Ruth took Mabel back to her bed to find out. *She held me in her arms and she kissed me. I wasn't so big. I was little, much smaller than I am now.* But nothing was resolved that evening. *I went to sleep.*

"Say the truth, Mabel."

It is Joan Nestle's voice that interrupts Mabel's story on the tapes. Joan is an interviewer who always presses down on the narrative to squeeze out something more. She met Mabel in 1950, at age twelve, when Mabel, already fifty-two, came to work as a domestic for Joan's mother, Regina. Decades later, Joan recorded this series of oral history interviews with Mabel, all before I was born. In a different life, I would have been able to hold the cassette tapes in my hands, to push

my pinky into the rollers, to wind and unwind Mabel's life. Now all the tapes, thirty-four in total, two sides each, holding just as many hours of sound, have been digitized, and I can listen in bed, pretending that it is Mabel, not the computer, who keeps the other side warm. Some of the audio has been ruined, the ribbon warped with voices loud and blurred, as impossible to read as Helen Gould's correspondence, written in cursive and housed at the New-York Historical Society. Mabel and her interviewers sound like they're calling me from the beach, sitting in the wind, rushing farther and farther from the mic to chase an umbrella tumbling down the shore. *I can't hear so good,* Mabel says, the sounds around her dulled by aging ears. "I can't hear you, either," I whisper back. She is interrupted by the *trill* of a phone, rotary, I'm sure, the yap of a dog, perhaps her own, Liberation. Libby, *I tell you, she's a bad girl.*

I listen intently on those dark winter mornings, a season spent falling in love, half of my heart to the woman who lived on West 122nd, now just a voice at my ear, half to the person, flesh and blood, lips and salt, who stood with me before the ghost of number 120. I rewind the tape to catch the name of a song, and again to discern the title of a play, to make sure I have recorded Mabel's actual words and not just the syntax I have come to expect. Sometimes, the voices end before the tape plays out. Stubborn in my search—for what, I don't know yet—I listen through to the end, ten, fifteen minutes of scratch and static, in wait of a flare as bright as the pink sun struck against the winter sky.

Joan is there on the tapes too. Mostly, she's the rudder, hanging at the back, keeping the conversation on course. She's even there in the black-and-white photographs that serve as archive album art. My favorite is of the two of them holding each other like ballroom dancers. It's Mabel's birthday, somewhere in her late seventies, and she's dressed as a sailor. Joan has thrown her a birthday party in her Upper West Side apartment, streamers hung across the frame. Joan wears

white slacks that come to Mabel's chest, and she smiles down as the birthday girl pulls a sour frown.

Once, Joan took up the microphone for a solo performance that fills up an entire B side. She was sick. Her head hurt too much to write. Doctors couldn't diagnose her. She worried she was coming to the end of her life and wanted to leave a final message. "I want to tell tales of a lesbian life," she says, her voice high and self-conscious where Mabel's is deep and restless. "I want to talk about the wonderful women I've known, and I want to talk about what it's meant to be a lesbian and how it was at the core of all I think that was best in me."

When Joan sat down to record this tape, she had already begun to collect tales of the wonderful women and lesbians she had known. In 1974, she cofounded the Lesbian Herstory Archives with Mabel Hampton and two other women dedicated to preserving lesbian culture before it disappeared. A year later, the budding collection of letters, magazines, cassettes, photographs, and books took up residence at Joan's Upper West Side apartment, where it would continue to grow for the next fifteen years, until the organization raised enough money to purchase a permanent home, a brownstone in Park Slope. Mabel was a fixture at the archives, regaling volunteers with stories of the Harlem Renaissance as they opened the mail.

Joan lived. She went on to record dozens more interviews with Mabel for the archive. Their relationship marked a fundamental shift in how lesbian history was set down and passed along. Until Joan and Mabel, the amateur sexologists who edited Mary Casal's memoir, the police who arrested women in male garb and the courts who put them on trial, and the newspaper editors who reduced their stories to lurid headlines filtered lesbian stories through the gaze of authority. Sheer accident preserved much of what we know, what I can know, about the lesbians who lived at the turn of the century. Their personal letters and pages of poetry left a record so riddled with holes it leaves room to either imagine lesbian stories or discount them entirely.

The state still has a jealous hold on parts of Mabel. The New York State Archives house her prison records: her intake forms, the results of her medical examination, letters in her sloping script that always begin "Just a few lines . . ." In these pages, the staff at Bedford Hills created a racist characterization of Mabel's body and mind, words I choose to redact, the way New York State blacked out the notes on her "General character of home and environment / Association and recreations" before sending me the pages.

By the time Mabel arrived in 1924, Bedford was no longer the site of the tortures and abuses laid bare in a March 19, 1920, *New York Tribune* exposé: "Bedford Cruelty Charges Against Officials Upheld." Not so long ago, women, Black and white alike, had been tied to their cots or handcuffed to their cell bars with their feet dangling inches above the ground. Even if Bedford had reformed, I doubt it was the *good time* Mabel tells Joan it was. *We made whiskey. We made wine . . . We had parties there. Each night you slept with a different woman if you wanted to. Me, I was havin' a ball.* Superintendent Barker saw Bedford Hills not as a center of surveillance, the panopticon of prison we know today, but as a benevolent institution of moral reform, a safe haven away from the dangers and carnal pleasures of the city that might lead any young woman astray.

After serving seven months, Mabel was paroled with a foster family in Jersey City and worked as a domestic nearby. Bedford's hold did not end here, though. The prison was a pipeline feeding domestic labor to well-off white ladies who lived outside the pull of New York City's whirlwind hedonism. Mabel's foster family reported her movements to Dr. Barker, and when she strayed into the City of Pleasure, she had to return to Bedford to continue serving her sentence. Then there was yet another domestic labor parole placement before Mabel's discharge papers arrived in October 1926. "I do not want you to feel that our interest in you ends with the mailing of these papers,"

Superintendent Barker wrote. "It is always my hope that should you at any time experience difficulties, there would be no hesitation on your part in getting in touch with the Institution."

To Bedford Hills, Mabel was always "wild and wayward," in need of reform. Their records are concerned only with the timeline—the dates of her incarceration and release—and the irrelevant facts they were asked to collect—a description of her nose, her IQ. An administrative accumulation we are told comprises a history.

To Joan, Mabel was an "icon," always *Ms.* Hampton, an address of respect never afforded in her prison records or by the wealthy white families, much better off than Joan's, that employed her. Joan tries to pin down the order of her hero's journey—"And what year is this, about? We always try and do the year so people know."—but that's not what Mabel wants us to remember. She can hardly remember it herself. The oral history is the kind of record I crave not for its attention to dates or names or accuracy but for the dialogue. Joan asks the direct questions I wish I could have posed to Mary.

Joan's interview style was shaped by a series of 1970s oral history workshops aimed at empowering people to record queer stories. She spent hours with friends drafting "questions that we thought would elicit the kind of history we wanted. What did you call yourself in the twenties? How did you and your friends dress in the forties? What bars did you go to?" These are not the questions of a doctor intent on diagnosis, or a sociologist intent on reform. If, for instance, W. E. B. Du Bois had drifted from 1890s Philadelphia to Mabel's doorstep while undertaking his 2,500-household survey, he simply would have asked if she was married, single, or widowed. Joan asks instead how Mabel liked to have sex, and Mabel responds with a series of gestures, lost to us now. "They can't see your hands," Joan says. I imagine the middle and pointer fingers of both hands spread wide like legs, meeting at the vertices, the international symbol for scissoring.

Or the same *V* held against her mouth, tongue poking through. But I'm getting lost in my own inventions. The Mabel I have come to know would never have been so lewd.

Joan brings to the tapes an awareness of her own bias, and a reminder of my own. She knows her presence in the room, the framing of her questions alone, shapes what comes out of Mabel's mouth. Joan was raised by a single mother, Regina, who worked as a bookkeeper, who was let out on parole after embezzling money to provide for her daughter, and who remained poor and overworked until the day she died. "I know what it was to be marginal," Joan says into the tape recorder, evidence that she shares some of Mabel's working-class background. "From every eviction notice that was tacked on the door, every time the men came with flashlights to reclaim the beds or the furniture." Still, Joan was first introduced to Mabel as the family housekeeper after Regina first met the "small black Christian woman" not at the Bronx Slave Market, street corners and intersections where Black women hoped to find a day's work cleaning the homes of the wealthy, but at a luncheonette in Bayside, Queens. When Regina couldn't afford the help anymore, the two women became friends and would go to the racetrack together. It was to Mabel that Regina turned when she suspected her own daughter might be a lesbian. "I'm gonna kill myself. My daughter is a lesbian," she said. "Regina," Mabel calmly replied. "What are you talking about? So am I. So am I."

When Joan grew up, she developed a friendship with Mabel all her own. It was a friendship marked by question and answer, call and response, Joan's attempts to understand the lesbians who came before and Mabel's insistence that Joan gets her story right.

"Mabel, I want to ask you a question."

*You already asked me seventy eleven! How many more you gonna ask me?*

~~~~~

I waded through the tapes in search of Mabel's first meeting with Lillian Foster. In the midst of my own messy love story, I yearned for someone else's clean beginning, the start of a love that ended only in death, a relationship held entirely in the embrace of the past tense.

First, though, I met Mabel Hampton at the start. She was born in Winston-Salem, North Carolina, on May 2. Bedford Hills recorded her birth year as 1903, but later in life, when Mabel petitioned the government for her birth certificate, she learned it was, in fact, 1902. How could Mabel be certain of the year when her own mother, Lula Simmons, passed away just a month after giving birth? Mabel never met her father, Joseph Rogers, either. It was her grandmother who passed along the family name Hampton, but that matriarch's first name is lost to history—*I forget right this minute, but I knew. Grandma*, with a little help from her younger daughter, raised Mabel on the family farm, alongside *pigs, vegetables, chickens, turkeys, all kinds of things.*

Shortly before Mabel's eighth birthday, her grandmother had a stroke that left her bedridden. *My Younger Aunt, I'll never forget it, was combing my hair, and I looked over at Grandma laying on the bed. It was in the morning, the sun was up and everything, and all the sudden, she never said too much, she couldn't talk, see, so I kept looking at her. I knew something was wrong with her, see. She looked at me, and I looked at her. My Aunt got through combing my hair. I kept watching Grandma in bed, so she went to see Grandma. Grandma had gone away.*

Mabel's grandmother was gone for good, and so, too, was Mabel's time in Winston-Salem. The deceased's eldest daughter, Mabel's Older Aunt, came down from New York City to pay her respects. When the time came for her to return to the big city—the place Mabel knew only as the origin of the packages that regularly arrived with frilly dresses tucked inside—the family decided that Mabel would go too. There was hardly anyone left on the farm to take care of her.

There's the little girl in the colored section of the northbound train, heels tucked under her bum, face pressed against the windows to soak

up her first glimpse of the world beyond North Carolina. By lunchtime, though, she has already tired of so much newness. She whines, and her aunt hands her a liver sandwich. The soured meat tastes nothing like what they had back on the farm. She wants to go home.

Mabel lasted only a few days in New York City. The Older Aunt lived in the Village at 52 West Eighth Street with her husband, George, a minister, who held services in their apartment. Uncle George *was tall, dark and had the most beautiful wavy hair*, but Mabel saw right through his good looks and righteous ways. She saw him for what he was. *In the back of my head, I knew he was no good, preaching the word of God and living something else.* He beat Mabel in the face with his shoe until *my mouth and things swole all that*, and then, one day when the aunt went out, *he raped me.*

That day, Mabel decided she'd be better off without any blood relations at all. *I said to myself, 'I got to leave here.'* Mabel walked out the door of her uncle's West Village apartment with only the jumper dress she had put on that morning. *And I walked and I walked and I walked.*

Mabel walked to the Hudson and Manhattan Railroad. A stranger gave her train fare. *That was a turning point in my life, that nickel.* She rode the train beneath the streets of Manhattan and under the Hudson River until the conductor shouted, *"All out . . . Jersey City! Grove Street!"* She hopped off. She emerged onto a new street in a new city and laid eyes on a familiar sight: a group of kids playing in the park. *I never had no pleasure since I left Winston-Salem, swing or do anything.* Mabel rushed to join them.

One of the other kids, an Italian girl, already a teenager, noticed Mabel, alone. *"Where's your people?"*

Mabel told the first lie that popped into her head. *"My Aunt told me to stay here until she come and get me."*

The girl turned to her brother. *"Tony,"* she instructed him. *"You go that way, and I go this way. You go after the cop, and I'll go out and see if I can find the Aunt."*

Mabel waited in the park, worried for a moment that it was Tony who would come back first. *I knew if the cop got me, he would take me back to New York, and I'd get beat very badly.* Luckily, it was the Italian girl who returned first, with a young Black woman in tow.

"Where you from?" asked the newcomer. Her name, Mabel would come to learn, was Bessie White. *"How you come to be here?"* Mabel repeated the story she had only just made up, that she was waiting for her aunt. *This woman carried me to her house and she says, "Mama, here's a girl that's got lost. Help her out."* Bessie's mother, Mrs. White, took Mabel into her Jersey City home and into her family as if she were one of her own. During the years Mabel lived there, she grew particularly fond of one of Mrs. White's daughters, Ellen, a *light-brown-skinned woman. She'd put her arm around me and hold me tight. That was grand.*

No matter where Mabel went, she was always getting help from strangers, and she was always crushing on some girl.

~~~~~

*After I met Lillian.* My body tensed on the couch, expectant. Here it was. The moment this larger-than-life woman who lived in my imagination would solidify into soft flesh and warm blood.

*After I met Lillian, I didn't go so much. Her and I was together, and I stayed home. I wanted to take care of her, and her and I be together.*

Before Lillian, there were parties. Before Mabel started a four-decades-long romance, she lived the life of a 1920s Black lesbian bachelor in New York City. Mabel was never a host herself, but she often attended parties at her neighbor's apartment on 122nd Street, where the women served *chitlins, pig's feet, sauerkraut, cole slaw, sauces, bread. They danced up a breeze. They did the Charleston. They did a little bit of everything.*

Sometimes Mabel traveled farther afield to meet other women *in the life.* Joan never asks for a definition of the phrase, but it's one

that crops up again and again to catch nearly everyone in Mabel's orbit. No one in her day used the word *lesbian*—*the words I heard it was women lovers and bulldikers, bulldikers and women lovers*— yet still they managed to find one another. They gathered at the home of A'Lelia Walker, who spent part of the inheritance from her mother, Madam C. J. Walker—the first self-made female million-aire, a fortune earned from her line of hair care products for Black women—on hosting parties in her house *up on the hill, beautiful* for her companions *in the life.* Mabel is flattered to get an invite because *you have to be known in order to get in. On the floor was nothing but pillows.* Mabel stands, though, up by the buffet to chat up the cool kids. There's cabaret singer Florence Mills with her *short, short hair,* who won't quit bragging about her upcoming role in *Shuffle Along* at the Lafayette Theater to anyone who will listen. *A very good-looking girl, see.* Next to her must be male impersonator Gladys Bentley in a white tuxedo and top hat, plate piled high with food. Mabel quickly realizes Gladys is too much of a womanizer to pursue, too much of a *stud* like herself, but could perhaps make a steady friend. Just as much a performer of masculinity offstage as on, Gladys might not even be a woman at all but is still firmly *in the life.* Next in line is Ma Rainey, fan drawn so no one will recognize her as the famous blues singer, so no one will ask her to sing "Prove It on Me Blues": "I went out last night with a crowd of my friends, / It must've been women, 'cause I don't like no men." The lines are a bit of a lie—she does like a man every once in a while—but the words just sounded better this way. If Mabel can stay out late enough, the performer Josephine Baker might drop in, face still done up in stage makeup from dancing in the chorus line.

*They had nice gay parties, and I went to them, but I didn't have to participate in anything they done . . . They wanna drink, get naked . . . That was their business! Not mine.*

Joan's words come to me: "Say the truth, Mabel." Even as the

custodian of her own archive, Mabel is not to be trusted. She polishes her record, blows dust from the grooves, keeps the juiciest parts up the sleeve. A Christian woman in her eighties with a microphone to her mouth, Mabel was slow to admit she *made love a coupla times* with Ruth at Bedford Hills, and now she is shy about her participation in Harlem's private parties of the 1920s. I want for her more than the life of a wallflower. Perhaps she worries that the man with the watch on his belt is lying in wait, just outside Joan's Upper West Side apartment, to set up an old woman for arrest. Perhaps she simply wants the privacy she is due.

Mabel knew she had risked another arrest back when she attended those parties. Queer women came under scrutiny from the moment they left their houses en route to see friends, and even their clothes were policed. *Very seldom that any of them had slacks or anything like that because they had to come through the street.* Like Mary Casal's contemporaries whose male garb made headlines and who were often arrested through an expansive interpretation of the Masquerade Law, queer women on their way to Harlem house parties were expected to wear skirts, dresses, and tailored suits.

Arrival at another queer woman's comfortable apartment wasn't a guarantee of safety, either. In 1925, Ma Rainey, that bisexual blues singer whom I imagined in the buffet line beside Mabel, had invited her chorus girls over for a party. The neighbors overheard the ruckus—the music, the laughter—and filed a noise complaint. When the police arrived, they discovered Ma and her chorus girls fleeing out the back door, struggling to get their clothes on. The girls escaped, but Ma fell on the stairs. The police arrested her for hosting an indecent party and threw her in jail. For those *in the life*, even the boundaries of the domestic sphere weren't a shield from police violence.

I like to think that Mabel was part of Ma's orgy that night, a chorine who got away. *Sometimes I have narrow escapes*, Mabel brags. *Somebody's having a party, Bulldykers party, and I always lucky I got out.*

*The dead takes care of me*, Mabel is fond of saying, *and the living*. She might say it at a moment like this, ascribing her ability to always escape a party on the brink of being raided to the watchful eye of someone who loved her. She never specifies who, exactly, does the caretaking, but when I hear her voice, I can see their faces. Her dead mother and father, nudging her out the back door of Ma's building just in time. *And the living*. Just as likely, it could have been a stranger with a sharp ear and a quick hand who pushed Mabel across the threshold. That stranger would have joined the ranks of the other women, often Black, often lesbians, who lent Mabel a hand. Every time someone steps into Mabel's life hell-bent on using her body for their own gain, from abusive Uncle George with his greedy hands to the man with the watch on his belt looking to make a quick buck, it seems a woman reaches out to lend a hand, to lift her up, to set her down on her feet again. The unnamed Italian girl, offering up a sandwich on the playground in Jersey City. The dykes locked up in Bedford Hills who promised *nobody's gonna hurt ya*. Joan, who shepherds Mabel's story along.

Mabel found another support network of Black women *in the life* when she worked for *a couple of months* as a dancer at the Garden of Joy, a nightclub *up on the hill* in Harlem, near where the Abyssinian Baptist Church still stands today. *They got me in the chorus there, and I could dance pretty good*. She quickly noticed that the clientele was primarily made up of gay men and women. *There were lots of girls there. They were lesbians*.

From a young age, Mabel had been a performer. Not even Uncle George could take that love away from her when he pushed her to sing in the streets for coins he later pocketed. As an adult, she took lessons for five years, and she finally got to keep her earnings. Mabel didn't *like dancing that much*, not nearly as much as singing, but that wasn't for lack of talent. As a girl, she had danced as part of a troupe on Coney Island, that group of four caught in a photograph as they rehearsed

on the boardwalk, one body held aloft by the others' knees. Then the Lafayette Theater in Harlem cast her as a chorus girl in *Come Along, Mandy* in 1924. Nearly a decade before she began attending Harlem's house parties, the theater was where she had first met beloved cabaret singer Florence Mills, who *danced very nicely. She was light-brown-skinned, and she tried to help all the other girls she knew, dark ones, light ones, anybody.* It was also where she learned the code to describe and distinguish the varied skin tones on the stage: *DC: Dark Cloud* for a Black woman, *SJ: Smokey Joe* for a brown-skinned woman, *OF: Old Fay* for a white woman. By 1933, with Florence dead and Mabel already working as a domestic, the Lafayette was floundering, until male impersonator Bert Whitman stepped in with her troupe of sisters to save the day. For all three—Florence, Bert, and Mabel—performing was a way to make money with their bodies that channeled far more joy and far more freedom than cleaning a white woman's house ever could.

Mabel and other women *in the life*, the living who took care of one another, could meet at Harlem's private parties or inside its public clubs. If Mabel had ventured farther from her neighborhood, she would have found a third space in the city to flirt with women, to kiss in the dark: the bars downtown in Greenwich Village. Joan keeps asking Mabel about her experiences at the bars in the Village, and Mabel repeats that she went there *very seldom*. She never says it outright, but Mabel might not have been welcome at the bars because they catered to a predominantly white clientele.

The racial divide between uptown and downtown spaces extended beyond the queer community. At the turn of the century, racial violence downtown had pushed Black communities uptown into Harlem, and from that violent root, poetry, blues music, and house parties flourished. While white queers had their own spaces downtown, lesbian historian Lillian Faderman documents how they also traveled uptown, tourists in the very neighborhood they had chased Black

people into, racists who left their manners and rules and morality behind in pursuit of sexual experimentation with people they cast as savage and liberated. Mabel invited a few tourists to Harlem's house parties. *I had a couple of girls, white girls, from downtown in the Village, and tell them about it and they would come up, see. They were white girls. And we got along fine.* For Mabel, Harlem was simply home.

<center>~~~~~</center>

*When I met Lillian.* I paused the audio, rapt but not ready. I am a rotten historian, consumed to my core by selfish motives. Mabel's life is my link to a wide community of lesbians, an era rich with our recorded history, but what I truly want is for her to guide me through the now, to be the dead who takes care of me, the living. I followed her intently from Harlem living rooms lined with plush pillows and rich buffets to performances at the Garden of Joy to dimly lit bars downtown. All the while, I was thinking of Lillian. I wanted this. I wanted a road map, a recipe for how to find someone who would tolerate me, decade after decade.

*When I met Lillian*, Mabel says, *I was an old woman.*

The two first met in the fall of 1932. She marks the date as September 22 on one tape, and sometime in October on another. No matter the month, Mabel was thirty in 1932. That was nearly my age when I met my frozen-fingered lover. I count it as an auspicious sign.

*I had a girlfriend when I met Lillian.*

Another auspicious sign. My lover had a girlfriend when we first met. My lover still had a girlfriend that snowy evening when we visited Mabel's apartment, a girlfriend who knew about us.

*I was living in New York, and I'd come from New York . . . every day to Jersey*, Mabel explains. *That's why I met Lillian, cause I went to look for another job so that I could stay in New York.*

After Mabel "was granted her discharge from parole" on October 5, 1926, life continued to be marked by the hunt for work. *Right*

*up until I pass away, I'm still working.* She worked as a dancer, and then at a garment factory, sewing on a machine.

(My father's Italian American mother, Diva, sewed zippers at the Pawnee Pants factory in eastern Pennsylvania. Her broad, wrinkled face often pops into my mind, unbidden, when my lover reaches for my waistband. Like Mabel, she loved the opera. When her husband left, she cut his face out of every photo, an index-finger-sized hole in the family archive.)

The day Mabel met Lillian, the garment workers were on strike. Rather than scab, Mabel looked for work elsewhere. She would find it a few days later at a button factory. But this fall day, whenever it was, was a day without work.

Clad in her customary *suit*, Mabel waits for the Lexington Avenue streetcar on a downtown sidewalk thatched with leaves turned gold by the alchemy of the season. She can't help but notice the woman in front of her. *She had on a skirt with a coat over top of it. She was smaller than me, shorter than me.* When the woman whirls around, Mabel looks down at her own *low-heeled* shoes so she won't be accused of staring.

The woman points at a pair of headlights trundling up the road. *"You want to get in that streetcar?"*

*"Yeah, sure I do."*

Lillian holds out a hand to pull Mabel on board. They find two seats tucked in the back and chat away as the street numbers climb. When they enter the hundreds, Mabel grows nervous at the thought of parting ways. Her stop arrives first. Before she gets out, Lillian asks for her address, and she gives *122nd Street* willingly. *She's alright,* Mabel thinks on her walk back to the ground floor apartment. *She's very nice.* It wasn't love at first sight. Mabel didn't just know. *I just live from one day to the other.*

I measured my own meet cute against Mabel's, as if the juxtaposition might reveal what future I could have with my lover.

I am certain it was September, two months shy of thirty. Chilly

tendrils held the sea in their grip, threatened to wind around my fin-
gers and toes, to snake their way into my lungs, but still, I was deter-
mined to swim. I biked to the beach, where I met up with a friend
for the last two miles of the season. Moments before we set sail, a
familiar figure in a purple and gray collegiate sweatsuit tumbled onto
the beach. I recognized them: the youngest coach on the team, the
one I had fantasized about for nearly two years as they loomed over
me on deck to explain the workout, the one who was much too young
for me, who already had a girlfriend. I guess it wasn't our first meet-
ing after all. Today, they had no one to swim with. "Can I tag along
with you?" My friend and I looked at each other, shrugged. It was the
meeting that mattered.

I could predict nothing of my own future relationship after that
swim. I had complained the whole way. It was cold. My friend and
my future lover were fast. I hated to lag behind because it reminded
me of high school swim practice, cast out for not keeping up. Tears
warmed my face and fogged my goggles. I popped up vertical to tread
water and consider the length of the walk back to our dry towels and
the sun-warm sand. But before my eyes could measure the distance,
I saw two swimmers, the both of them, waiting to shuttle me back
through the sea.

We came ashore to shiver on the sand and eat snacks in the sun.
I watched as my future lover struggled to eat sports gel from a foil
pouch, licking their fingers. That crass vulnerability gave me the cour-
age to put my number in their phone, the modern version of sharing
your address with a stranger on the streetcar in the hopes that they
were *in the life* and might show up at your doorstep. I didn't know
what was possible between us, but I knew I wanted to know them
more.

Mabel hardly thought of Lillian after the bus ride. *Two days passed.
I had kinda forgotten a little bit.* She went about her life, unchanged.
*One evening, I think I was reading.* A noise interrupted her solitude.

*The lady upstairs, she answered the top bell. I heard her say like, "Miss Hampton lives downstairs. C'mon, I'll take you down."*

Footsteps on the stairs. Lillian, small and steady, at her door. *"Hello,"* she said.

*"Hello,"* Mabel replied. *"How did you find me so fast?"*

*"I was thinking about it."*

*"Well, let's pull off your coat and hat, rest yourself awhile."* She reached for Lillian's stylish jacket. *"You had supper?"*

*She spent the night.* It was as uneventful as that. *And we got together.*

Four weeks later, Lillian went to live in those three rooms on 122nd Street, since demolished. Like Mabel, she had first called the South home and had been swept up north to New York City by the Great Migration. Born in Norfolk, Virginia, Lillian grew up alongside two sisters, a brother, and a tolerant set of parents who knew their daughter had struck up a romantic and sexual relationship with her schoolteacher. Mabel was surprised by how experienced her new lover was. Lillian *knew more about it than I did, and I was supposed to be a big cheese.* After all, Lillian's relationship with the schoolteacher had lasted a year and a half. Mabel might have also been surprised to learn how the relationship had ended—*"You can have Lillian,"* her father said, *"but you can't beat her. I'll take my Winchester and kill you."*

*Men are funny. If you had color, they were after you.* Mabel had suffered at the hands of men, like Uncle George who beat and assaulted her, who insisted on the kind of "seance" Peter had tried to hold with his own wife's sister, Mary Casal. Even Mabel's arrival in Jersey City to live with the White family was not the refuge it had first seemed. Mrs. White *had a bitchy old husband. All he wanted to do was put his hands up your dress.* Then there are the men who go unnamed on the tapes, the ones who tried to touch and grab her. *Everywhere I went some man was trying to force his advantages on me.*

Women could be *funny* too. Queer relationships were not a guaranteed escape from the violence and sexual assault Mabel had run from

during her youth. When Mabel and Lillian moved from Harlem to the Bronx in 1945, they befriended their neighbors Billie and Francis. *Francis come down and spoke to us, and I said to myself, hmmmm . . . I looked at Billie. Billie had on pants and everything.* Mabel realized this couple next door was also *in the life*. They could never be role models, though. Billie *beat the hell out of Francis because Francis was fresh.* Mabel, however, wanted to break the chain. *I never hit nobody at all.*

Still, Mabel and Lillian borrowed from the script written by generations of straight couples. Mabel *liked to dress like a boy, I liked to dress like a fellow with pants and shirt, tie. Nobody know what you was when you had a suit on and flat, low-heeled shoes.* Mabel only ever took to the stage as a dancer, but on the streets she performed her own kind of male impersonation, in the spirit of Gladys Bentley.

But Mabel wasn't a *boy*, or even a *fellow. I didn't think that much about men to be wanting to be one. Why should I, why should I want to be a man and don't like the men? That don't make sense.* Instead, she called herself a *stud*.

Lillian, on the other hand, *she never wore pants . . . She was a real girl. She was real wifey. She was a fashion plate and I wasn't fashion nothing.* Lillian even worked in fashion, as a presser, ironing clothes and costumes for theaters. *She made more money than I did . . . She loved it.*

This was not a relationship modeled after Mary and Juno's romantic friendship, where both women melded masculine and feminine, both in their style of dress, the tailored suit, and in their roles, wooing and working. Instead, Mabel and Lillian were stud and wifey. Butch and femme. It was a script rehearsed by the people who surrounded them *in the life*, from their neighbors in Harlem to the two women they saw married by a gay reverend who still used the words *husband* and *wife* in his ceremony. *That girl looked so much like a fella you couldn't tell her apart.*

Perhaps someone walking the streets of Harlem at dusk spotted

the pair walking hand in hand—Mabel small, Lillian smaller—
and mistook them for husband and wife. If the wind was right, the
stranger might have heard Mabel whisper *Little Duchess* in Lillian's
ear, her first nickname for her love, or, later on, *Little Bear*. The *Little
Bear* to Mabel's *Big Bear*.

Prison culture was a possible root for the gendered roles performed
by queer women of the era, according to Faderman. Jail was a space
where women paired off not just for sex, as Mabel witnessed and ex-
perienced, but also to forge alliances and protect one another. After
their release, women may have brought their prison identities—mama
or papa—back home to their communities.

Black women in particular were pioneers when it came to invent-
ing relationships outside the traditional family. When denied the pos-
sibility of maintaining traditional families, as Hartman outlines, and
instead earning their own salaries for the domestic labor white women
demanded but did not want to perform, Black women seized the oppor-
tunity to write their own futures. They borrowed from the heterosexual
dynamics they witnessed playing out all around them, at times out of
necessity, to gain access to the institution of marriage, and at times out
of pleasure, the pleasure Mabel took in putting on a pair of low-heeled
shoes. Quotidian gender play was amplified on stage by the male and
female impersonators Mabel watched perform in the mid-1920s, like
her friend the womanizer Gladys Bentley, or later, in the 1950s, Stormé
DeLarverie, part of the Jewel Box Revue that performed at the Apollo
Theater, billed as "25 Men and A Girl," and no one could guess who the
"real girl" was. *The women wore pants and the men wore dresses.* Descen-
dants of Johnstone Bennett and Ella Wesner, Gladys and Stormé kept
alive an art form that would continue to grow and endure for decades
to come, even after Stormé threw the first Stonewall punch.

Through ten years of dating women, I had rarely played the
femme. Now, with this lover, I auditioned for a new part in the gen-
dered script. I rolled on tights, clamped shut the buttons down the

front of my dress, rewinding a seduction. I clomped my way through Brooklyn and across the bridge to Manhattan in a pair of low-heeled boots, clumsy as a colt. When I arrived at their East Harlem apartment, ankles intact, they lifted me off the ground and carried me into bed. Hours later, emerging onto the streets, I let them hold open doors, place our order at the ice cream counter.

Some nights, we swapped roles. They cooked dinner in nothing but a blue apron while I waited impatiently on the couch, beer in hand. They sewed a pair of pajama shorts out of fabric printed with tiny whales and left them folded on top of my pillow. We'd studied our parts, rehearsed the lines until they came out whispered in our sleep, but after years of frustrated auditions, we opted instead for our own messy improv.

We climbed on the subway back to Brooklyn, and my lover spread their legs wide as a man marking his territory. A busker crooned at the far end of the car, and we nodded in time to his song, sleepy and sated. The train careened to a halt. He stumbled in front of us, hat outstretched. My lover tucked a dollar inside. The busker looked them in the eye and said, "Thank you, ma'am," before moving along to the next set of seats. He wheeled back around. "Are you a woman?" My lover tensed. The whole train stopped to listen. What did this stranger see? Body burritoed into a coat. Beanie squashed over a head of short hair. White cheeks sandwiched in between. They weren't a ma'am. They weren't a sir either, except sometimes, in bed. They were both. They were neither. They wanted to write their own story.

No matter where Mabel went, she always found others *in the life* who invented new roles. *When you find one, you're bound to find everybody else.* Whether she was working in the theater or befriending neighbors or serving time for a crime she didn't commit or climbing on the streetcar, she was surrounded by people who created new configurations not just of gender, but also of family.

Mabel was an orphan in the world. I listened to her tell of her

mother's murder. *She was poisoned with an apple, and the poison was put in a hypodermic needle, and that was injected into the apple, and she ate it.* The murderer was her own sister, the Older Aunt Mabel went to live with for a few days in New York City. The motive was jealousy over Mabel's father, Joseph Rogers. *I never seen him, but they say he a good-looking man.* All she knew was that he was from Lynchburg, Virginia, born to a family of five brothers, all bootleggers. One day, I'm not sure where in the timeline, one of her aunts, I'm not sure which, got in touch with Joseph and told him about Mabel, born out of wedlock. *He gets on the train and on his way he took with a heart attack, and they rushed him back, and he died, so I never seen him.* The relations she did have left betrayed and abused her. *I don't have any family.*

Yet there was always someone around to look out for Mabel. *I have a spirit that walks around with me and guides me. I got people that looks after me and gives me advice and teach me different things, you know. I'm really a lucky and fortunate woman, see. I got people who loves me, both white and colored.* There was the White family who took her in when she ran away to Jersey City at age eight, and also Joan, who made a home for her story. Without children, without Lillian, this new generation of lesbians who interviewed Mabel—there's Joan, and also Pam and Morgan, who make their subject "pamcakes" for breakfast while chatting, Madeline, too, and other anonymous voices against the scratch of the tape—became her family, pestering, prodding aunts gathered around the table at Thanksgiving.

Joan latches on to these moments of community connection and asks Mabel to unspool each one, to describe the spaces where queer people gathered, the outfits they wore, who was a stud and who was a femme, who was white and who was Black. I recognize in Joan my own impulse to prove that we were there, a pin in the map, a flag on the moon, that people loved and touched each other outside of heterosexual marriage, regardless of whether anyone actually used the word *lesbian* in the 1920s.

Joan rarely asks for the day-to-day details of life with Lillian. Perhaps it was because Joan knew them as a unit, witnessed their love up close. Lillian and Mabel even went to live with Joan and her then-partner, Deb, after a fire tore through their Bronx apartment— another moment when the living took care of Mabel. *We played and we sang and we ate and it was marvelous. I will never forget it.* Or perhaps it is because these things—a life built together over shared dinners and petty arguments, a life imagined into being, some pieces borrowed from straight relatives, others from gay neighbors, and others wholly invented—do not feel like the stuff of history, fall outside the bounds of what Joan was taught in those oral history workshops. "Letters are built of longing, which means that archives run on longing," writes queer archivist Isaac Fellman. "You make less of an archive once you get what you want."

I long for a turn at the rudder, a chance to diverge from the course, run us into shallow eddies where, yes, we might get stuck, but we'd also have the chance of an intimate moment with the fish swimming those murky waters, a chance at my rotten, selfish questions: Who started more fights, Mabel or Lillian? Who was the better cook? Who left dishes in the sink? Who was the big spoon? Who hogged the covers? Did either of them snore? Who was better in bed? Who had a wandering eye? Who loved more?

~~~~~

Things could not last between me and my lover. They were six and a half years younger, and yet already they were ahead of me when it came to the study and practice of adulthood. In preparation for their weekly visits, I made the bed with my only set of worn sheets, tugged my too-small curtains together as if they might finally meet in the middle, and scrubbed the stains at the bottom of the toilet bowl. We ran into my friends on the street, and I flubbed the introductions. I silenced phone calls from my mother. "So what you're saying," they

asked, "is that I might never pull it together?" Still, they called me Professor in bed.

Their age was a problem, but so was the fact of their girlfriend, a woman who lived in another country and was, somehow, okay with us. I tried to make friends with the idea of her, that other woman, the real girlfriend, to be as okay with her as she was with me. She was a pair of lips planting a kiss on my lover's face in a Valentine's Day post, a name that popped up on their phone screen when I rolled over in bed to turn off the alarm. A flimsy sheet of paper with the words *Useless Lesbian* in shaky script hung on their bedroom door, a sign she had held up at the foot of the airport escalators as if she were a chauffeur waiting for a business executive. The two of them loved the word—lesbian movies, lesbian memes, lesbian novels—but neither could fully embrace it.

I didn't know what to call my lover. They couldn't be my girlfriend. They already played that role for someone else. Besides, they weren't a girl at all. We came up with other words, each worse than the last. Boyfriend. Paramour. Beaux. Female Companion. There weren't any role models for us. Still, we carried on through the seasons, without a label. They sent me dispatches from Mabel's block. In winter they went there to cry, a tea kettle letting off steam. In spring, I received a picture of the view Mabel might have seen sitting on her stoop, watching the neighborhood pass and listening to the rattle of the streetcar. The block covered in blossoms I still don't know how to name.

Romantic love, my middle school English teacher told me, is, by definition, the thing that is felt for just one person. She sensed I was in love with both my rebellious classmate and his brilliant older brother and gave the only kind of advice she knew: words, definitions. She drove me along the river, past industrial parts of the city that had faded but refused to disappear. Rusted cranes, train tracks covered in knee-high grass, shuttered stores. I couldn't look at her, my eyes locked on the dashboard clock, but I took her words to heart. She was

still happily married to her high school sweetheart, so she must have known a thing or two. From that moment on, all my relationships—with men, with women, with both and neither—were monogamous, faithful. My one and only. An entire future, from marriage to a shared gravestone, laid out before us. I was looking for someone to commit to, a life partner, the Lillian to my Mabel.

"Was Lillian passionate?" Joan asked.

I guess she was. She was running with Helen.

Helen. I wasn't expecting you.

I skipped around the tapes until I found more. Mabel and Lillian first met Helen, *mulatta* with *beautiful hair*, at a house party in the Bronx. She was divorced and worked as a nurse to provide for her two children. *She used to come to the house and sleep and eat, cause I worked almost all the time.*

I asked Helen what's going on. Mabel's voice grows soft around the name, as if it still might prick her. *She lied to everybody but me, didn't lie to me. I said, I'll catch you anyways.*

Mabel never names what there was between Helen and Lillian. What did she *catch* her doing? What was it to *run* with another woman? I am tempted to call it an affair, infidelity. I had idealized Lillian and Mabel's relationship when, in fact, it was spoiled at the center, green with rot and jealousy. Spoiled by someone. Helen. My own self, reflected back to me.

Through the stolen seasons spent sharing a bed with someone I would never call mine, I often woke at four in the morning, heart running from the fear that this person beside me would forever remain a stranger. I would never possess them. I would never build an archive that could contain them because those private future moments shared with someone else—the wedding, the first day with a new husky pup, the argument that kept them up late and left them unable to answer my messages—would always elude me. It was this I was jealous of. Not of *her*, of the daily nudes she sent as reminders of her six-pack and biceps.

Not of her status as The Girlfriend who met the parents and appeared in adoring social media posts. Not even of her time with my lover, their unmeasured quotidian rhythms. I had arrived here in defiance of my middle school teacher, in pursuit of every possible experience, an experiment in living. When I uncovered Helen, I became jealous, jealous that I would never get a starring role in the narrative. I would be only the footnote, the dirty secret in someone else's epic love story.

Mabel, always one step ahead, warns me against this easy interpretation. *Didn't bother me,* she insists, her words a refutation of her tone. *I wouldn't tell you why it didn't bother me—because I don't like jumping down people's throats for every little thing they do. You can't stop me for having passion for that girl over there or feeling for that girl over there. You can't stop it! So you might as well forget it! That's how I got along. So many years I knew her and Helen was going together. Didn't bother me.*

Mabel had her own *passion,* did her own *running,* and perhaps even had her own relationships with other women while partnered with her *wifey* Lillian. *I had a good time on the sly, you know. When I got home I was the perfect husband.*

"How many women?" Joan asks.

Get outta here! Mabel shouts. *I had enough. Didn't bother me. White, black, green, or yellow, didn't bother me. I liked them all. All the little dears I loved! . . . I just suppose I wanted everybody liking me. That's all.*

Later, Mabel guesses that in her eighty-plus years, she slept with twelve women. If I did my own inventory—the married lady Mabel slept with at age nineteen, whose husband came home unexpectedly, forcing Mabel to jump and hide under the bed; Mabel's first love, another married lady and also her employer in domestic work, *when she kissed me I fainted dead away*; another employer, this time one who kept her around for three years for both her housekeeping and her affections; Viola, the woman she was out with when she got arrested;

Ruth, the woman she *made love* with in Bedford Hills; the unnamed woman Mabel was dating when she met Lillian; Lillian herself; Chris, the new love Mabel found after Lillian passed—I bet the count would come to something higher than twelve. This list doesn't even include the women Mabel insists she turned down, like Lillian's niece, *a nasty woman*, and Helen herself. What am I to believe? A new kind of lacuna opens, different from the simple forgettings, the names and dates that have eroded over time. Mabel wants to maintain her privacy, her dignity.

If I could get a moment alone with Mabel, I'd scrap my other questions and ask just one. "You and Lillian," I might begin, readying myself to defy all the rules of my own undergraduate oral history course. "In your own relationship, you borrowed a lot from straight relationships. One of you wore slacks, one of you wore dresses. One of you was a stud, the other a wife. Were you also as jealous, as possessive, as heterosexual couples?" *No*, I need her to say. *I loved Lillian, and I wanted her to be free, happy.*

Mabel didn't have the word *lesbian* until later in life, but that doesn't mean she didn't spend her life loving women. The vocabulary for polyamory wasn't around back then, either. (It is new to me too.) Even without the word for it, Lillian, and perhaps Mabel too, experienced many loves and gave each other the space to explore their emotions and identities outside the bounds of their relationship. They didn't own each other. Being *in the life* wasn't just about who you loved, but also how you loved.

~~~~~

The New York City property tax office photographed every tax-paying house and building in the five boroughs in the early 1940s. Taken by anonymous photographers, the black-and-white collection was fully digitized in the 2010s. Each photo has a black sign with white letters in the foreground, marking the block and lot number of the building,

an indexed archive of the city. I ordered a physical print of 120 West 122nd Street without sneaking a peek at the digital photo.

I recognized the cardboard envelope from the words DO NOT BEND stamped in red across the front, sitting in the hands of the postal worker. I tore open the seal, lifted out the matte print. Two little Black girls stood outside 118, their faces wrapped in hats and hoods. It must have been winter. Next door, at 120 West 122nd Street, someone had just taken out the trash. The bin sat at the foot of the staircase, next to the two windows looking into the garden apartment. Mabel's apartment. This was the building that no longer was, the block where my lover and I had kissed in the snow, the basement Mabel moved into when she got out of Bedford Hills, the staircase Lillian had walked down to find the mysterious stud she had met on the Lexington Avenue streetcar. Was the identical brownstone next door, 122, where Mabel went to the lesbian parties? Or was it where the woman who cautioned Lillian lived, the one who told her, *Don't bother with Mabel cause Mabel after every woman she knows?* By the time the photo was taken, Mabel and Lillian had already moved to 111th Street. By the time the tax department took the next set of photos in the 1960s, their brownstone had already been torn down.

Mabel and Lillian eventually settled in the Bronx at 639 East 169th Street, a building that still stands today. After living there for over twenty-five years, Mabel wrote to New York City's mayor John Lindsay to ask for assistance finding better housing for her and her "sister" because there was no heat in the building and the housing authority was no help. Joan has kept the letter in her archives and cites it in her essay about her friend's life, "The Life of Mabel Hampton as Told by a White Woman."

"Mabel," Joan asked on the tapes, decades before she published that essay, "in those years, did you ever feel oppressed—do you know what I mean by the word *oppressed*? Did you ever feel people were

cruel to you 'cause you were Black and because you were a lesbian? Did you ever feel prejudice?"

*No, no, I never did. With the lesbian part, no. Uh uh. Cause they treated me so nice until I couldn't think of people being cruel.*

"And what about being Black? Did you feel people were cruel to you sometimes or unkind?"

*Tell ya, Joanie, I didn't go around those type of people. I didn't go around those type of people.*

It would be easy, comfortable even, for me, another white Jewish lesbian stumbling onto Mabel's stage, to take her at her word. To believe this story she is spinning of a life suffused with song and community, romance and sex and mutual support in equal measure, a life punctuated by loss and loneliness and trauma but still unmarked by racism.

And yet. Even if people treated her *so nice*, if her Black communities in Harlem and the Bronx opened a space where she could avoid cruel people, Mabel still cannot keep the marks of structural racism and class oppression out of her story. They are present when she speaks of her work as a domestic for a string of white families, and when she slowly opens up about her wrongful arrest and the time she served in Bedford Hills. They are there in her letter to the mayor of New York, politely asking for help getting a place to live that has heat in the winter, and in the illness that took Lillian in the end, likely brought on by the unventilated back rooms where she ironed clothes for actors and the city's wealthy theatergoers.

These currents are familiar. Our city, mine and Mabel's, much less our country, is far from eliminating the white supremacy built into its foundations. We're even further from offering any kind of repair. Arriving in Jersey City on the edge of age eight, Mabel already feared the cop that might come to the playground and send her back to Uncle George. Complete strangers offered her more help than the state ever could. Black New Yorkers continue to face the same housing

discrimination and false arrest that marred Mabel's peace. There's a straight line from the man with the watch on his belt who set up Mabel to be arrested on prostitution charges to the daily harm the state continues to inflict on Black lives.

I don't buy that Mabel didn't face racism in her lifetime, but she doesn't want it at the center of her story. It's not what propels her into mine. Her life was too big to be contained on the page.

Mabel lived, and fell in love with Lillian, at a time when women who loved women began to realize that they were not alone. It's not mere happenstance that this burgeoning sense of community among queer women is so visible at its intersection with the Black community. In her analysis of the lives of queer women in the 1920s, Faderman attributes the flourishing of a Black lesbian subculture in Harlem not just to the relationships formed in prison but also to the neighborhood's relative acceptance of homosexuality, at least in comparison to the intolerance found elsewhere in the city. Joan's own writings dig deeper into history to draw a connection between the mutual aid networks of Black women in and around New York City that caught and held Mabel and the community support that emerged among Southern Black women in the era of sharecropping.

I borrow from each of these lesbian historians, and I layer my own interpretation on top. I see these communities of *lady lovers* and *bulldikers* taking root to fill in the gaps when the state failed to provide for Black women and, in some cases, to care for those that the state had harmed. New York City in the 1920s was marked by the push and pull between morality and pleasure. The people who chose the side of pleasure didn't just pursue the pleasures of the flesh, parties and drink and the touch of a stranger's lips. They also found pleasure in caring for one another, their dead and their living. I want to fold Mabel into my own queer community. I summon her as the dead who takes care of me, the living.

I imagine Mabel on her stoop in winter. A light snow dusts her

block in East Harlem. She watches me and my lover kiss. Did they have the nod in the 1920s, the one we get when we hold hands in Prospect Park, from companions in this life we don't know yet but could? The Mabel I have resurrected knows that my lover and I aren't each other's one and only, but she doesn't ask, "What if you want them all to yourself?" or "Are you being safe?" the way my mother does. Mabel can't give us a name for what we're building, but she can give us a role model, a history.

Mabel is still watching when I end things with my lover, not for lack of love but because I want more, more than once a week, more than something kept secret. Mabel watches as I buy my own apartment and move my things into three rooms: a giant living room, a junior bedroom, a galley kitchen with an ice machine built into the refrigerator door. A secure home where no one can raise the rent. The down payment alone is more than my parents spent to buy their entire house, that down payment, in turn, more than my zipper-sewing grandmother couldn't pay for her house, the five-thousand-dollar mortgage still not finished with after thirty years. This is the kind of upward mobility our whiteness affords. I soak in the morning light, the solitude of things that remain in place until I move them, but for all its pleasures, I can't imagine living here alone for the rest of my life. I can't imagine how a place like this, an investment, a piece of real estate, would have changed Mabel's life.

I hesitate to keep calling up Mabel for favors, for advice. "Telling Mabel Hampton's history forces me to confront racism in my own relationship to her," Joan writes, a role model for me in her own way. Her relationship with Mabel began with Mabel as the caretaker, the underpaid domestic, but somewhere along the way it became its own love story. In November 1960, Joan wrote Mabel a postcard from Basel, Switzerland. "I am going to buy a mountain here for us," she said. "Would you like to live in the Alps?"

The story ended with Joan taking care of Mabel. As Mabel aged,

losing her hearing and some of the feeling in her fingers, Joan brought her to live in her Upper West Side apartment, where she cared for her hero's body, and also for her story, one she would tell in essays and speeches long after Mabel was gone. "The loss to me personally is too huge to even talk about even after all these years."

Following Joan's lead, I tend to Mabel's story. I dig around for the moments tying her to those *in the life* in Harlem in the 1920s and '30s, the cruelties they suffered at the hands of the state and the unbridled joys they found in each other's arms. I also dig for the more intimate moments that make her my own personal hero, a lesbian who came out of hardship and rewrote the ways we can love one another, not just our Lillians but also our neighbors, strangers, transient lovers, everyone *in the life*. I speak Mabel's name in the snow, those syllables a sweet something to whisper in my lover's ear. I nod back to let Mabel know that I smile when I see her, laugh when I hear her. I want a monument on her block, funded by lesbians, but for now I will settle for this, the kiss of snowflakes and streetlamps, of lips that repeat her name back to me.

"You have lots of stories to tell, Mabel," Joan says.

*I don't have nothing.*

Another day, another interview session. Mabel changes her mind. *Somebody should write about me and what I think.*

*What I wanted out of life was to be with a woman and stay with a woman.*

*When you're in this life you know everybody and everybody knows you.*

## Extracts | PULP NOVELS AND OTHER BOOKS HOUSED AT THE LESBIAN HERSTORY ARCHIVES

*I gave Joan over three hundred novels . . . All of them is about women loving each other. I read some very beautiful stories about the women.*

> *Dominating Dyke* by Justine Aumond
>
> *That Other Hunger* by Sloane Britain
>
> *Lesbians in Prison: Actual Case Histories from a Women's Prison* by Wilma Y. Cleevendar
>
> *Left of Sex* by Stacey Clubb
>
> *The Delicate Vice* by Sloan Britton
>
> *Dyke Diary* by John Dexter
>
> *Her Raging Needs* by Kay Johnson
>
> *The Evil Friendship* by Vin Packer*
>
> *Sea Madame* by Jon Parker
>
> *Vixens Pageant* by Jon Parker
>
> *The Making of Susan* by Julie Rowe
>
> *Punishment for Passion* by Sylvia Sharon**
>
> *Stranger Lovers* by John Trinian
>
> *Another Way of Love* by Joe Weiss

*Vin Packer was a pseudonym for Marijane Meaker.
**Sylvia Sharon is thought to be the pseudonym of male writer Paul Little.

# 3.

## A Golf League of Her Own:
## Babe Didrikson Zaharias and Betty Dodd

*(1950–1956)*

MILDRED IS IN LOVE WITH THE GAME. SURE, BRENTWOOD
Country Club is more posh than any place a daughter of two Norwe-
gian immigrants would have been allowed back home in Texas, and
sure, her rough charm and wit spark bright against the four sports
writers who invited her out to play, but it's the challenge that really
hooks her. Everything else has come easy. Her Olympic gold in the
eighty-meter hurdles? No different than jumping hedges with her sis-
ter Lillie back home on Doucette Street in Beaumont. Besides, as if
her speed weren't enough, she knew how to clinch the deal by raising
her arm to signal victory to the judges as she hit the finish line side
by side with that Hall girl. The javelin throw? Another gold, and the
Olympic record by eleven feet. And the high jump? Stolen from her
with the unfair ruling that her Western Roll wasn't legal. She'd had to
settle for a half gold, half silver medal, the only one of its kind. Still,
she had already achieved her goal, *to be the greatest athlete that ever
lived*, and she was only eighteen. Well, twenty-one, but what woman

hasn't lied about her age? *Most things come natural to me, and golf was the first that ever gave me much trouble.*

Mildred pretends it's love at first sight. August 8, 1932. She feigns ignorance, asks pro Olin Dutra to show her how to swing a club, makes a big show of hardly knowing, even though she played in high school, the 1929 Beaumont High School yearbook proves it, and so does her bitter teacher who swore, "She never did beat me on the Beaumont course."

Today they're playing two on three, or match play, as it's called. Her and Grantland Rice—Granny suits him better—against those other boys: Westbrook Pegler and Braven Dyer and Paul Gallico. For a moment, it seems like they might beat her and Granny, and she can hardly bear the thought. The rest of them may be boys, but at the end of the day they're sports writers, not athletes. Her drives are long and powerful, two hundred and fifty yards off into the horizon, but what her Olympic training has given her in strength and muscle she lacks in consistency and accuracy. Her reputation has attracted a little crowd of spectators. She'll have to win this thing the only way she knows how.

"Hey, Paul!" she goads. "Paul? I bet I can beat you up and down that hill. Wanna race?"

His eyes light up at the challenge. He hands off his club to Granny, their unofficial referee.

Granny counts down to give the mismatched pair their start. He laughs as he watches the launch. Mildred's dress flutters in the wind, clutters up the space around her ankles. Still, he knows she will win. Paul may be a man, but he's no Olympian. He's a bespectacled, sedentary writer. This is why women belong in the Olympics, ancient Greek no-girls-allowed tradition be damned. Maybe next time around, the officials would allow women to enter more than three track and field events after seeing the kind of stamina athletes like Mildred had. Maybe they'd allow women in the eight-hundred-meter,

the decathlon—even add other sports, like basketball, where Mildred had gotten her start. Women could best men. They just needed the opportunity to try. Granny can only beg people to believe what he writes. Mildred, she can show them the truth with her body.

Mildred arrives first, arms held aloft in victory. Paul wheezes. *He was so winded he had to lie down on the grass and catch his breath.* The plan had worked. *Granny and I won the hole and the match.*

Mildred hopes one of the boys will write about their day together out on the golf green. Granny's invitation was meant as a pick-me-up, something to distract her from her failure to sweep all three Olympic gold medals, but what will really make her feel better is to see her name in print, to watch her fame grow. When they write about her—they must—Mildred hopes they call her Babe, maybe they'll even say it's after Babe Ruth and not just some family nickname, the sixth child, the youngest, for a moment, of the ones born in America. That is, until Bubba came along and couldn't say Mildred to save his life. She'd settle for Mildred, though, so long as they don't call her the Texas Tomboy or a muscle moll. Later, after another bout of "love at first sight" on the golf green in 1938, she would become Babe Didrikson Zaharias, Babe D. Zaharias, Mrs. Zaharias, of Rainbow Manor in Tampa, Florida. For now, just Babe, please. Babe Didrikson, with an "o," not the "e" her parents used back in Norway. Babe Didrikson of Beaumont.

When Paul's piece hits newsstands two months later, it's like a pro baseball pitch right to the stomach. At least he got her name right in the headline—"The Texas Babe"—and her reputation right with that opening line calling her "the world's champion lady athlete." He cements the myth that she is only nineteen, that she had hardly ever played golf before, but she barely notices those details. There are thirteen—she counts them all—jabs at her for being "like a man," "like a boy," a "strange nineteen-year-old girl-boy child." If it were just her muscles, that would be one thing, but it's her entire body under

scrutiny. "There is a light fuzz on her upper lip, her face, her neck . . . Her legs are powerful and hirsute." Was this her punishment for beating a man both in a footrace and a game of golf?

The piece is not enough to shake her love for golf. She loves the game not just for the challenge, not just because she could probably beat a male pro or two. She loves it because the sport might just help her become a lady.

~~~~~

I tried to ignore Babe. She was arrogant and self-aggrandizing, a shameless self-promoter. Truth be told, golf bores me. The game bores me almost as much as Babe's future husband, George Zaharias, the wrestler promoted as "the Crying Greek from Cripple Creek." On principle, I refused to learn the golfing vocabulary that clutters her autobiography, *This Life I've Led*, as told to writer Harry T. Paxton on a series of audio tapes. My eyes gloss over words like *fore!*, *bogey*, *birdie*, *eagle 3*. Harry describes her as "too well known to require any introduction," but frankly I've never even heard her name before. What's more, I swore to myself I would never pursue a lesbian like Babe. She never calls herself one in the book, or even admits to a romantic relationship beyond the one she shared with her husband, *without whom there never would have been a life to lead.*

As one of the greatest athletes in history, named the ninth-greatest athlete of all time and the second-greatest female athlete of the twentieth century, Babe led her life in the public eye. She left not just a self-narrated account of her life, in the tradition of Mabel and Mary, but also a trail of secondary sources richer than her lesbian ancestors could have ever wished for. I hoped that somewhere in these reflections and refractions of Babe—press interviews, film reels, a movie cameo alongside Katharine Hepburn, multiple biographies, a television special, and even a full-length musical—I might find the real Babe, a confession of love outside the bounds of heterosexual marriage.

Instead the wealth of biographical detail buries and obscures her. The more the press covered Babe, the more opportunities she had to peddle her mythology and bury the truth. If she had altered the spelling of her family name and lied about both her birth year and her previous experience with golf, what else was she hiding? *The stories about me*, she writes, as if in anticipation of my question, *sometimes get a little tall in the telling.*

If Babe were here today to take a swing at telling the unfiltered version of her story, she would still brag about her achievements, the records she set in track and field, the length of her golf winning streak—heck, she might even tack on an extra tournament or three, but as her publicist (mind you, a publicist always on the brink of getting fired for nudging her client back toward the truth) I would jump in to remind her to mention her true legacy. She was an unparalleled athlete, sure, in golf and track and field, and also tennis, baseball, basketball, bowling. Name a sport and she was probably great at it. More important, though, Babe changed the game for female athletes. She was mostly in it for herself, but her advocacy and her participation in the formation of the Ladies Professional Golf Association paved the way for women to actually earn a living in sport, to make money with the very bodies that were supposed to belong to their husbands. Fellow pro golfer Patty Berg said it best: "Our sport grew because of Babe." I'd doctor her quote a little for the press release: Women's sports grew because of Babe.

Perhaps I'm unable to ignore Babe because I once had my own athletic aspirations. My fourth-grade teacher, a gay man I adored so much that I once asked my parents for a pet iguana to match his, gave us each a standard-issue blue composition notebook. Each week, we were supposed to write an entry for him to read. A diary without any privacy. I wrote that I wanted to qualify for the Olympic trials in swimming. That was before. Before I realized I wasn't all that fast, or even fast enough to compete at the Junior Olympics hosted by the

local university each summer. Before the other girls in the locker room began to tease me for the stubble nestled in my armpit and the hairs that poked out of my swimsuit along my bikini line. I can't remember which of these things happened first, whether one led to the other with the kind of cruel causality that only teenage girls have mastered. I wasn't girl enough to fit in, or boy enough for the fast lane.

The International Olympic Committee had opened swimming events to women back in 1912, sixteen years before they would allow track and field athletes like Babe, but permission alone wasn't enough. I would also have to qualify. My teacher, bless him, didn't have the heart to crush my dreams. My parents got me a Chinese dwarf hamster for Christmas instead.

Gallico—the rat, who asked for his thoughts?—identified eight sports that were suitable for women, including shooting, riding, and skating. He was on the fence about swimming. *Vanity Fair* gave him two full pages, and a hefty fee, I'm sure, to weigh the question: "Babes in the Drink," January 1936. I don't recognize the names of the women who competed back then or the distances they swam—220- and 440-yard backstroke, a rough imperial approximation of today's Olympic 200- and 400-meter races—but his judgments are familiar. What, Gallico wondered, attracted so many spectators, including himself, to women's swimming when "the gentlemen of course can swim rings around them"? It might be true that "a damp young lady in a black silk, one-piece racing suit is an eye-filling piece of baggage for the spectators," and many of the competitors were married to boot, but even with their sporty sex appeal and personal decorum they still couldn't stack up to "the greatest free peep show of the age, the public beach (and even better, the private beach)."

Golf didn't make Gallico's list either.

Babe had the press, that sometimes friend and often foe, to police her appearance. At the turn of the century, readers had thirsted for newspaper stories about people who transgressed gender, like *female*

husbands and male impersonators. Now, journalists slaked that same thirst by writing about female athletes—their achievements and glory, but also their clothing, mannerisms, and all-around comportment. Babe was labeled as the dreaded Muscle Moll, a "derogatory term for women athletes," adapted from just plain old *moll*, the name for either a gangster's girlfriend or a prostitute. One *Austin American-Statesman* columnist called Babe a "Sapphic, Brobdingnagian woman," lifting from both ancient Greek lyric and Jonathan Swift's *Gulliver's Travels*. No newspaper would ever write up my swim races. Still, I had my teammates to keep me in line.

The Jewish Community Center locker room was governed by the same set of unspoken rules as the yellow bus that took us on high school field trips. Popular kids in the back, where our chaperones couldn't see their mischief; unpopular kids up front, an audience for the backseat antics. At school, I was always a middle-seat kind of girl, and with a boyfriend at my side, I might gain entry to sit a few rows closer to the back than where I was allowed on my own.

In the swim locker room, though, I was always on the fringes. The girls who stood at the center, an amphitheater of benches spread out before them, had it all: Juicy Couture velour tracksuits, Razr flip phones, straightened hair, and faces heavy with makeup. While I spent Friday nights watching art films with my boyfriend, they snuck alcohol into school dances and bragged when they got caught. While I prayed I wouldn't be DFL (Dead. Fucking. Last.) in my events, they always qualified for Junior Olympics, for national meets, for athletic scholarships.

It must have been one of them who messaged me on AIM one night after practice, my hair still slack with the weight of the water. She wasn't ready to identify herself, but she knew me from the pool, she said. Perhaps, I thought, with a thrill that brought my shoulders out of their tired slouch, this anonymous cool-girl wanted to be my friend.

"how was practice?" I typed.

"kicked my buttttttt." There was a beat. I prayed my parents wouldn't ask me to disconnect the internet so they could make a phone call. I waited while she typed more, barely breathing. "i always know its u in the pool. ur pubes are always sticking out of your suit lolololol."

The conversation continued for a few more volleys. I can't remember her words, only the acid burn in my throat. Then, a final message appeared: "You've been tricked! The original messages were written by a human, but everything after has been generated by a computer."

I was used to little form corrections from our coaches. Every week was governed by five days of swim practice, two days of dryland exercises, one day of lifting, and one lesson in technique. Twelve hours, a part-time job that didn't pay. Coach, belly as hardened by age as the medicine balls we held while doing our crunches, told me that my left hand crossed over the midline when I swam freestyle, that if I could see the Hebrew flags on the ceiling when I turned my head to breathe, I had turned too far. He squeezed his thumb into the spot where my shoulder had curved from exhaustion to correct my seated posture. He had me stand against the wall with my hands held aloft in a streamline and ordered me to tighten my abs until he could no longer fit his hand between my back and the blue tile. "When the other girls can't bench press their weight," he said to me, "I tell them to lose a few pounds. You, you're too skinny. You just needed to get stronger."

I absorbed those anonymous AIM messages like they were just another one of these corrections. Determined not to shed a tear, I walked to the bathroom, pulled my razor and my father's shaving cream out of the closet, and started the tap. Part of me still clung to that fourth-grade Olympic dream, and if not the real Olympics, then at least the Junior Olympics. And if I wanted to make it, then I had to train my body. Not just to swim faster, but also to conform.

Nearly twenty years after her victory at the Brentwood Country Club, Babe falls in love on the golf course all over again. This time it's not the game that makes her heart pump in time to her record-setting feet but rather the freckled redhead, nineteen to Babe's thirty-nine, who dares believe she can beat Babe at the Miami amateur tournament. Betty Dodd is a golfer but also a fan. If it were a different era, not the 1950s but the 2010s, an era replete with lesbian sports heroes like tennis champion Billie Jean King and soccer stars Abby Wambach and Megan Rapinoe, Betty might have hung posters and magazine cutouts on her bedroom walls. Instead, she'll have to settle for joining Babe's gallery after her own elimination from play. She's late to the narrative, breathless and disheveled, a frown of concentration set into her face.

"Couldn't hit an elephant's ass with a bull fiddle today," Babe shouts after a particularly rough hole. The words send a tingle up Betty's spine. She wants to kiss that rough mouth, has wanted to ever since she read Babe's secret to success in the papers—*You've got to loosen your girdle and really let the ball have it!*—ever since she first laid eyes on Babe at the Red Cross charity exhibition in her hometown of San Antonio back in 1947, when Betty was just a high school junior.

Babe's mouth might still be rough, but she looks different now than in her Olympic days. I can just barely recognize her: the angular set of her jaw buried beneath shoulder-length hair, the musculature of her hurdling legs hidden behind an ankle-length golf skirt, and her thin-lipped smile under a mask of lipstick. Now, reporters dub her a "magnificent specimen of athletic womanhood."

The decades between the 1932 Los Angeles Olympics and that surely soggy Miami day when she met Betty had been spent trying to master just two things with the same furious focus: golf, which she practiced until her hands blistered and bled, and womanhood, which she rehearsed until she could perform in her sleep. She was desperate

for golf, but the high society ladies on the tournament circuit wanted nothing to do with a crass, working-class tomboy. *They didn't want me to beat the rich dames.*

If Babe wanted to pursue golf seriously, she would need money for lessons, travel, hotel, and tournament fees. The other women on the amateur circuit, the ladies who blur together in my mind until they become a chorus of interchangeable voices—Betty and Betsy and Peggy and Patty—were bankrolled by their husbands and families. That wouldn't be an option for Babe. Whenever she had money, she had always sent as much as she could back to her family, her parents Hannah and Ole and her six siblings. That had been the case ever since she had gotten her first job cleaning figs in a trough of acid water at the local packing plant for thirty cents an hour. No matter the job, she always dropped as much of her wages as she could into *Momma's sugar bowl*, until she left high school just a few months shy of graduation to work as a secretary for the Employers Casualty Company.

Babe, who had never excelled in school the way she had in athletics and lacked a high school diploma, was probably a lousy secretary. The Employers Casualty Company didn't care. They had hired her after watching her play basketball for Beaumont High. The job, with a salary of seventy-five dollars a month, was just a ruse. It created an opportunity to pay Babe to play ball with the Golden Cyclones, one of many women's company teams across the country that served as "traveling advertising campaigns for the companies that sponsored them," while still allowing her to maintain her status as an amateur athlete, a requirement if she still wanted to achieve her dream of Olympic glory. Company teams were one of only a few avenues available for women to earn livings as athletes.

Fresh off her track and field Olympic medal wins, Babe returned to Texas and faced a dilemma: to continue with the Golden Cyclones and her seventy-five dollars or to turn pro and cash in on her Olympic success? Seventy-five dollars was already a small fortune during the

economic free fall of the Great Depression, especially when compared to the women in New York City garment factories in 1934 earning less than ten dollars a month.

For some women, the very idea of working during the Great Depression was out of the question. At a time when a quarter of the workforce was unemployed, it was seen as unpatriotic for middle-class white women to accept jobs that should be left open for their husbands, or someone else's husband. Without the possibility of economic independence, few of these women could afford to live as lesbians. However, working-class women kept both their jobs, the kind of menial tasks in factories and homes that men would never stoop to do, and their freedom to live as they pleased. *The Depression didn't bother me*, Mabel Hampton insisted. *I stayed on my jobs.* She continued to make forty-five to fifty dollars a month. Even she was outpaced by Babe.

Still, Babe suspected she could make even more if she was willing to give up on the Golden Cyclones and the possibility of a second set of Olympic medals.

In the end, the decision was made for her. After a photo of Babe midstride appeared in a car ad—an ad for the very same car she hadn't paid a cent for before driving off the lot—she was declared a pro and banned from amateur competition. Who's to say if she truly did plan to pay for that car in monthly installments, if she never did give her permission for that photo to be used? She was insistent on both points as the Amateur Athletic Union reviewed her case. Hours before the AAU would overturn their decision, though, Babe gave in. There were whispers that the *rich dames* who wanted to keep her off the golf green had pushed for the decision in order to throw yet another obstacle in her path, and she refused to let them hold another victory over her. She would go pro. (Later, perhaps in that disputed car, she killed an old man in an accident, but she wouldn't want you to know that either.)

With basketball and track and field already in the rearview mirror,

Babe could focus completely on golf. She talked her way into free lessons from pros across the country, many of them men. One of the most important lessons she got, though, was from lady golfer Bertha Bowen, who sheltered Babe from the cruelties of her other competitors and offered her a Pygmalion-style makeover.

The working-class family and community that raised Babe in Beaumont, Texas, had done little to shake her out of her tomboy ways. Now with national attention came national scrutiny. The moniker *muscle moll*, the very thing that Paul Gallico had accused Babe of being after she bested him in a game of golf, was a bit like the early twentieth century's *invert* in that it failed to make any distinction between gender identity and sexuality. Any woman who rejected traditional femininity became a lesbian. And any lesbian who perfected the art of femininity could fly under the radar.

I can picture Babe's transformation in montage: Bertha throws out Babe's ratty old checked blue dress and buys her a new evening gown. When she pulls it out of the closet before yet another country club party, Babe bolts down the stairs. "I'd rather go naked than wear that *sissy* thing!" she shouts. Bertha has no choice but to chase the Olympian until she is cornered in the kitchen like a nervous foal. After Babe submits to the gown, Bertha sits her down in front of the vanity. She drapes a string of pearls around the girl's neck and runs her fingers through the close-cropped hair. "You're like the daughter I never had," Bertha croons. She tugs, as if that could make this boy's cut grow into a ladylike wave overnight. "Ouch! B.B., that hurts!" Babe cries. When Babe finally teeters into the party, the chorus of country club women falls silent.

Over time, the hair grows and softens. Babe's demeanor is still rough, and she hardly talks to the other women on the circuit except to taunt them. It's progress, though. Enough progress that Bertha can't even scold her on those nights she wakes with a start to the racket of laughter and billiard balls, the sound of Babe hell-bent on defeating

Bertha's husband R.L. at the pool table. Bertha smiles before she falls back asleep. There is a certain charm to the parts of Babe that have yet to be smoothed over. Perhaps, Bertha thinks, they never should be.

Babe's transformation is near complete. She tears a photo of herself printed alongside yet another one of Paul Gallico's demeaning stories out of the 1933 issue of *Vanity Fair*. There is something oddly flirtatious about her posture back then: shorts as small as underpants worn beneath an oversize sweatshirt, hands sandwiched between her back and the wall, one knee bent forward to support her lean, all topped off by the stern fire of her gaze. No matter, that's not the woman she is anymore. She sets her lighter, the one she hides alongside her pack-a-day habit, to the edge of the photo and watches it burn. Now she's a lady.

This newly minted lady—the one with the straight-silhouette pastel skirt and the chin-length waves tamped down under a visor—was still ostracized. When Babe entered only her second golf tournament, the Women's Texas Amateur Championship, the Country Club Chorus tried to bar her from competition with the claim that no country club would grant membership, a requirement for entry, to such a tumbleweed. Babe had her Beaumont Country Club card to prove them wrong. She played what I have heard were several sensational rounds of golf—though you'll have to look elsewhere if you want a stroke-by-stroke record—and she won the Texas trophy by a margin of just two holes, whatever that means. The mean girls became even more desperate to kick Babe off the amateur circuit once and for all. One woman stood up from her chorus chair, turned to the U.S. Golf Association, and insisted that if Babe was a pro in track and field, then she must be a pro in all sports. Two weeks later, the USGA banned Babe from amateur competition. The Country Club Chorus got their wish and seemingly put an end to Babe's golfing career even before it began. Babe responded with the kind of graceful acceptance Bertha had worked so hard to teach her.

Their idea is that I used to be all tomboy, with none of the usual girls' interests, and then all of the sudden I switched over to being feminine. Babe wants to correct the reporters and biographers, to trick me into deleting that montage, erasing all she had been. *But I was always interested in the women's things around the house, like cooking and sewing and decorating.*

There is more that the Country Club Chorus took away from Babe, more to the story than what she can speak into the recorder, what she can admit on the tapes she has to hand over to Harry so he can write her autobiography, something more that the press can't have because they would turn it into something sordid, into *quite a rhubarb*. For instance, there's that day in Miami, 1950, after she's waited out three years of paying pro gigs and earned back her amateur status, after she's found a husband who finally lends legitimacy to her lady act, that day when she spots Betty in her tournament gallery and recognizes something of her old self. The short hair. The unselfconscious way she stands. The jerk and bounce of her gait, her hunger for the game. Babe wants to hold her arms around Betty's narrow hips and guide her swing, callused hand over callused hand. She waits a few more stops on the tour, until they get to Atlanta, to ask her father, General Dodd, not for Betty's hand but to take the girl back to Tampa, to help Betty come into herself not just as a golfer, but also as a lady.

~~~

Just six years after I vowed to give up swimming, I found myself on the starting block at the Piscine Georges Vallerey in Paris, built to host the 1924 Olympics. It wasn't the Olympics I had dreamed of when I filled in my fourth-grade diary, but it was the closest I would ever get.

When I had moved to Brooklyn after college, I swore to give up the water. I would become a swammer, past tense. What had the sport ever given me, anyhow? I had pulled and kicked and breathed, spun and churned and spat for more than five thousand miles. Had I sailed

that distance, I would have earned a swallow tattoo. Instead, the only badges I had to show for the journey were a permanent one-piece tan, a signature shoulder slouch I couldn't shake, and a lasting concern for the maintenance of my bikini line. Swimmers had policed the lines of my exposed body, told me what kind of girl I could be. I threw my old suit into the back of my underwear drawer. In this anonymous city, I was resolved to become someone new.

New York was an island in motion, and New Yorkers ran to keep up with it. They chased down cabs, sprinted after subway cars, beat a steady rhythm against the road in Prospect Park. If Babe had grown up here, she would have practiced her hurdles over hot dog carts and bike racks, not a quiet row of hedges. If I wanted to become a New Yorker, I would have to learn how to run. I bought leggings and a sweatshirt, a solid pair of shoes. I joined the throng, three days a week, three miles a day. I ran with my eyes on my feet, grimaced at the concrete. Without the water to wipe away my sweat, my skin bristled and stung. Sure enough, my body was in motion too, just barely keeping time with the thrum of the city, but this motion was nothing like the snowed-in quiet of an early morning swim.

A whiff of chlorine greeted me each morning when I got dressed, the perfume of an old lover. The temptation to pull out the old suit and press it to my nose grew. My will wasn't very strong. All it took was one unsettled, sleepless night just a few months after my move for me to give in. The elastic straps had grown brittle. Somehow, the suit stretched without breaking. It still fit. I just needed somewhere to wear it.

Over half a dozen adult swim clubs, master's teams, vied for my membership with their slick websites and paid subscription packages. Back in the 1930s when Babe wanted to learn golf, organized athletic teams for adults in search of leisure competition were unheard of. Now, I faced too many options to make a decision. There, that one with the orange logo. Orange was my favorite color, and that seemed

as good a reason as any. Besides, this particular team, Team New York Aquatics, didn't require members to compete. I blushed at the thought of returning to the pool without returning to competition. Maybe I wasn't giving in to an old lover who took from me more than they gave back. I was starting up an affair, one that could afford me the support and space I needed to blossom.

I noticed the gay men from my first TNYA practice. They kissed each other in greeting on deck, called each other *bitch* and *honey*, as in, "That bitch is in a *mood* today." They left me a women's locker room all to myself where I could host naked dance parties for a guest list of one. I had been here long enough to know that gay men had found refuge in so many pockets of New York City—refrigerated trucks in Meatpacking; Broadway stages and audiences; the bars and dance clubs of Hell's Kitchen; circuit parties that never stayed in one place for too long; the Rambles in Central Park, ripe for cruising in any season; live drag shows and *RuPaul's Drag Race* watch parties. Was the pool theirs too?

The first time another woman entered the locker room, I pounced. "It's nice to have some company in here for once," I said. "Why is this team full of nothing but gay men?"

The woman, who stood naked save for a pair of pink plastic flip-flops to guard against the mildewed tile, laughed. It had none of the bite of the laughter from those girls on my high school swim team. "It's an LGBT swim team," she said. "Didn't you know?"

"Of course," I said. If there was a gay swim team, how had I never heard of it? Why didn't it say so on the site? "I just meant, where's the *L* and the *B* and the *T*?"

She laughed again, something soft like water in the sound. "The women don't always stick around," she said. "But you're staying, right? Don't let those boys scare you off."

TNYA, I learned when I went back to study the website beyond the color of the logo, was part of an entire league of LGBTQIA+

teams, International Gay and Lesbian Aquatics. *Aquatic Lesbian.* That seemed like the right description of my identity. The team had been founded in the late 1980s by queer swimmers who wanted to train for an event that attracted an even bigger community of queer athletes, the Gay Games, which began in San Francisco in 1982. Dr. Tom Waddell and his co-conspirators had conceived of the Gay Olympic Games, as it was originally called, after he competed in the decathlon at the 1968 Olympics as a closeted athlete. (Women still cannot compete in the Olympic decathlon, a ten-event series that includes hurdles, javelin, and high jump.) Dr. Waddell took the best parts of the Olympics—he even tried to borrow the name until the real Olympics sued—and introduced three core principles intended to foster a better environment not just for queers but for any athlete who wanted to escape the performance pressures of the real thing: "Participation, Inclusion, and Personal Best." (Babe was only in it to win, at all costs.)

Not long after I joined the team, I met the pale, gangly middle-aged man who had founded it on the pool deck: Charlie Carson. His voice still carried the twang of Tennessee, where he had grown up closeted and worked as a manager for the men's collegiate swim team. He moved to New York City in 1977 and came out a year and half later. When Charlie joined the Gay Men's Chorus (where was the Gay Women's Chorus?), the other singers told him great things about San Francisco, so he decided to make the trip out for the very first Gay Games in 1982, even without a team to support him. He loved the experience so much that he returned in 1986. The swimmers and divers grew impatient at having to wait every four years to see their friends, so they formed their own league with an annual international competition, IGLA. It wasn't until 1990, the year I was born, that Charlie and the other New York swimmers found a space to practice and officially formed New York City's queer team, TNYA. Since then, Charlie has been to every Gay Games ever held, and even organized the aquatics portion of Gay Games IV, which attracted ten thousand

athletes to New York City in 1994. TNYA is now one of the largest queer swim teams in the world, with more than two hundred registered swimmers, divers, water polo players, and synchronistas. Charlie still uses a flip phone.

Had Gallico been given the opportunity to write about my first weeks on the team, nine hundred words for *Vanity Fair* tentatively titled "Lesbian in the Drink," he might have called me hirsute. Before practice one morning, standing at the edge of the pool in the hopes that the water might miraculously get warmer before we jumped in, one man lifted my arm to inspect the hair nestled in the pit. "It's longer than mine!" he shouted, loud enough for everyone to hear. Another man, by way of starting a conversation, asked, "Why don't lesbians have any sense of style?" I had hoped the team would provide the kind of safe haven Dr. Waddell had dreamed of, but my body was still judged every day, and still found wanting. My new teammates held the same barbs as my old ones, the weapons sport had given us.

At the Gay Games 10, Paris 2018, those very same men, the catty ones and the old-timers alike, marched by my side as we entered the stadium for the opening ceremonies—yet another borrowed tradition, one that had been in place since the 1932 Los Angeles games. *We all had to wear special dresses and stockings and white shoes that the Olympic Committee had issued to us*, Babe remembered in her autobiography. *I believe that was about the first time I'd ever worn a pair of stockings in my life.* Babe found these traditions, the girlie uniform and the pageantry of it all, stifling. *And as for those shoes, they were really hurting my feet.* After over an hour of *speeches and things*, Babe slipped off her shoes. One by one, the other girls followed suit.

I didn't stage a revolt in Stade Jean-Bouin. I stood beside the other New York City athletes—runners and volleyball players and an entire basketball team—in my TNYA shirt, as bright orange as Babe's Golden Cyclones uniform, and we walked across a platform raised over the stadium grass to the tune of Lady Gaga. I kept my sandals

on. I threw my hands in the air and danced. Charlie wrapped his arm around my shoulder and took a selfie. Back home, it was easy to take for granted that I could move freely from space to space, from bar to bookstore to pool, without question or comment, without the fear that I might be thrown out or spotted by the press or, worse, arrested for prostitution. On someone else's soil, with the team's founder by my side, it suddenly seemed remarkable and hard-won. Paris had been the site not just of the 1924 Olympics and the 2018 Gay Games but also of the first International Ladies' Games, held in 1922 to give women a space to compete in track and field at the highest level before they were allowed to enter the Olympics in 1928. For a moment, the comments the younger men had made evaporated into the hot August air, and I felt enveloped by the team, protected and free, feelings Babe had never known at a single one of the hundreds of events she competed in throughout her life.

The unfettered joy of the opening ceremonies buoyed me along through my swim races, the part of the sport I had always dreaded. At the worst moments of my high school swim season, I had vomited up my nerves. The atmosphere in Paris, right out of Dr. Waddell's vision, left no room for anxiety. Most of the men showed up to the pool exhausted and hung over, still smelling of party. I could hear my teammates cheer and whistle from the concrete stands. I looked up to see C. A. Hutton—one of Charlie's old friends from the Gay Men's Chorus and the early days of the team, may he rest in peace—in a shirt that read NOBODY KNOWS I'M A LESBIAN. I laughed and looked down at the pool. "Take your mark." I grabbed the edge of the starting block and waited for the horn.

~~~

Ever since the moment Babe was first declared a pro athlete in 1932, she'd had to become a show pony. Luckily, she had always been something of a performer. At age thirteen, Babe and her older sister Lillie

ran off to join the circus, where the two girls learned to walk the
tightrope, perform trapeze tricks, and balance in a headstand on the
back of an elephant.

As an adult, she sang on Chicago's vaudeville stage. She played ex-
hibition basketball. She pitched for major league baseball players. She
joined the House of David baseball team, a group of hirsute men who
played against major and minor league teams. In one game, they ran
the bases on donkeyback. At another, a woman in the crowd shouted,
"Where are your whiskers?" Babe replied, *I'm sitting on 'em sister, just
like you are!*"

No matter what she was doing, Babe was always playing to the
gallery. *I just love a gallery.* That was the only bit of golf vocabulary I
picked up from my time with her. She knew that if she could continue
to draw a crowd with her feats of strength and rough wit, then she
could make a living as an almost-athlete, with money enough to buy a
car for her father and a wicker bedroom set for her mother.

I want to know the Babe that emerged when the gallery left, the
woman underneath the performance. What did she do after Ruth
McGinnis, the unmarried queen Billiard Player of the World, de-
feated her at the Capitol Billiard and Bowling Academy? Perhaps tick-
led by the legendary combination of their names, they went to a bar
in Greenwich Village, the kind Babe had only heard whispers of, or
went slumming uptown in Harlem, where Mabel had just brought
Lillian to live at West 122nd Street. There is a photo of Babe and Ruth
cozied up against the pool table's pocket, all collars and close-cropped
waves, a pair of leather gloves sticking out of Babe's wool coat, and, if
I squint, they could become any two dykes playing pool at Ginger's in
Brooklyn, where the signup chalkboard is, as far as I'm concerned, the
only billiards tournament that matters.

I am suddenly suspicious of every athletic woman who crosses
Babe's path. Before Babe tried her hand at billiards, she had played
women's basketball, which didn't become an Olympic sport until

1976, for the Brooklyn Yankees against the Long Island Ducklings. Did those players who roughed Babe up on the court look anything like her old teammates on the Golden Cyclones? *Large feet, and large hands. They were really husky.* Babe and Ruth will meet again on another exhibition basketball team, a detail left out by Babe and many of her biographers. Did they pick up their relationship, whatever it was, right where they left off? Even Bertha Bowen, a proper lady golfer, becomes suspect. Does she call Babe her surrogate daughter to hide the true nature of their relationship, the way that Mabel listed Lillian as her sister, even on her death certificate?

I scrutinize these women because looks alone are not enough to make Babe a lesbian. The press is relentless in its cruelties, calling for a "gender test" to determine whether she is, in fact, a man or a woman. They have not yet mined the distinction between gender and sexuality. What could make Babe a lesbian is not her appearance but the way her body clacks against others in her life, the way it brushes up against Betty.

~~~~

Babe and Betty, I must choose to believe, were happy for a spell. They ignored, as best they could, the specter of George in her Tampa house, a three-hundred-fifty-pound drunk who kept a tight grip on Babe's career.

*She's like a daughter to me,* Babe wrote. Babe never did have a child of her own, though at least one miscarriage, a *swimmer* who got away, suggested she had wanted one. *George and I see a lot of her.* Now, among the ladies of the hostile Country Club Chorus, she had a coconspirator and confidante, *my buddy,* someone to eat dinner with after a long day of play, someone to sing along to the tune of her harmonica.

Babe and Betty's happiness is palpable in a photo of the two performing side by side. A harmonica obscures Babe's expression. Her

hair has been set by curlers and her free hand, held aloft, is bound by a wedding ring, but I can still tell she is smiling from the crinkles around her eyes. Betty, in an oversized white blazer and a newsboy cap, serves as a reminder of who Babe used to be. There's a guitar slung over her shoulder, and her face looks skeptical of the camera. *Bertha made a lady out of me*, Babe scolds later in the evening, *and I'm gonna do the same thing to you.*

This photo—much like the photos of Babe and Ruth at the billiards table—never appears in her biographies, so I am unsure when exactly it was taken. The photo agency insists on 1948, but that was two years before the pair struck up a relationship. Perhaps it was captured on that day in 1953 when they recorded two songs for Mercury Records, Babe's harmonica solo on the A side and a joint performance, Babe on harmonica with Betty on vocals, of "I Felt a Little Teardrop" on the B side. There was so much pressure, from the era and from the media, for Babe to keep any romantic or physical aspects of the relationship private, to excise tender, intimate moments from her autobiography, to hide them from the cameras. *They say our love was just a lie*, Betty croons. I danced alone in the living room to the mournful tune, careful not to slip on the wooden floorboards in my socks, and felt, somewhere between needle and vinyl, a record of their lesbian love.

Maybe the photo was taken on August 16, 1953, when Babe and Betty performed Cole Porter's "Begin the Beguine" together on the *Ed Sullivan Show* in New York City. To Babe it might have been just another gig—she was paid fifteen hundred dollars for the appearance—but for Betty it was a rare moment in the spotlight. She doesn't care that she only got three hundred and fifty, less than a third of what Babe was given. Babe is older, the more famous one. She's the one who draws the audience, runs the show. She'd never ask for Betty's input on what song they should perform, but that's okay. Betty is just along for the ride, to keep Babe company from the passenger seat, to tune the radio and point out landmarks along the highways.

Or perhaps the photo was taken at a more private affair, a dinner after yet another round of golf that Betty has won. The other women find Babe less insufferable now that she has taken Betty under her wing. There is something softer about her now. Sure, she is still hellbent on winning, but there is a new humanity to her, a vulnerability. After the plates are cleared away at the club, one of the women brushes by that table where Babe and Betty are seated—George is said to be in California "on business," but everyone has their own suspicions about his absence after overhearing the couple's last public fight—and stops for a moment to say, "Oh, won't you play something for us?" The two oblige without hesitation. Sure, Betty isn't in the driver's seat, how could she be with such an accomplished woman twenty years her senior, but *this* is why she does it. Everyone—George, the Country Club Chorus, the press, the gallery—has laid claim to a piece of Babe, but only Betty gets to see the quiet moments, Babe's private self.

Cayleff is the only biographer of Babe's to study her romantic relationship with Betty and to acknowledge that Babe could finally let her guard down around her *buddy*. Cayleff had the opportunity to interview Betty just a few years before she passed away in 1993, at a moment when she felt "empowered by a changing cultural climate" to open up a little. Still, it was a "coded conversation," and the aging golfer never described herself or Babe as a lesbian. Betty asked Cayleff if she was a lesbian, and when the writer said yes, the former golfer seemed to relax a little bit. I called Cayleff because she was now my closest link to Betty and to that private side of Babe.

"It pained me," Cayleff said, both to read Babe's "heterosexual inventions" in her autobiography and to know there was a lesbian love story she never had the space or security to tell. "We're always looking for images and reflections of ourselves."

When she conducted other interviews for the book, Cayleff always asked, "How would you characterize Babe's relationship with Betty Dodd?" In response, one aging golf pro flipped over a table at a

country club. After Cayleff published the book, she received an eight-page letter written in "elderly scrawl" that attacked her for writing and publishing a book that identified Babe as a lesbian. The letter writer had not signed her name, but she did include a return address that revealed her to be another aging golf pro. The Babe Didrikson Zaharias Museum in Beaumont, Texas, does not sell copies of Cayleff's book.

It pains me, too, to know that I will never get a firsthand account of what existed between Betty and Babe because everyone who witnessed their relationship has taken their story to the grave. We know that Babe and George called each other Romance as a pet name, that they married in St. Louis the same year they met, that they honeymooned in Australia, a working trip for Babe, that George turned her dream house, Rainbow Manor, into a reality. This is the story each biography—*Whatta-Gal, Wonder Girl, Babe*—must tell. No one has written *Whatta-Dyke*. Babe and Betty remain unreachable, unarchived.

Because Babe had access to the word but never used it in her countless interviews and press conferences, I am hesitant to call her a lesbian. I want to claim her for the masculinity that brought her nothing but derision from the press; for her achievements in sports, even when I don't understand them; for the joy she shared with Betty, caught in photographs and vinyl grooves. When these facts alone are not enough to quiet my discomfort, I turn to another piece of her legacy: the LPGA, the Ladies Professional Golf Association.

When Babe was declared a pro golfer at the behest of the mean girls in the Country Club Chorus, there was only one tournament she was permitted to enter. Bertha Bowen created a second when she opened the Fort Worth Women's Invitational to pros in 1935. She did it just for Babe. It was not nearly enough. Babe was tired of a life spent earning a living as a performer and wanted to return to real competitions. She decided to wait out the three-year probation period required for her to be reinstated as an amateur. The idle time was made easier by

World War II, which canceled many women's golf competitions, and by the annual six figures George earned as a sports promoter, which allowed Babe to turn down tournament purses, endorsement offers, and exhibition play. After she was finally reinstated as an amateur in 1943, she clocked an unparalleled seventeen-tournament winning streak before she returned to life as a pro in 1947. By 1948, there were seven pro tournaments for Babe to play. Still, it wasn't enough.

Like George, golf often seems a distraction from the real story. For a moment, though, the sport presents the full lesbian love story Cayleff couldn't get out of Betty. The Ladies Professional Golf Association—or the *Lesbian* Professional Golf Association, as I like to think of it—began in 1949 with the mission of creating a professional tour for women, something male golfers had had for two decades. George wanted to take credit for the idea, but in reality it came from the president of Wilson Sporting Goods, who had the money to fund each tournament's purse. They had to use the *L*-word because *Women's* Professional Golf Association was already taken by an earlier, failed endeavor.

One thing is for certain: it was never Babe's idea. Cayleff was quick to remind me on our phone call that Babe never took up the feminist mantle or used her fame to become an advocate for women in sports. She was, as ever, only in it for herself. Before the LPGA became "the most successful women's sports association in the world," before the annual prize money topped six figures spread out over nearly two dozen tournaments, Babe insisted she be paid an additional one thousand dollars just for showing up. *Well* I'm *the star and all of you are in the chorus*, Babe reminded everyone. I *get the money and if it weren't for me, half of our tournaments wouldn't even be.* By 1951, she became the first female athlete to bring in six figures a year.

Babe wasn't the brains behind the operation, and she wasn't going to win Miss Congeniality on the tour either. She brought the brawn. The LPGA was formed because she showed the world the need for it,

and she left behind as her legacy the opportunity for other lady golfers to earn an independent income through sport. The women who followed her wouldn't need to strike an unsteady truce with someone like George. They wouldn't need to bury the story of their love for a girl like Betty. They would be free to live their lesbian lives in the light.

~~~~~

At one point, as she tried to sort out how to make money through sport, Babe bragged that she was going to swim the English Channel, like Gertrude Ederle before her. In the summer of 1926, Ederle became the first woman to accomplish that feat. A lot of good it did her. Unable to turn her warm reception, complete with a ticker tape parade through lower Manhattan, and the publicity that followed into a viable career, she died anonymous and unmarried, a few years shy of seventy.

I am seriously considering taking up long distance swimming in a big way. It's nearly impossible to sort fact from fiction, to know how good a swimmer Babe really was. *The stories about me,* she is quick to repeat, *sometimes get a little tall in the telling.* In LA, she had goaded one of the women on the Olympic swim team: *I'll cut two seconds off* your one-hundred-meter time *next year.* After her Olympic victories, Grantland Rice helped create a video to show off her skill in over half a dozen sports. Babe dives into a pool and swims freestyle down the lane. There's a bit of a wiggle to her stroke that could be corrected if she engaged her core. Were I to coach her, I'd give that pointer, free of charge. "The Texas Marvel is only a fraction of a second back of the world mark for one hundred meters," says Granny over the flicker of film, with no evidence to back up his claim. "There's hardly a flaw in her style." In her own autobiography, she later admits, *I didn't care too much for just swimming,* but insists she could have made the Olympic diving team *if I had concentrated on it.*

More than the swimming, I recognize Babe's restless pace. Two

of her biographers have attributed her "versatility" to "the lack of opportunities for women in sport." Yet each time she picks up a new game—basketball, golf, bowling, tennis—with the same ease and determination, my sense grows that her movements are fueled by more than a simple desire to win. There is a disquiet at the heart of her relentless training, a truth that cowers behind her gallery quips. You only run like that when you are running *from* something. She is unsettled in her body, ill at ease as she stands on the golf green. Gendered, sexualized, she is something to be owned, by her husband, by the media, by promoters and agents. In motion, though, she has a chance at escape. She is strength, grace. She doesn't have to decide what kind of woman to be, whether she wants to even *be* a woman. She becomes her body.

Those mean girls couldn't keep me away from the pool. I returned day after day, year after year, to feel my body in motion, what it could do no matter how I groomed or dressed myself. I could never give it up. I wouldn't let them take that away from me.

I expect to play golf until I am 90.

~~~~

I entered the Parisian pool with the dive I had been taught as a child, before I learned to ride a bike. It could have been any race. Today, it was the four-hundred-meter freestyle.

I hardly remember a moment of that race, of my time in that historic pool. It blurs and fuzzes against the hundreds of other races I have swum, all over before my mind could register what my body was up to. Not the blur of speed but of monotony. I can't recall my time or what place I came in or whether I won a gay medal. It was the least memorable moment of the entire trip. Gay swimming, as it turns out, is still just swimming. The uniform and regulation of it. The competition. The heats sorted into men and women. The coded language of the official's whistle: three short blasts for silence at the start, one long

blast to climb up onto the block, and a long, loud horn to start. The competition, where someone always has to come out on top.

I could never tell Charlie.

~~~~~

Babe didn't get to play golf until she turned ninety. It is a tragic love story I am telling. In 1953, she was diagnosed with colon cancer. She was only forty-one. The doctors told George before they told Babe, but it was Betty who stood by her side through the disease. Betty had played the roles of daughter, travel companion, devoted fan, and even confidant when Babe's pains got so bad she confessed only to Betty that she suspected cancer. Now, she would play the role of nurse too. This was yet another role that both George, who often saw Betty as an unwelcome visitor in his marriage, and the prying eyes of the press could accept.

When Babe finally learned the news herself, she gave her golf clubs away to Bertha's husband, R.L., her one-time billiards opponent, because she feared she would never play again. It was Betty who brought them back to Babe's Beaumont hospital room. It was Betty who slept in Babe's Galveston hospital room where she awaited a colostomy. George was away on business. *It was good having Betty in the room with me at night, so I could talk to someone when I felt like it.*

The surgery meant Babe would no longer be able to pass solid waste on her own, and she was convinced that it meant the end of her golf career. For the rest of her days, she would live with a small bag attached to her stomach, one that would need to be cleaned every day. After a successful operation, it was Betty whom Babe trusted to help clean her colostomy bag, and it was Betty whom the doctors trusted with the news that they had been unable to remove all the cancer. It was news that she and George, now bound by a secret, could never tell Babe.

Betty watched as Babe recovered. Babe, eager to launch herself

back in motion, was a terrible patient, who thrashed so hard she nearly ripped out her stitches and her IV drip. Only Betty could calm her. *All she had to do was just touch my finger.*

Back at home, Babe played one hole of golf at the Tampa Golf and Country Club, which she and George now owned. Then she played nine holes. Just fourteen weeks after the operation, she competed in the LPGA's All-American. She didn't need just her strength back to play. She also needed Betty, whose presence combated her fears that she would have an accident on the course, in front of the gallery. Betty put her own golf career on hold so she could stand by Babe's side. Less than a year after the surgery, Babe won her first tournament since the diagnosis.

Betty watched as Babe became an outspoken advocate for cancer research, the kind of advocate she had never been for women in sport. She helped Babe pack to attend President Dwight Eisenhower's kick-off for the annual Cancer Crusade. She even agreed to perform with Babe on the *Ed Sullivan Show,* following a brief interview about her recovery. Betty flinches to think the disease is not yet done with Babe.

The pain and fatigue returned, mysterious and sharp. Doctors searched for the source. They removed a herniated disk in her back. They accused her of having an addiction to pain pills. Betty once again gave up her game and returned to sleep in Babe's hospital room, perhaps haunted in her dreams by the terrible truth she had been asked to guard. A little over two years after her original diagnosis, doctors admitted to Babe there was more cancer.

When Babe was hospitalized for the last time in March 1956, age forty-four, Betty was no longer at her side. Did Babe finally want to let her live, or could Betty no longer face the secret she had kept from the one she most adored? Betty last saw Babe, unrecognizable and unrecognizing, eleven days before Babe died in the early hours of September 27, 1956. Babe had asked that Betty skip the funeral, and she kept her promise. "I never wanted to be away from her," she told

Cayleff years later. "Even when she was dying of cancer. I loved her. I would have done anything for her."

Betty won her first LPGA title a month after Babe's death. She continued as a professional golfer, never nearly as good as Babe, but it was a career path her old lover had carved out for her. She never married. She lived to see the great tennis star Billie Jean King come out as a lesbian, but she wasn't around to watch U.S. women's soccer player Abby Wambach kiss her wife on the field after she won the 2015 World Cup. She wasn't around to pass the six-foot-tall Nike ad outside Penn Station featuring Abby's soccer teammate and equal-pay advocate Megan Rapinoe holding hands with her girlfriend, basketball champion Sue Bird. Betty and Babe weren't around to see the first openly transgender athletes compete in the Olympics in 2021, the same year several female athletes were banned because their natural testosterone levels were deemed too high by the same set of gender regulations. No doubt Babe and Betty would have stayed out of the debate, even though journalists had wasted years in pursuit of the true nature of Babe's gender identity, and would have tested her testosterone in a heartbeat, if given the chance.

Who was to say if sports attracted lesbians, or if it made them? (I bet Paul Gallico would want to opine on that, if given the column inches.) But there was intention in the road Babe built for these other lesbians, Betty included. She was a trailblazer who opened a path for women to earn money with their bodies, not as sex workers or as wives who would surely never see a penny of their own dowries but with strength and autonomy. "I could even have strangled George," Betty said to Cayleff, her hands strong from massaging Babe's feet. After Babe, athletes could earn money enough to live without men.

~~~~~

Charlie Carson lives. He lives longer than Babe. Charlie lives, still, in one of his first apartments in the city, a rent-stabilized three-bedroom

in SoHo with a modern facade and video intercom that lead into a unit stuck in the 1980s, complete with peeling ceiling paint and a swinging bathroom door that looks more suited to a bar than a home. Charlie lives long enough to join me for a swim one snowy Monday night at an indoor pool so old that when he enters, he says, "This takes me back fifty years," and means it, because that's how long he's been a swimmer.

He invited me and several of our other teammates to his apartment for the Second Annual Potato Chip Party. For the past year, he had gathered every unusual variety of potato chip he had spotted on the shelves of grocery stores and corner bodegas. Friends brought him bags from Canada (*Ruffles All Dressed*), Australia (*Smith's Chicken Flavour*), and Thailand (*Lay's 2 in 1: Grilled Shrimp & Seafood Sauce Flavor*). Now we were invited to sample them. "*The ceremonial opening of the bags will be approximately 9:15–9:30,*" the invitation read. I had to go.

The foil bags of potato chips had been laid out across a card table like winning poker hands. I walked right past the display and into the living room, which held a piano, a sectional, corner windows, and room enough left over for me to twirl without knocking anything out of place. A Manhattan palace, the kind Charlie could never afford were he to move here today. Just off the end of the living room, the door to Charlie's bedroom stood open. Everyone was preoccupied by the chips and the hunt for a flavor that offered something more than chemical chaos. No one would notice my absence. I slipped inside.

Charlie's bedroom was cluttered with the archives of our queer swim league. He sleeps beside trophies and ribbons, screen-printed GAY OLYMPICS T-shirts, photos in a stack next to the digital scanner, binders filled with event lineups and results from every annual championship. Charlie is the sub-sub librarian of this collection. He guards these items as closely as Herman Melville's character guards whale facts.

The sub-sub librarian himself appeared behind me. He steered me

back into the kitchen, toward the table laden with chips. "What's your favorite flavor so far?" he asked.

The night wore on. We drank vodka and Coke to wash the sour salt fuzz out of our mouths. I chatted with my teammates. I met Charlie's old friend, James Ballard, in from LA, who explained to me that he hosts a similar party back home in West Hollywood, except in place of potato chips, he served his guests elaborate desserts that required a week's preparation. I didn't care much for conversation. I itched to sneak back into Charlie's bedroom, to be left alone with the paper trail left by the community he had built.

Unable to get that cluttered trove out of my mind, I began to email Charlie every now and again with an innocent question or two about the team. In response, he sent me old photos and digitized issues of the league newsletter, *Wet Notes*, which had been put together in the days when cut and paste could only be performed with scissors and glue. I never asked directly, but I wanted to understand why the league still existed in an era when queer people could participate in the *real* Olympics, when most queer people, I assumed, were like me and didn't care much for competition at all.

Eventually, perhaps weary of my questions, Charlie invited me to join him and a few of his old buddies back at his apartment to watch a documentary about the first queer swim team, formed in West Hollywood after the 1982 Gay Games. Sitting there watching the movie with some of the team's original members—men who had supported one another through the AIDS crisis, men who had competed in the real Olympics from the confines of the closet—I began to understand the importance of Team New York Aquatics. It was more than an opportunity to swim while gay. It held within its history resistance and community organizing, sanctuary and freedom. It was the kind of community Mabel might have celebrated even though she never learned how to swim, one where the dead seemed to take care of the living, and the living looked out for each other.

Yet there was still something missing for me—a body that would never know the fear of AIDS; a body that had never lived, closeted, in the limelight, haunted by the threat of exposure; a body that did hurt from constant critique and scrutiny; a body that failed, by my own design, to live up to the standards of femininity.

Back at home, I flipped through *Wet Notes* again, in the hope I had missed something that might connect me to a team that rarely felt like my own. A headline in the 1993 issue caught my eye: "Lesbians Who Swim." The short article was written by a woman who swam with Philadelphia's queer team, the Fins, and had been the only lesbian member for three years. When another lesbian joined, she was excited to have the company, but then immediately disappointed to realize they were still two lesbians short of a full relay team. Even though mixed relays, two men and two women, were a staple at IGLA, they were not offered in Chicago that year. "To my dismay," she wrote, "I realized sexism was alive and well in my gay community."

When I read those words, I realized that if I wanted a swim league that felt like my own, I might just have to stop searching for it and, with Babe as my inspiration, create it.

*Extracts* | INTERNATIONAL GAY AND
LESBIAN AQUATICS TEAMS

À Contre-Courant | Montreal, QC
Atlanta Rainbow Trout | Atlanta, GA
Different Strokes Swim Team | San Diego, CA
District of Columbia Aquatics Club (DCAC) |
   Washington, D.C.
English Bay Swim Club | Vancouver, BC
Glamourhead Sharks | Melbourne, Australia
Liquid Assets New England Swimming (LANES) |
   Boston, MA
Orca Swim Club | Seattle, WA
Out to Swim | London, England
Paris Aquatique | Paris, France
Philadelphia Fins | Philadelphia, PA
San Francisco Tsunami | San Francisco, CA
Subversive Sirens | Minneapolis, MN
Sydney Stingers | Sydney, Australia
Team New York Aquatics (TNYA) | New York, NY
Toronto Triggerfish | Toronto, ON
West Hollywood Aquatics (WH20) | Los Angeles, CA

# 4.

## On the Island of Lesbians: Sappho and Anactoria

*(floruit 595 BC)*

I PLUCKED THESE LESBIANS, MARY AND MABEL AND BABE, like violets from a field. They grew separately, entirely unaware of one another, but I pulled them together in a bouquet, an imitation of Mary's gift to Juno, tied together with just one word.

That same word had come into my own life as an accusation before I even knew what it meant or where it had come from. I heard it crackle through the telephone when my neighbor, the one who drove me and her own daughter to swim practice on summer mornings so hot they glued us to the faux leather seats of her minivan, called up my mother. I had just come home from a taffy afternoon stretched sticky across the rooms of their house: a snack in the kitchen, a serenade on her brother's new guitar in the basement, and, finally, arts and crafts at the dining table. We decorated our new team water bottles with an assortment of Sharpies and slogans we had picked up from a season of swim meets. EAT MY BUBBLES! SWIM FAST!! KICK BUTT!!!

My neighborhood friend added our initials to her own water bottle, linked by a plus sign and surrounded by a heart.

"How dare!" My neighbor's voice now came through the phone. It was the same tone she used to tell us to quiet down in the backseat of the van or to finish up our salmon before we left the dinner table. "Your lesbian daughter is a bad influence, and I won't have her in my house. How dare you let her lead our kid astray." She had already scrubbed her daughter's bottle clean, as if whatever I had might be catching.

These first three lesbians in my collection found the word to be a burden too. The heavy label had often been affixed to their names and stories by outsiders who inspected them through a glass. (I offer it to them as if looking in a mirror.) They wore the word *lesbian* alone, held it in solitude. Soon, though, the word would be celebrated as a gift with the power to unite. It would become a rope. If you held fast to it in a storm, soon enough another would pull you onto the shore. Lesbian became a culture and a community.

Before I gather up this next generation of lesbians, a generation who embraced their shared identity, my gaze is called back to the woman who gave us the word. Lesbian is born from another *violet-weaver*, an ancient Greek singer who was just one Lesbian among the many residents of the island of Lesbos, the patron saint of today's lesbians: Sappho. Her story has been told countless times, by scholars and pulp novelists, by poets and playwrights, but little of her biography is known with any certainty. The poetry she composed and performed to the tune of her lyre is even more uncertain, fragmented by time. Taken together, though, the conflicting accounts of Sappho's life paired with the verses she wrote in the mood of a forlorn ballad could resurrect the Lesbian who gave us our name and forge a myth strong enough to bring us together.

~~~~~

Sappho knows she is a *soft woman*, her life full of *refinement, the splendor and the beauty of the sun*, a life lived in radiant color: purple

wine and *white goats*, *honey*, and *chickpeas more golden than gold*. The *rosy-fingered* flesh of her lovers who lay with her on *soft beds* to *satisfy* their *longing*.

None of her lovers had been like Anactoria, though. When Sappho shuts her eyes, she is greeted by the vision of her beloved the way she was just the other morning, the last time they would ever see one another. Anactoria, a *rejoicing bride* with *delicately woven garlands around her tender neck*, her *bridegroom* at her side.

When she shuts her eyes, all Sappho can see is all that she must soon leave behind. *Goodbye, bride. Goodbye, respectable bridegroom.* The Cleanactidae are finally sending her away to Sicily. The prominent family claims it is for her family's politics. But she knows, her husband Cercylas knows, maybe even little Cleis knows, that it is for her love. For the way she interrupted the wedding ceremony to tear the violets from Anactoria's head. When they dragged her away, she beat her own breast, tore her garments so that someone else might understand her pain.

"*You cooled my heart that burned with desire*," she sings against a simple tune. She is tired of being asked to write wedding songs. She refuses to sing about the gods, about great men and their histories, as the other poets do. She will sing about what she loves. "*Honestly, I wish to be dead. You, who I treated so well, have harmed me the most.*"

It isn't true, the part about death. She doesn't care what happens to her body, but she needs her words to live on, to make her immortal. Live on they will. All she had to sacrifice was love. Aphrodite promised Sappho that if she never let anyone love her as much as she loved *immortal Aphrodite*, then her words would endure for as long as civilization could last. Love seemed a small price to pay. Today, it is too much to bear.

"*Oh, Aphrodite, release me from anguish and distress, from cruel cares*," Sappho sings. She wants to forget the angry words Anactoria spoke to her at her door the night before the wedding, the last they

would ever exchange. *"How unhappy we have been, Sappho. Against my will I must leave you."*

Now it is Sappho who is leaving. Leaving her house, leaving her island, all that she knows. But she is leaving behind something of herself too, something that will never be forgotten. *"When you lie dead, there will never be any memory of you,"* she cries, the last lament of Lesbos. *"Go and goodbye, and remember me."*

~~~~~

The French philosopher Jacques Derrida reminds me that the word *archive* comes from these ancient Greeks. I can't say I understood much of his book *Archive Fever*, but the title offers an apt diagnosis of my affliction. Our modern *archive* is a descendant of the ancient Greek word *Archeion*, the home of the ruler, the place where laws are stored, the place from which they are enforced. Today the word calls to mind the place where books and papers are stored, the physical or digital space where they are preserved. Charlie Carson's bedroom collection of swim team memorabilia. The fictional room where Herman Melville's Sub-Sub Librarian stored his assemblage of whale quotes. The New-York Historical Society. The Lesbian Herstory Archives.

*Archeion* also evokes Roman Emperor Hadrian's library on the north side of the Acropolis in Athens, Greece. I made my only trip to the country as an adult, without my classicist father. "I'm really more of a Latinist than a Hellenist," he explained.

One summer back in high school, when the rest of my classmates were at the beach, he took my mother and me on a research trip to England to hike Hadrian's Wall. The seventy-three-mile fortification was built to span the width of the island's waistband, to defend Roman Britain from the "barbarians." I wrote nightly reports to my then-boyfriend: *Mom shielded my eyes from naked statues at the museum. My father took lots of notes for his lectures. I suspect he has a thing for Hadrian.* From Greece, I had to send my father a photo of his darling

emperor's other erection. Or at least what's left of it. The marble steps leading up to the library curve beneath centuries of feet. Fluted columns shoulder a roof that could no longer provide shelter. While the western wall has been restored to its former glory, the eastern wall—where papyrus scrolls were stored in small cubbies—is now just a pile of rubble.

If I turned my gaze away from the ruin of Hadrian's library and squinted into the sun, I could just maybe imagine a series of papyri there, tightly wound and tucked into the recessed shelves of that eastern wall: *The Complete Works of Sappho in Nine Volumes*. Is that a woman I see climbing the solid steps, shooing the cats begging at her *shining ankles*, sneaking by the scholars to reach past Ovid, past Homer, toward Sappho? Maybe those scrolls were destroyed by Herulian invaders. Maybe her work was never there at all. Maybe the library only ever housed words written about Sappho, volumes and shelves filled by all we cannot know about her, an entire collection of lacunae waiting for an imagination to sound their depths.

"Archivable meaning," writes Jacques Derrida in *Archive Fever*, "is also and in advance codetermined by the structure that archives." It is easier for me to understand Derrida when I picture this fallen library, a structure that archives. Of those nine volumes of verse attributed to Sappho, only around two hundred fragments and one full poem remain. Recorded history is not a straightforward representation of what happened but rather a portrait of who had the power to make the recording, of what those in power selected for the rest of us to remember, of how even the tools at hand—the lyre, the papyrus plant, the printing press, the library, the computer—shaped what was set down. In other words, what remains of Sappho's poetry and her life story says more about the systems and the people that preserved those fragments than it does about her. My father's life work in classics has been the study of the system that failed to preserve Sappho.

I texted my father updates from my trip. I loved the nation of islands

for its *salt sea*. I felt a kinship with the place, as if I had been forged from the scrape of ocean salt against my skin, from the blast of wind that carved out handholds in the cliffs, from the rake of currents across the seafloor, from the volcanic heat that brought desire to the surface. I asked my father if there might be any Greek in our Italian blood. No, he told me definitively. His brother had done a DNA ancestry test.

I sent him photos of the cats that littered the island. Cats so hungry you could count their ribs, so dirty you can't distinguish their mottled calico markings from the mud and clay matted to their fur. "Cats," according to two other French authors, Monique Wittig and her partner Sande Zeig, "are among the companion lovers' favorite bed animals." This line comes from their own foundational lesbian myth, filled with plenty of ancient Greeks and Amazons, as told through a series of fabricated dictionary entries published in the 1970s, *Lesbian Peoples: Material for a Dictionary*. Monique and Sande use the phrase *companion lovers* in place of the word *lesbian* to describe "those who, violently desiring one another, live/love in peoples, following the verses of Sappho, 'in beauty I will sing my companions.' The companion lovers gather from lesbians all of the culture, the past, the inventions, the songs and the ways of life." In Sappho's day, though, it was horses, not cats, who ran wild on the island.

My father must have known that I sought some sort of connection with Sappho, a clear line to trace our lineage. After my trip, he mailed me a stocky little edition of Sappho's poetry published by the Loeb Classical Library, the green standard of classical studies: *Greek Lyric I*, translated by David A. Campbell. The house I grew up in is filled with these books, which pair original Latin (red jackets) or Greek (green jackets) text on the left-hand page with the English translation on the right. I accepted my first—a rite of passage, an inheritance—with pride. I wanted to know Sappho just as much as I wanted to know this side of my father. I texted him questions about Greek grammar and history, finally taking a shine to the discipline decades after he

had given up on our Greek alphabet lessons at the dining room table. *Alpha. Beta. Gamma. Delta.* At age seven I had drawn a series of shaky letters, capital and lowercase, once or twice on sheets of newsprint before walking away in frustration.

Campbell was to be my guide now. I imagined him something like my father, a white man who littered every room of the house with piles of books and covered little scraps of paper with crawling cursive and arcing coffee rings. In his annotations to the text, Campbell calls the Lesbian poet simply S., and I soon began to think of her that way too. Not the Sappho of history, but a secret epistolary friend, one whose letters often get lost in the mail because she forgot to affix enough postage. The words that do arrive endear me toward her. There is something of the melodramatic simplicity of pop music in her verses. I am left to wonder which of her tabloid romances inspired the latest album. She is easy to forgive.

Campbell relies on a series of biographical notes to set the stage before our mutual friend walks on to sing. They read like a gossip column, the society pages, holiday bickering among a set of great uncles who want to prove who knows S. best. In truth, they are historians, grammarians, and poets of the classical period who reference S.'s life and work for their own purposes, whether it's to write an adoring letter or to give an example of a particular type of poetic meter. One of the first entries comes from the *Suda*—"a Byzantine encyclopedia," my father explained, "a precursor of Wikipedia, where you can find more information about it"—which contained two conflicting sketches of S:

*First Notice*

*Daughter of Simon or of Eumenus or of Eerigyius or of Ecrytus or of Semus or of Camon or of Etarchus or of Scamandronymus; her mother was Cleis; a Lesbian from Eresus, a lyric poetess;*

*flourished in the 42nd Olympiad (612/608 B.C.), when Alcaeus,*
*Stesichorus and Pittacus were also alive. She had three brothers,*
*Larichus, Charaxus and Eurygius. She was married to a very*
*wealthy man called Cercylas, who traded from Andros, and she*
*had a daughter by him, called Cleis. She had three companions*
*and friends, Atthis, Telesippa and Megara, and she got a bad*
*name for her impure friendship with them . . .*

*Second Notice*

*A Lesbian from Mytilene, a lyre-player. This Sappho leapt from*
*the cliff of Leucates and drowned herself for love of Phaon the*
*Mytilenaean. Some have said that she too composed lyric poetry.*

From these scraps of text a portrait of S. begins to emerge. So does a
portrait of how knowing is made within classics. It is a field of study
where we can be certain that little to no new information will turn
up. There is no one left alive who can tell us which of those men listed
in the *Suda* was actually S.'s father, or what, exactly, made her friend-
ships with the women—Atthis, Telesippa, and Megara—impure. For
centuries, scholars have created new ways of decoding what little re-
mains, of wringing new meaning from it. It is a methodical art of de-
tection, of collation and cross-referencing, a careful study of grammar
and etymology, an obsessive hunt, a degree in taking illegible notes
and precariously stacking books.

Take, for instance, the question of when S. lived. The Greek verb
translated here as *flourished* could refer either to when she was born or
her *floruit*, when it could be proven that she was alive and at the height
of her career. Classicists are left to scour additional texts and histories
to pinpoint the timeline of other notable events in her life, like an
unexplained exile to Sicily with her daughter, Cleis, in tow, as well
as the dates those other men, Alcaeus and Stesichorus and Pittacus,

"were also alive." Since her exile was known to be before 595 BC, here scholars read that S. was already flourishing by 612 B.C. It is all an exercise in close reading, a labor of loving obsession.

S.'s husband's name, Cercylas of Andros, also begs a closer reading. At first glance, my eyes skate over it, a collection of vowels and consonants as cumbersome as the names of her brothers Larichus, Charaxus, and Eurygius, as tricky as the Greek letters I traced as a child. I'd rather ignore him. He stands in the way of the uncomplicated claiming of Sappho as a queer icon. "The case-history," Campbell writes, "is complicated by the evidence, usually neglected, that she was married." But I am told her husband's name was an unusual one, unusual even to those who can read Greek as easily as the tail wags of a beloved dog. Campbell translates the name as "Prick from the Isle of Man," and lesbian classicist Ella Haselswerdt takes a more contemporary stab with "Rod Johnson from Dudesville." His name is a joke, and a dirty one at that. It's the ancient equivalent of fans who write imagined queer romances into the Wikipedia pages of their favorite television shows, only to see their work removed by moderators overnight. Still, they won't be deterred from trying to rewrite the narrative, over and over again. Who snuck Rod Johnson into the *Suda*, and what story were they trying to cover over with his invention? Was the author making the joke or simply repeating one they had heard told over and over again?

The second entry in the *Suda* evokes another version of S., a woman who loved a man, Phaon, so much that she threw herself off a cliff still known today as Sappho's Leap by the locals of Lefkada. Campbell explains away this entry as pure make-believe: "'The other Sappho' was almost certainly the invention of a scholar who wished to save S.'s reputation."

"Reputation as what?" I would ask if he were with me in my living room, rendered rosy by the winter's sunrise, arid by the radiator's rattle. S.'s reputation as someone who, according to the first entry, struck

up "impure friendships" with her female students and companions? Campbell has laid out for me how to read the gaps in our knowledge of ancient times, the vagueness of verbs, the perverse puns hidden in plain sight, but he cannot tell me how to read this, the potent contradictions within a text said to have the veracity of an encyclopedia, the eyesore in S.'s life that someone, or many someones, tried to cover over by creating men for her to love.

The facts presented in S.'s biography may or may not have happened. She comes to me distorted, disfigured by those who brought their own motives to her representation, her voice filtered through thousands of others. But that's not the same as saying there's no truth to them. I must study not just the fragments and whispers of her that remain but also the whys and hows of their preservation. None of the individual details about S.'s life that I collect—the name of her husband, the cause of her untimely death on a distant, rocky shore—can be taken as fact, but together a tiled image begins to form, vague as a face on a black and orange Attic hydria.

To use Derrida's words, the myth of S. is "codetermined by the structure that archives." Its truth comes not from the details but rather the way each one reveals the hands constructing S.'s archive. The hands of "a despicable public administrator" who stole a statue of S. from the city of Syracuse on his way out of town and into exile, leaving behind only the plinth, which read THE TENTH MUSE. The hands that changed the pronouns in her verse to excise her love of women. The hands that copied her lines about the *apple branches*, their *quivering leaves*, on a vase. The hands that discovered a broken piece of that vase on a dig in Egypt.

"Who was S.?" I ask Campbell, I ask my father, because I cannot ask her.

"Here is the structure that tried to capture her," they might reply. "This is what it succeeded in capturing."

Hundreds of years after S.'s *floruit*, an Alexandrian scholar

collected her work into nine papyrus scrolls, arranged according to their meter. One of those books, it is said, consisted entirely of wedding songs. While at one point her words were well enough revered to be housed in the Library of Alexandria, many of the pieces that made it to us were discovered in cartonnage, an ancient plaster used to wrap mummies and bind books, with papyrus used as gauze. Some of S.'s lines turned up at the end of the nineteenth century in the garbage dump of an ancient town on the Nile, Oxyrhynchus—meaning literally, according to my father, sharp-nosed—among hundreds of discarded papyrus texts in various states of preservation. Fifteen lines were discovered on a broken piece of a clay pot, a potsherd.

The explanations for the loss of S.'s work range from the actively destructive—the church set fire to her words because of their erotic nature, or they were burned during a pillaging expedition—to the more passive ravages of time—a diminishing interest in and understanding of Aeolic, the ancient Greek dialect spoken on Lesbos; an upgrade in the technology of the book from papyrus scrolls to parchment codices bound at the spine, like the books we carry today; floods; forgetting. "Destroyed," Wittig and Zeig explain in their fantastical dictionary, "by the enemies of lesbians."

Some of S.'s verses made it to us not through the accidental preservation of discarded bits of the original text but rather because certain lines were archived by ancient scholars, who cited S. in the following documents: Letters attributed to the Roman Emperor Julian. Hephaistion's metrical *Handbook*. Marius Plotius Sacerdos's *Art of Grammar*. Apollonios Dyskolos's treatise *On Adverbs*. *A discussion of the use of garlands. A discussion of chickpeas. A discussion of hyperbole. To comment on the spelling of the word for* egg. *An unusual word for* sleep.

From grammar to garlands, these men had truly varied interests, but none of them were working to archive S.'s love of women. In fact, that may have been exactly what they were looking to bury. To me, the fact that S.'s desire for Atthis and Telesippa and Megara, for

Anactoria, calls out clearly from such an accidental archive makes the thrum of desire beat all the stronger. If no one set out to preserve the love in her verses, there must be even more of it in the thousands of lost lines.

Scholars have been inventing S. for centuries. I'd like to try my hand, to pluck the lines from her poems that will form a catalogue of queer desire.

Other parts of S. have been made immortal. She lives on as the tenth muse, the female Homer. She is credited with the invention of the *pektis*, a type of lyre, the *plektron*, to pluck the lyre, the *adonius*, a metrical unit, and the *Mixolydian mode*, a tragic lyric tone. Some of the things she left behind have been named for her too. Sappho's Leap, the cliff on the island of Lefkada where some claim she jumped to a rocky end; the Sapphic hendecasyllable, a line of eleven syllables; the Sapphic stanza, consisting of four lines. The people of her hometown of Mitylene (rhymes with *zucchini*) put her face on their coins. She also gave us the word *Sapphic*, full stop, not a meter but perhaps a cadence, the rhythm of loving beyond the grasp of men.

The word *lesbian* as we use it today, of course, comes from S. and her rumored "impure friendships" with women, several of them thought to be her students. The path, though, from S.'s biography—a figure praised as a Lesbian singer, a capital *L* for the homeland that briefly exiled her, and derided as "masculine Sappho" by the poet Horace—to our modern idea of a lesbian is unclear. The ancient Greeks didn't declare sexual identity. During the classical period, which began around the end of S.'s life, the Greek verb *lesbiazein* meant to give head, the rumored fetish of the women of Lesbos.

It wasn't until 1732 that we have a record of the English word *lesbian* (adjective) used to describe a sexuality. That year, William King, an Oxford don, published *The Toast: An Epic Poem in Four Books*. It is a revenge rhyme written to get back at the duchess of Newburgh, who had bested King in some kind of financial dispute. King satirizes

the duchess as Myra, a witch, a hermaphrodite, and, last but not least, a lesbian, recognizing the word's power to tarnish a woman's reputation. S. might have left behind the word *lesbian* as an inheritance, but it was King's character Myra who got to live as one of the first lesbians (noun) off the island. At least, she was among the first women to be named so, even if it wasn't of her own choosing.

The word *Lesbian* appears four times in the book, though never in the verses themselves. My favorite is perhaps the footnote explaining the origin of Myra's name: "A corruption of *Myrrhina*, a famous Courtesan of Athens, who first practis'd and taught in that City *Sappho's* Manner and the *Lesbian* Gambols." Once, the word is misprinted as *Lisbians*. Still, it thrills me.

Myra, on those rare occasions she appears in the text, thrills me even more. There is something in her I recognize. She carries a masculine strength and masculine features. She is as fluent in the art of witchcraft as she is in the art of seduction. "She daily practiced that unnatural act the *Spaniards* call *Donna con Donna*." King's character reads a whole lot like someone my middle school classmates might have come up with if pressed to write a story about a lesbian, except their witch would be wearing a pair of vegan leather Dr. Martens.

In this pause before the word *lesbian* became imbued with the power to pull people together into a community, I chased S. across time and language and ocean because I thought she would define it for me. She could not. Neither could Myra. They were nothing more than hollow fantasies.

I knew, at the very least, that I was part of the definition. It was a word I heard more and more as I grew into myself. I heard it from people who sensed something in me I could not yet name. Or maybe they were just mean. It wasn't the girls I shared tents with at Girl Scout camp, the ones I wrote letters to long after the summer ended, long after they stopped responding. It wasn't their mothers, either. It wasn't even my high school best friend, a girl cut with the smooth skin and

curved figure of a Greek statue, whom I had asked out at the Shins concert. Our friendship marched on, unchanged by her rejection.

"Lesbians," the word (plural) hurled at me by two senior girls when I held hands with my statuesque best friend.

"Ignore them," she encouraged me as soon as we were out of earshot.

I wasn't worried. I had a boyfriend who complicated the case history, and the hickies to prove it. When the other girls in my grade started to pair off, I set my sights on a boy who seemed the most sensible choice for me. I couldn't drive, didn't have cable, and was rarely allowed junk food. This boy, though, drove his own car, carried his own cell phone, and had already had his braces removed to reveal a set of straight, white teeth. An obvious choice. When he picked me up from swim practice, none of my teammates or their mothers dared called me a lesbian anymore. I was equally impressed by his personal DVD collection and the contents of his parents' refrigerator. We spent Friday nights in his attic bedroom devouring reruns of *Scrubs*, Papa Johns pizza, and Scooby Doo push-up pops that glowed brighter than the screen.

I never got to date the statuesque best friend who held my hand, but now we had so much to share when she gave me a ride home from school: how some boys smelled so good you wanted to keep their shirts in your locker, where to find the best blow job tutorials, when was the right moment to say "I love you."

"You know," she said to me one night, brakes slammed hard against the base of a hill, "love isn't just making out with your best friend." She suspected the relationship was an arrangement of convenience. Endless junk food and late-night rides in exchange for the wet of my mouth, the bragging rights to my virginity.

I tried out other words.

"Do you think you're bi?" The most popular girl in our grade stood ahead of me in the lunch line, a sharpened version of my own

reflection with a powder blue Lacoste polo in place of my navy Target knockoff, flat-ironed hair in place of my frizzed curls.

"Yes," I said without hesitation. There was the fact of my boyfriend, but also the fact of something new waking up inside me.

The popular girl laughed. "Pinky swear it."

I stuck out my pinky, all bluster and confidence. I did it for the challenge, for her uncomprehending look, to see her wonder whether I had had any experience with women. She could never ask me to prove it. I didn't need any experience to know. "If you have ever been a lesbian," writes Jordy Rosenberg in his novel *Confessions of the Fox*, "you will never even have to touch a woman to know that."

I finally picked the word *lesbian* for myself in college, on the pool deck. I sat with an injured teammate, bags of ice balanced on our shoulders to cool muscles that *burned* not with Sappho's immortal *longing* but with the mortal curses of over-rotation and tendonitis.

Our new coach walked by and gave us a nod. Her haircut was too short to be considered a professional bob, and her polo fit too poorly to hide the outline of her sports bra. There was only one thing she could be.

We giggled. The shake of our shoulders set the ice clacking. We were smitten. Smitten with Coach, yes, but also with the physical trainers, the women who always wore their hair up, who told us to lie down on the vinyl-covered table so they could examine our joints, diagnose our bodies. Mostly, though, we were smitten with the girls our own age, the ones on the dance floor and the rugby team, the ones in the dorm and at the dining hall.

"Do you think Coach knows?" my injured teammate asked, cheeks as rosy as the flush that spread from the frozen bag.

"Knows what?"

"What we're laughing about. Our crushes. That we might be lesbians." The word was handed to me like a bouquet of violets to lay across my lap, violets passed down from S., the goddess of lesbians.

We were theoretical lesbians, future tense, all words and no deed. By all accounts, we didn't measure up. Neither of us had slept with a woman. Truth be told, I didn't know much more about lesbians than what the middle school girls had whispered, than the myths and legends, than the hiss of the word spat out at me. Still, something about the label felt right. It described the space we had carved out on the slick tile floor for ourselves, a space we shared with Coach and our trainers, with the images of the crushes we conjured.

Lesbians of the generations to come wrote a lot about their identity and how they chose to define it. Most of them agreed that a lesbian was a woman who loved only women. Take, for example, Wittig and Zeig's dictionary entry for the original definition of lesbian: "Lesbian meant she who was interested by 'only' half of the population and had a violent desire for that half."

This purist definition is still in circulation today. The Gold Star Gay, in modern parlance. Someone who has never had sex with some-one of the opposite sex. "I'm a Platinum Star Gay," a friend once bragged over dinner, his lips moving invisibly beneath his beard. "I was born by C-section, so I've never touched a vagina." It stops me in my tracks as I scroll through Lex, a queer community app that tries to recreate the charm and anonymity of personal ads:

HOOKUP
Full blown lesbian only please text me ###-###-####

Would S. and Myra be eligible to send a text? (Who could be more "full-blown" than our founding mother and father?) Did Myra have a "violent desire" *only* for women? No. That's not a standard she can live up to. She had male Gallants who left her "unsated." She had a husband too: Ares, the god of war. Perhaps she kept him around for the free rides in his horse-drawn chariot, for the Friday night pizza and rainbow push-up pops. Who can say now? All the record can tell

me is that Myra, like Sappho, didn't love only women, and yet still she was a lesbian. I didn't have to renounce my boyfriend, to insist I never loved him, to claim the word as my own.

*You will never even have to touch a woman to know.*

Woman. So often the first part of any lesbian definition. The "she" of Wittig and Zeig. An unspoken qualification for the full-blown lesbian hookup that anonymous person, probably a woman herself, was in search of on Lex. It is a qualification on the mind of more than just one Lex user. I scrolled through the personal ads set against a teal blue background and stumbled across another post that evokes S.

### TOUGH TIME WITH LABELS
Any other Agender, Non-binary, or otherwise nonconforming Sapphics have a tough time with referring to themselves as "Lesbian"?

There's been a resurgence in the use of the word *Sapphic* in an effort to bring people who don't identify as women and people who don't exclusively love women all under the same tent, alongside those mythical women who love only women. But, at its start, the word *lesbian* was that inclusive too. Myra, the original specimen, is not a woman. The poet derides her as a hermaphrodite—a mythological being, at once both a man and a woman—because the gods changed her into a man to settle their own dispute. In spite of her male side, like "masculine Sappho" she is still, irrevocably, a lesbian.

We no longer refer to humans as hermaphrodites, but there is still an important nugget of truth here. A specific gender identity, or set of genitalia, played no role in this moment of lesbian invention. An agender, nonbinary, or otherwise gender-nonconforming person could be a lesbian, so long as they have the "violent desire" for it to be so.

This big-tent, come-one-come-all view of lesbianism is still held by at least one other person I know of: Canadian rapper Drake. In

"Girls Want Girls," he sings, "Yeah, say that you a lesbian, girl, me too." I am so tickled to hear the word *lesbian* in a song that I don't even care my neighbor woke me up blasting it at 3:00 a.m. It would be easy to dismiss Drake's lyric as something voyeuristic, the objectification of two naked women, thought in the act. That would let me ignore the resonance of his words. Drake wants to relate, to announce that he, too, loves those who have been traded, and, hopefully, he has no desire to trade them.

I am reminded of the words Wittig wrote in another one of her books, *The Straight Mind*, the very ones that helped me define *lesbian* when I began this collection: "'Woman' has meaning only in heterosexual systems of thought and heterosexual economic systems. Lesbians are not women."

There's one thing I am certain of in the midst of all that clouds S.'s biography: she constructed her life outside heterosexual economic systems.

Respectable women of ancient Greece, translator Anne Carson tells me in a series of endnotes to S.'s poetry that read like a cohesive essay all their own, were expected to cover their heads in public as a display of modesty and sexual decency. Only a prostitute would go without. I read this *many-colored headband* as a sign that women were property, an outward mark of their worth to men.

(My father did not name me for Amelia Earhart or Amelia Bedelia. I am named for the daughters of the Roman general Lucius Aemilius Paullus Macedonicus, who were all called Amelia, meaning daughter of Aemilius. To distinguish one girl from the next, they were numbered according to their birth order. Amelia 1. Amelia 2. Amelia 3.)

In an era that left us with so many stories about the heroic deeds of men and gods, S. sang about women, and she sang with them. *Maidens all night long.* Women are not just the "I" of her poetry and the "you," but also the "we," the first-person plural that is so common in ancient poetry, composed for a chorus.

S.'s pursuit of poetry didn't exempt her or her daughter from the currency of head coverings, but it did push her outside traditional womanhood. "'Masculine Sappho,'" Campbell quotes from a Latin grammarian who lived over half a millennium after S., "either because she is famous for her poetry, in which men more often excel, or because she is maligned for having been a tribad." Like that other early lesbian Myra, and even the Muscle Moll of Babe Didrikson's day, S. was described as masculine not just on account of her relations with women but also for her defiance of a social order that could only conceive of her in relation to men. "Masculine Sappho" because S. made space for women at a time when we were expected to be property.

The meaning of words expanded in the presence of S. to capture what could exist only beyond the confines of heterosexual economic systems. Classical grammarians archived the way she spelled *egg* and her word choice when singing of *sleep*, but it was other words that caught my eye. S. describes the goddess Leto and the mortal woman Niobe as *hetairai*, a word translated as friends or companions. It was the word, my new companion Carson tells me, men used for courtesan or mistress, but outside their trade it was used among friends. Perhaps S. meant it exactly the way Wittig translates it, companion lovers.

A commentary on Sappho written over half a millennium after her *floruit* describes one woman as another's "yoke-mate," a phrase whose meaning, Carson admits, is blurry. It has been used to describe married couples, pairs of fish, and comrades but rarely, in the examples left to us, two women. Perhaps they are held together by the yoke of their own invented version of marriage, a kinship connection not brokered by men. Not a wife, defined by Wittig as "a being who, in a state of servitude, was set under the yoke." Not sisters, daughters one and two, and not mother and child, but something lesbian, long before there was a word for it.

"What did Sappho of Lesbos teach her girls," Ovid wrote, "except how to love?"

~~~~

Now the goddess is asking for more. If S. truly wants to be remembered, to escape the destruction of the years to come, of flood and fire, the forgetfulness of scholars, words will not be enough. She must act.

She has seen the man in town, pointed out not with a celestial finger but with a warmth in her heart that could easily be confused with love or, at the very least, desire. The ferryman Phaon. She has seen the way women flirt with him. To make a public declaration would only make her look foolish, as foolish as she had been in her youth at Anactoria's wedding. She is old enough now to be his mother, grandmother, even.

Aphrodite came to her in a dream. To be remembered, she said without a word, S. must show her love for Phaon, show that she is willing to risk it all for him, even if he does not feel the same in return. She wakes with a start, heat pricking her skin even before the sun has risen over Mytilene. *"I know not what to do,"* she whispers, *"I have two minds."*

She senses a trick. Aphrodite already rewarded the man with *youth and beauty* for his kindness in ferrying her, a stranger, divinity buried under the guise of an old woman, across a strait. S. wonders if Aphrodite intends to give him the poetess of desire as another of his rewards.

There was a desperation in the goddess's request, as if she had begun to realize that power is not forever, not even the power of an immortal. More men will come, and they will bring more gods. Aphrodite alone cannot make the world remember S.

In the blaze of the day, S. makes a plan. She will leave her island again, this time never to return. Cleis is old enough to no longer need a mother, and Cercylas grew bored of her long ago. She will sail to the high cliffs of Lefkada. There, she will stage her own death, a jump, a swan song, her dress snagged against the rocks, fluttering in the wind,

no body left to fill it. Aphrodite and Phaon and the generations still to come will get their myth and, in exchange, she will get to live out the rest of her days undisturbed. Perhaps she will bring the girl, the one without shyness, and together they will live on *lonely mountain peaks*. *Death is an evil: the gods have so decided, otherwise they would die.* But S. is determined to be ruled by a different fate.

> *I shall love.*
> *Into desire I shall come.*
> *Sweet-speaking desire*
> *streams over your lovely face,*
> *and I will lay down my limbs*
> *on a soft cushion.*
> *I say someone in the future*
> *will remember us.*

~~~~~

I dream in song.

*I don't think any girl who sees the sunlight will ever have your wisdom.*

I write S.'s words back to her as proof that she is remembered, that this pact she has made with Aphrodite, this pact I have imagined for her, was worth the heartache.

*No day will ever dawn that does not speak the name of Sappho, the lyric poetess.*

I set off down the path with S. in tow, the mother and father of lesbians, the husband and wife, teacher and student, poet and lover. The patron saint of lesbians, violets clutched in her lap, a bride and goddess out of one of her own poems. Scholars—men, the lot of them—will continue to debate not just who her father was or how she died but also the nature of her desire for the women in her songs, whether she even sang about her own life at all. They will construct arguments

out of what little evidence remains, arguments that suit their needs, further their own careers. I have defiantly joined them, arguing for the lesbian ancestor I need.

I rarely say her name. It is like a snake caught in the throat. When released, it is nothing more than a puff of air, as intangible as her image. The word *lesbian*, though, is one I can't get enough of. Lesbian bar. Lesbian movie. Lesbian romance. Lesbian sex. Lesbian feminist. Lesbian separatist. It is a word that the lesbians still to come in this collection will use more often as they seek each other out for dates and for solidarity. Always an homage to our patron saint, to our namesake, as full of contradictions and inconsistencies as the rest of us.

*Extracts* | LESBIAN USAGE EXAMPLES FROM
THE OXFORD ENGLISH DICTIONARY

1597 BP. J. King *Lect. Ionas* i. 1
Aristotle liketh better of the wine of Lesbos, then the
wine of Rhodes; he affirmeth both to be good, but the
Lesbian the more pleasant.

1732 W. King *Toast* ii. 67/2
This little Woman gave Myra more Pleasure than all
the rest of her Lovers and Mistresses. She was therefore
dignified with the Title of Chief of the Tribades or
Lesbians.

1844 H. G. Robinson *Odes of Horace* i. xvii. 69
Here shalt thou quaff . . . The unintoxicating bowl Of
Lesbian.

1808 *Edinb. Med. & Surg. Jrnl.* 4 477
The disease seldom proceeds so far except in women
who have indulged in Sapphic and Lesbian habits.

1940 'G. Orwell' *Inside Whale* 132
Gruff-voiced Lesbians in corduroy breeches . . . could
walk along the streets without attracting a glance.

1947 E. Taylor *View of Harbour* x. 170
'I think I look like a Lesbian,' Beth said doubtfully.

1965 *New Statesman* 9 Apr. 570/2
Why does it matter so much to them whether lesbians
use a dildo or not?

1983 A. Walker *In Search of our Mothers' Gardens* 282
Until recently there has been almost nothing
written by or about the black lesbian in American
literature—a void signifying that the black lesbian
was a nonentity.

2003 *Times* 28 Apr. II. 3
The female inhabitants of the Greek isle of Lesbos . . .
can't all be lesbians, even if they are all Lesbians.

# 5.

## Who Wears the Pants?
## Rusty Brown and Terry

~~~~~~~

(1951–1979)

RUSTY BROWN MADE HER LIVING, FOR A TIME, DRESSED IN men's clothes. First as a civilian who worked for the navy during World War II; then, after all the boys came back home, in a factory at the Brooklyn Navy Yard, where she used her grandfather's name to masquerade as an orphaned boy; and finally, as a male impersonator who performed on Coney Island.

One night after the show, Rusty walks inland with her bud John and they stand on the *curb*. They've got a good thing going with their *take-off on Ginger Rogers and Fred Astaire* as played by a male and female impersonator. Her as Fred and him as Ginger, and still, they do a convincing number with all the tap and twirl of Hollywood's most famous dance partners.

Tonight, though, just this once, pretty please, John has convinced her to swap costumes on their way out of the sideshow theater. Even across that short expanse of concrete, though, Rusty could not *walk on high heels worth a damn*. She has already grown frustrated with the

skirt of her *evening gown*. It should flow liquid around bird-boned ankles but instead it stumbles and spits against her crooked gait. Her *hairy muscular legs*.

As Rusty and John wait for a cab to come along, a police officer across the street squints at the pair. To him they must look drunk or, at the very least, like a pale refraction of the glamorous, poised movie stars they pretend to be. Rusty should have never let John talk her into this. They're much more convincing the other way around, her in a suit, him in a dress. *He walked like any woman would walk in high heels.*

Two headlights, brighter than anything Madam Tirza could afford for her Wine Bath burlesque sideshow, catch the performers in a circular frame. John stretches his cane out into the street to hail down the checkered cab. In that moment, a coin drops in the payphone of the officer's mind, and he can finally hear what the voice in his head has been trying to tell him. That woman is not a woman. The calves are just too big. The officer stubs out his cigarette against a brick wall. He crosses the street, toward the oddball couple. As he gets closer, he can make out the hair on her *legs sticking out through the stockings*.

"All right, buster, you're under arrest."

Rusty elbows John in the ribs. "*Oh Christ*," she whispers. "You *finally got caught*."

"What's your name, ma'am?" It's her the officer addresses.

"Rusty," she says. Could it be that the officer has mistaken her for a man dressed as a woman?

"Rusty, you're under arrest for impersonating a woman." She tries to reason with him, but he's unwilling to believe her unless she undresses right there on the spot, and that's one indignity she won't suffer. The officer reaches for her shoulders, spins Rusty around, the dress giving a proper twirl now, and locks handcuffs around her wrists against the passenger door of the Checker.

After he drops Rusty off at the men's jail, the officer doesn't stick

around long enough to hear the other inmates shout, *"Bad enough you got us in this jail, you have to put this damn fag in here with us. Get him the hell out of here, we don't want him in here with us."* He isn't there to notice that Rusty never, not once the whole night, uses the toilet in the corner of the cell. And he's long gone by the next morning, when Rusty's boss comes to bail out his dancer.

"Jesus Christ," the manager of Madam Tirza's club shouts when Rusty walks out into the station. He hardly recognizes her in that dress. *"You had to go and do it, didn't you?"*

"I don't know," Rusty says, *"how I let* John *talk me into getting one of his evening gowns on and a pair of his high heels . . . We were going to go somewhere."* She gives her first proper twirl. *"I look like a fag in drag."*

"Did you have to listen to him?"

"I got busted, for wearing women's clothes. And I can't believe you came to bail me out."

"Fifty dollars to get you *out on bail . . . A hundred and fifty for* your *fine."* He sticks his hands in his pockets, as if to see whether the money might still be there. *"For the sake of seeing* you *in an evening gown and high heels? . . .* I'm *willing to pay it."*

For a night, Rusty was a *female* female impersonator. *I haven't had a dress on to my knowledge from that day to this.*

While this night was the only time Rusty Brown was mistaken for a man dressed as a woman, the story of her life could, in fact, be told through a montage of moments when she was seen as a man.

She remembers once, at the Sheraton Hotel in '58, '59, the *bellboys* sent her and the other male impersonators *to the men's room. None of us could use the standup urinal if our life depended on it.*

And the night she took her girlfriend Terry out to the Zebra Club, *a perfectly straight club. I was wearing white tie and tails, and she was in an evening gown. There was no problem. Nobody questioned.*

Even at the factory, the man she *worked with once tapped* her *on the shoulder* and asked, *"Are you a man or a woman?"* Her reply—*"Why*

darling, what do you think?"—had him convinced she was a *fag* and made him so *mad he threw a hunk of steel across the room.*

At this stage of building my lesbian collection, it's easy to spot the familiar motifs in Rusty's story. Like Mary Casal, she grew up playing with the boys. And, like all the other lesbians in my collection—Mary in a tailored suit, Mabel in her *flat, low-heeled shoes*, Babe the "Muscle Moll," even *masculine Sappho*—she adopted masculinity in her style of dress.

Previous generations, though, had approached their gender expression as a private joy and a public burden. For them, being a woman meant not just that they could be traded in marriage but also that they must wear a skirt or a dress, a norm upheld by the police and the media. Their options were confined, for the most part, to being a woman or being a failed woman. *Lesbian* became another word for failed woman, for a masculine woman, regardless of her sexuality. Those who did risk it all to live as men, from female husbands to male impersonators, rarely left behind detailed accounts of their motives, whether they put on pants to earn a better living, to legally marry a woman, to match their outward appearance to their internal identity, or some combination of all three.

Rusty and her generation could finally revel in gender play, whether in a sideshow act or on the factory floor, out on the town or in the privacy of their own homes. World War II created new job opportunities for women and made it socially acceptable for them to wear pants. The rise in club culture, where the heirs of Ella Wesner, Johnstone Bennett, and Gladys Bentley performed as male impersonators, gave them a public stage to try on different clothes and identities, and new lesbian bars opened a space where butches and femmes could perform gender for a smaller audience. As ideas about what work women could do and what they could wear expanded, there were more choices beyond just "woman" or "failed woman." There was more space to articulate gender identity as separate from sexuality,

to weave masculinity and femininity together, to be a femme lesbian or to live full-time as a man.

Rusty should be remembered as one of the forefathers of contemporary drag culture, of the drag kings who are direct descendants of male impersonators. She and her generation pioneered an exploration of the distinctions between gender identity and sexuality beyond the theater, before they had the language to articulate it. They showed us that all the world's a stage, ready and waiting for gendered performance.

~~~~~

"Five. Six. Seven. Eight."

The music started, and I walked to take my place in the ragged kick line fanned out across the mirror-lined room. I stretched my arms to hug the broad-shouldered men at my sides. To my left, a chest as chiseled as a Greek statue, covered in hair coarse as chain mail. To my right, a brown one gone concave with age above the ribs.

The Rockette who led our rehearsal lifted her leg past ninety degrees. Mine could only go up to seventy-five. And there, at the end of the line, a pair of veiny white legs that couldn't tilt past thirty-five. I was in rehearsal for the 2019 International Gay and Lesbian Aquatics Championship, to be hosted on my home turf in New York City. We were to hold competitions in diving, water polo, speed swimming, synchronized swimming, and an open-water race hosted at Coney Island. Today, though, I was training for another event entirely. The Pink Flamingo, an aquatic drag performance that combined dance, lip synch, and synchro that would be judged by a panel of local celebrities.

"Stop. Stop. Stop," said our teacher. She shook her head at us, and her braid, cinched at both ends, swung from side to side. I was already jealous of her. The articulation of her arm muscles, the neat sweep of her dyed blond hair and the confident stroke of her eyeliner, the fact that her thighs didn't meet when she brought her feet together.

"Here, I'll tell you a little Rockette secret. The way to get your kick line straight is to look at the chest of the person standing two spots to your right. Take a look and adjust as needed."

I turned my head to the right. A platinum blond wig hid the face of a man whose legs extended into knee-high leather boots with three-inch heels, a shoe I would never dare try on my own feet. I turned my head farther and caught the man's face in one of the mirrors: Charlie Carson again. He was the founding mother and father of our swim team, of the meet we were about to host, and also of the Pink Flamingo.

The event, the only queer-invented competition to be featured at IGLA, brought together several informal traditions. Charlie brought the drag component. When he hopped on the plane to San Francisco for the first Gay Games in 1982, Charlie brought with him a yellow polka-dotted women's one-piece, elbow-length gloves, and a pair of white sunglasses in the style of Jackie O. It wasn't until the meet's after-party at The Oasis, a bar with a swimming pool in the center, that he found the perfect moment to don his Esther Williams drag. Using his medals from the meet as leashes, he led two men on hands and knees across the deck. Then, he jumped in the water to perform a solo routine in the style of the actress and swim star. The crowd cheered.

The first Pink Flamingo took place at the 1987 Northwest Gay and Lesbian Sports Festival hosted in Seattle. It was a relay race that required swimmers to carry a lawn flamingo, an idea that the English Bay Swim Club members from Vancouver got from a popular home improvement TV ad, across the pool, and then hand it off like a baton. In March 1987, the New York team married drag and competition at a different meet when all four relay swimmers dressed as Lady Liberty, complete with spiked crowns and long dresses that were sure to slow them down in the water. "We actually won our heat," said John Goodwin, the costume designer, "which really pissed some people off."

By 1989 the Pink Flamingo was a staple of gay swim competitions. Pru Sowers described it better than I ever could in the souvenir booklet for Gay Games IV, which Charlie digitized: "A Freudian delight, ripe with sexual stereotypes, gender disorder and an unquenchable desire for the spotlight. It's addictive. It's imaginative."

By 2019, the Pink Flamingo had already morphed from relay into choreographed skit. Charlie had been cast in the role of superhero Quicksilver in an eighteen-minute extravaganza that told the story of the Stonewall Riots and the origin of the Pride March in honor of their fiftieth anniversary, complete with pole-dancing Spider-Man, voice recordings of interviews with elders present at the Riots, an Iwo Jima–style raising of the Pride flag, and, of course, our kick line as the grand finale.

"Do you know the other thing everyone always gets wrong about a kick line?" I searched the room, worried I should have already learned the answer. The mirrors reflected back everything I already suspected was wrong about my body, my failure to construct an image of a woman as recognizable as the Rockette. My face was bare because I had never learned how to apply makeup. My hair came loose from my bun because I had never learned how to braid. My thighs ballooned out of my bike shorts because I had never cared to diet or to spend money on expensive athleisure. Unlike the men around me at rehearsal, I didn't dare take off my shirt. I have always been embarrassed by my breasts. Not the bulk of them, or lack thereof, but the skin just above. For years I have picked the acne there, a nervous habit, to the point of scarring. My body, devoid of grace.

"The other thing everyone gets wrong about kick lines is that you don't actually kick on the first count," she continued. "You jump down on one, kick up on two. Down on one, up on two." She slid easily into a practiced toy soldier, arms akimbo and smile stretched taut across her teeth. The mask fell a beat later. She returned to the doe-eyed dance teacher I had just met this afternoon. "Let's try it one more time. Count it out. One two three four. Five. Six. Seven. Eight."

I was jealous of these men with their wigs and their glitter, heels so high they would topple me. They were, it seemed, better women than I could ever be.

~~~~~

For Rusty, the pants had started quite early.

I was raised in the country, so wearing pants for me was easy 'cause we had did it up on the farm. But when my grandparents died, and I had to move to New York with my family, my mother and my father, it was like a culture shock. Dresses? Bows? Shoes and socks? I mean, it's summertime, what do I need shoes and socks for? And what the hell's this damn dress? I can't do the things I want to do with a dress on. But I did them anyway, to my mother's horror. I'd come home looking like anything but the little lady she sent me out.

I can see little Rusty wearing *god damned ribbons and bows and flounces,* leaving her scolding mother behind in San Juan Hill, what we now call Columbus Circle, to hang out with the men who worked the freight trains at Grand Central. She did little errands for them, *running getting coffee and doughnuts, and they'd give me a nickel . . . God, the candy I could get for a nickel. And a dime, that would keep me in candy for a week!* The men were so *accustomed* to the sight of a little white girl with hair *so blonde, it was almost white* in a stained dress with *flounces* that they told no one when she hopped on a freight headed south. They still didn't tattle the second time she did it, or the third. *Once . . . I got a little bit outside of Washington, D.C. That was the last time, and that was when I wound up in the, in the home and got sent away.*

If Rusty's adult life was a montage of gender play, then the story of her childhood could be told through a photo album of the institutions for poor, wayward children that she passed through. The same reformist impulse to clean up the streets of New York City in the 1920s that led to Mabel Hampton's wrongful conviction pushed

Rusty through the doors of these homes. Founded at the turn of the century to uplift runaways, prostitutes, and unwed mothers, often through religious teachings, these homes were the legacy of white philanthropists like lesbian Nobel laureate Jane Addams and Mary Casal's employer Helen Gould. Their promise of aid and education was, at its heart, as hollow as the feigned concern the superintendent of Bedford Hills Correctional Facility held for Mabel Hampton.

I count the number of homes that sheltered Rusty, write down their names in an effort to construct a timeline of her movements across the city: *the Society for the Prevention of Cruelty to Children*, where she was sent at age eight; *the Edwin Gould Foundation*; *Five Points House of Industry*, which she left in 1939, the first solid foothold Rusty offers me; *the Florence* Crittenton *Home* for unwed mothers and prostitutes; *the Salvation Army home*, and the *Bellevue* Hospital psychiatric ward. Before the age of eighteen, Rusty had passed through too many institutions for me to count on one hand.

Strangely enough those were the happiest years of my childhood—largely because the idea of homosexuality just never occurred to the people who ran the home.

Institutions should leave paper trails, case files and intake forms, but if any record of Rusty's time in these homes remains, I could not find it. Polite archivists wrote to me that their search hadn't turned up any results. They broke the news to me gently, as if the wait staff had failed to find a child's beloved stuffed animal. Some children, they explained, stayed with them so briefly that no file was ever opened. If I had a date of birth or a death certificate or any nicknames or aliases she used, they might be able to conduct a more thorough search. I didn't have any of those. For all I knew, Rusty was just a nickname for a girl whose blond hair had turned a brassy copper as she grew. The trail went cold.

Instead, I got the story straight from Rusty's own lips. She was interviewed by two queer oral historians in her lifetime, once by Len

Evans, who visited Rusty, already well into her sixties by the time he arrived at her San Francisco home on July 7, 1983, and once by Dr. Marcy Adelman, who was inspired by Studs Terkel to put together an oral history of aging lesbians, *Long Time Passing: Lives of Older Lesbians*, to learn what the future might hold for her. When I played the tapes in my empty apartment, I heard a cat cry out to be fed, and I rushed into the other room to check. Mine was fast asleep on the back of the couch. It was another cat crying, maybe even more than one, a cat as long gone as Rusty.

When she was first placed in a home, eight years old, perhaps after she ran as far away as D.C., *the first thing I heard them say is Hey, we got another dyke. And I turned around and looked at them and I says "I am?"* She had never heard the word before, or understood why she'd rather play with the boys, why she grew embarrassed around the girls. The four books she had read on the subject—who knows, perhaps *The Stone Wall* was one of them—had only warned her that a queer life would be filled with suffering. *The first time I had a name for it. And I breathed a sigh of relief. I'm not alone, maybe I'm not crazy after all.*

At another home, Five Points House of Industry, *there I got my education.* Founded by the United Methodist Church on the principle that vocational training could save souls better than religion ever could, Five Points gave Rusty shelter at 69 Madison Street in what is now Chinatown. The building still stands, with a plaque to commemorate its mission "to minister to the needs of immigrant and underprivileged peoples of New York City." *Not quite what they had anticipated, but let's say I graduated* cum laude.

Rusty went to *bed with every girl over the age of twelve, and at least two of the school teachers.* By the time she left, *they had on my record I had homosexual potential.* Oh, what it would be like to get my hands on those records. Homosexuality was rarely the explicit cause of Rusty's institutionalization, but, once she arrived, it gave her a sense of community, and perhaps made the young runaway feel less

alone. Just as the women's colleges of a previous generation provided a campus where white middle-class women could smash and spoon far from the prying eyes of fathers and would-be suitors, these homes were spaces, bunk beds and dorm rooms and cafeterias, where poor young women could exist outside of their dresses and could even take each other to bed.

There was even room for romance. *I tried to stay in contact with* two of the older girls at Five Points, *but our letters got waylaid.*

Rusty may have lucked upon a chosen family within the halls and the beds of institutions that saw her as just another body passing through, but why had she run away from her blood family? Had it been her mother's strict dress code, all *bows* and *dresses*? Or was it her father's suspicion that she might rub off on her sister? When he read about her *homosexual potential*, he grew nervous that Rusty was going to *corrupt* her own sister. When *things got bad at home*, what choice did she have except to run *away again*? At age sixteen, when Rusty's mother discovered the girl hadn't gotten her period yet, she dragged her daughter to the doctor. He—it must have been a man—discovered that the young woman's hymen had been broken. It could have been anything, really, he explains, rigorous physical activity, roughhousing with the boys, that broke it. Rusty's mother didn't hear a word of it. All it meant was that her daughter was no longer a virgin. She *blew a fuse* and took Rusty to juvenile court. Was it anything more than the shattering weight of family expectations? Did she share any of Mabel or Mary's history of family abuse? Rusty is a clam, holding fast to a mouthful of family secrets.

My best guess is that it was after the discovery of her broken hymen that Rusty ended up in the Bellevue Psychiatric unit, the first of the institutions that did not even pretend at benevolence. *I found out they were going to give me shock treatments.* She had never heard of this particular method of curing *homosexual potential* before. She *wandered into another ward* and asked the nurse what, exactly, was

going to happen to her. *Oh, no, they don't,* she thought when she heard the answer. *I found a nurse's uniform in the closet, I put it on and I just walked out of the hospital.* Rusty always did seem to understand the power of a uniform, how clothes grant us access to bathrooms and jobs and gender roles, allow us to pass by unnoticed in a hospital or heterosexual bar, to stand out on stage.

~~~~

I never had cause to run away from home. My mother never insisted on bows or dresses. She never said much of anything about my clothes, except to whine that the items I borrowed from her closet looked better on me. As a child, I was grateful she never wasted time teaching me how to apply makeup or set a straightening iron to my hair. I never thought of my mother as anything less than a woman or suspected her of being a lesbian.

When I started my first adult job, though, I felt ashamed that I had never learned the basic rites of femininity. All the women in the office wore the same uniform. Their blow-dried hair, gel manicures, stiletto heels, and glossed and shadowed faces conveyed authority in a way that my actual job performance never could. They were as mean to me about my mismatched orange corduroys and navy polos as the girls in the swim team locker room had been about my body hair. As much as I wanted to fit in, I couldn't imagine sinking my time and my new salary into my appearance. Everything they wore felt as exaggerated to me as a costume, as drag. I was born at a time when women have more rights than ever before and no one, not even my mother, expects me to get married. Yet, in the corporate office, women still held less power than men, and a woman who refused to conform somehow had even less.

"Women and drag have never really mixed," swimmer Sowers wrote in an article about the Pink Flamingo, "The Flamingo's Place in Herstory." Me and drag have never really mixed either. I don't go

to drag brunch or drag queen story time. I do not join my teammates for Thursday night *RuPaul's Drag Race* watch parties. That same jealousy I felt at the Pink Flamingo rehearsal rears its ugly head every time I come close to a drag performance. What if the queens are better women than I could ever be? What if the contrast between us exposes me as a fraud?

I reached out to veteran drag journalist Elyssa Goodman for an introduction to the 1940s and '50s drag culture that fostered Rusty Brown's Fred Astaire impersonation. She suggested we meet at a dive bar in Chelsea to watch the latest episode of *All Stars* with the crowd that assembled every Thursday night.

Elyssa doesn't identify as queer, but she was immediately drawn to drag as a solitary child in Florida raised on a steady diet of Disney princesses and 1950s movie musicals, all technicolor and sparkle. She has become used to gay men who question her presence as a photographer, writer, and fan at parties and performances, and she has developed her own effervescent charm to deflect their unease. It's an act she can take on and off, like drag, an act inspired by the fearlessness of queens, their exaggeration of words and gestures, their camp. The shield of a persona. She channeled the queens, too, when she got ready for work in the morning, back in the day when she held an office job.

The evening was emceed by a local drag queen, the winner of a recent competition. She asked if anyone in the audience was a *Drag Race* virgin. I refused to raise my hand. To my right, one of the few other women in the audience shot hers straight into the air. The queen called her up on stage.

"What brings you here tonight, honey?"

"I'm here on a date with my girlfriend," she said, then pointed to a woman in a polo shirt who shared her long, straight hair and boxy shoulders.

"I love lesbians!" the queen shouted. Everyone broke out into

laughter. The joke needed no punchline. "How long have you two been together?"

"We're both professional hockey players out in Jersey. We met on the team, and now we live together. I think it's been two years now. Right, babe?" The girlfriend nodded.

I continued to ask Elyssa questions over the noise of the show, the electronic buzz of its theme song: "Start your engines. May the best woman win." I wanted to know why male impersonators had faded into the background while female impersonators had given birth to drag queens who sat on a throne of incredible mainstream success. Elyssa's bubbles popped against the spear of my question. She instructed me not to rely on one reality TV show to capture every facet of an art form as rich and storied as drag.

Male impersonators, she explained, had given birth to drag kings. True, they hadn't made it as big as RuPaul's queens, but they had their own vibrant scene out in Brooklyn. I was struck by the force of my own ignorance. I had never even heard of drag kings, much less been to a show. What's more, I had always imagined that if I were to put on a gendered costume, it would be one designed to make me look more feminine, not one that would highlight the masculine features—my jawline, my chin hairs—that had brought me so much shame. Why had drag kings never made the big time? Why had I never considered embracing such exaggerated masculinity?

~~~~~

Rusty waits in the *engine room* of a U.S. Navy ship bound for home. Tucked behind one of the *turbines*, her body is as impatient as the hiss of the machines, as hot with expectation as the exhaust that warms the room. It had been easy to slip away from her welding work, to shout to no one in particular that she was needed in the engine room. Still, *keeping secrets on ship isn't the easiest thing to do.*

She hears the tap of black pumps along the *main corridor*. Then,

a sigh against her ear, the scratch of blue wool against her neck. Her lover grabs her from behind. Rusty whirls around. She tugs at the mushroom cap buttons of the jacket, the knot of the navy-issue blue tie around her neck. There isn't time, there's never enough time. They hug and kiss. They share in *a little foreplay*. The threat of discovery is its own presence in the room, alongside the rush of turbines and the bite of machine oil. It is what brought a fire between her legs when she took off her apron and leather gloves, removed her face shield, before heading to the engine room. But it also keeps her hands from ever reaching below her lover's skirt. *We never did get down to brass tacks. If word had gotten out she would been thrown out of the military.*

World War II brought Rusty and the women around her new job opportunities. I learned about the women who played in the All-American Girls Professional Baseball League from the movie *A League of Their Own* and about the lesbians in the league from the documentary *A Secret Love*. Around three hundred thousand women also joined the military service, seizing on the avenues the war opened for a woman, even one without a college education, to independently earn a living.

Rusty's lover was in the navy, a WAVES woman. Women Accepted for Volunteer Emergency Service. Her uniform had been designed by New York fashion house Mainbocher.

Rusty wanted to enlist too. *I was old enough and I had enough intelligence.* When she finally broke free from the orbit of Manhattan's institutions in *March of 1941*, Rusty first found a job *on a chicken farm in New Jersey*. It had been a bit of a *problem, getting a job without a high school diploma. I hadn't been really trained for anything.* Pretty soon, though, *I could see World War II was coming*, and along with the war, the possibility to get away from all the feathers. She failed the army physical because *one, I'd been in a home for delinquents; two, I had a heart defect.* Rusty became a civilian employee for the navy instead. She left New York to earn her welding certificate on Treasure Island

in San Francisco. *I got to do all the stuff I wanted to do, worked with all the tools and machinery I wanted.*

I had no problem finding companions wherever I went. First Rusty was sent to Hawaii and then, after Pearl Harbor, on to the Philippines for ten months. She met women in the service, both civilian and navy. She met women at bars and coffeehouses and *a friend of a friend of a friend's house.*

Lesbians worked for the military, and lesbianism worked for the military too. Much like women's colleges that fostered romantic friendship in Mary Casal's day, or correctional facilities that unknowingly brought together communities of *dykes*, or even Christian institutions and homes that afforded the privacy for Rusty to hop from one bed to the next, the army both attracted people who already identified as lesbians and those who would discover new companions and new words during their time there. There is no accurate count of the number of lesbians who served. Anyone who asked a servicemember to disclose her sexuality was just looking for a reason to discharge her.

Across an ocean and a continent, cautionary tales of lesbians thrown out of the military reached Mabel Hampton in Harlem. Mabel's friend's daughter had enlisted in the WAC, the Women's Army Corps, to serve alongside over one hundred and fifty thousand others. (Even Babe Didrikson had considered joining the WAC after the attack on Pearl Harbor, when George became so furious that he wanted to enlist, but the army wouldn't take him or his bulk, transversed by varicose veins.) When Mabel says WAC on the tapes, it comes out like the word *wax. Somebody squealed on them . . . They were all lesbians, every one of 'em . . . It was a damn nasty scandal.*

On the other hand, if a woman was willing to be discreet, then the military was willing to look the other way. In her history of American lesbian life in the twentieth century, Lillian Faderman documents how the military tolerated homosexuality among its ranks during World War II out of necessity. If the military started a witch hunt and kicked

out all the lesbians, there would be hardly anyone left to serve. There were certainly enough of them that WAC officers were cautioned not to accuse women in their units of lesbianism without solid proof. Through "a printed series of Sex Hygiene lectures, officers were" given strict guidelines about when "to take action against lesbianism" and reminded that "any officer bringing an unjust or unprovable charge against a woman in this regard will be severely reprimanded." When women were needed in the workforce, it was easier to overlook their personal lives, leaving room for queer relationships to take root.

Lesbians participated in the war effort on the home front too. Mabel Hampton was deputized as an air raid warden. *At night time I'd go out and other girls, other women, would go and watch, supposed to be watching, see.* They'd watch the night sky and prepare the neighborhood for an aerial attack.

The Lesbian Herstory Archives holds the records of Mabel's service: the 1942 statement that appoints her deputy sector commander in the Air Warden Service, citations from the War Finance Committee, and a Citizens Defense Corps card, which lists Mabel as age forty-one, four feet eleven inches, 123 pounds. They also preserved her air raid warden cap. I found it in a long, flat box perched high on a shelf in a climate-controlled storage room on the second floor of the old Park Slope brownstone. I had to climb a ladder to pull it off the shelf. On my way back down, Mabel's box balanced in my hands, I read the names on the boxes that had sat beneath it: Adrienne Rich. The Lesbian Avengers. They would have to wait for another day.

I set the box down on the reading table gingerly, as if it held her ashes. The army-green hat sat on top of a stack of faded magazines. I unfolded it and discovered it was cut from the same pattern as the sailor hat she wore to her birthday party years later. I was overcome by the temptation to try it on. This wasn't the New-York Historical Society with a staff paid to observe me, to scold me when I shifted documents off the wooden table and into my lap. I had already taken

liberties with my solitude. I had lain down against the cool wood floor to read Mabel's letters on a hot summer day. I had taken more than one folder out of the file box at a time. But I couldn't bring myself to wear the hat. I want to take care of the hat, of Mabel, not because someone is watching but because I want her record to endure.

Rusty's civilian naval records, like the institutional records of her teenage years, elude me. The only lead I had was Dr. Marcy Adelman, the lesbian who interviewed Rusty for her anthology *Long Time Passing*. "I get the most phone calls about her," she told me over the phone. "Rusty was amazing." Most of the lesbians Marcy featured in the collection weren't writers, so she interviewed them, then edited the transcripts alongside her subjects. She visited Rusty in her one-room apartment to conduct her interview. While they spoke, Rusty pulled a set of weights out from under the table to show off her exercise regimen. "She was so butch and in such good shape," Marcy said, her voice tinged with the same love I've felt for lesbians I've never met. In no time, she's the one asking me questions. "I'm so glad you're interested in understanding lesbian history. We're slow to document our lives and each other's lives."

I am tempted to claim Rusty and her companions as lesbian war heroes because it's a distinction easily accepted by historians. It would be an easy argument for why her life, and the lives of other lesbians who contributed to the war effort, should be documented. I could say that every time I see the famous image of Rosie the Riveter and her encouraging slogan "We can do it!" I imagine the face of Rusty the Welder beneath that red bandana, staring sternly back at me.

I can't give in to the temptation, though. I'm not one for war. The military is an extension of the other institutions that tried to trap and reform lesbians, from the Bedford Hills Correctional Facility to the homes for runaways where Rusty spent her youth. It attracted people who had few other options to earn a living and dangled the threat of expulsion to push their loving relationships behind turbines. It used

their labor to fuel a nationalist project, to take lives. I find it hard to stand with those who fight for gay people openly serving in the military. My vision of lesbian love, of liberation, has no place for the military.

What is remarkable to me about Rusty is that she made the most of it. She earned a living. She wore pants. She found and loved other lesbians, and they created pockets of refuge within the confines of yet another hostile institution.

~~~~

I quickly gave up on trying to conform to the unspoken dress code of my new office. In a fit of rebellion, I cut off all my hair. Who would expect me to style it now? To pin or braid or straighten it? What were they going to do, fire me? I hoped my short hair would signal to my coworkers that they should let go of their feminine expectations. I could not walk in heels. I would not get a manicure. I will not join the office diet.

My new haircut only attracted more attention. When I registered the surprise on my coworkers' faces, they were suddenly forced to come up with something to say, anything. Their comments hovered somewhere between compliment and insult. Hair fell in my eyes, blurred my vision.

Strangers noticed the difference too. A cashier at the grocery store called me sir. I flinched. I had failed at traditional femininity, but that didn't mean I wanted to be a man. I wanted to be my own kind of woman.

~~~~

Rusty was rewarded for her service in the navy by getting fired as soon as the men returned home. She had been working at the Brooklyn Navy Yard *when the Japanese signed the surrender; 150 of us were told that in two weeks our jobs would be through.* The jobs had to be

returned to their rightful owners: male veterans, returning home as heroes.

Rusty knew immediately she wanted another factory job. *I get along better with machines.* There was just one *little problem: I was female.* The solution came to her in an instant, dredged up from the same well of inspiration and necessity as her plan to steal a nurse's uniform to make her escape from Bellevue Hospital's threat of shock treatments. This time around, Rusty created the character of Henry, named for her own grandfather. She envisioned him as a sixteen-year-old, *too young for military conscription*, and too young to raise any questions about why she couldn't grow any facial hair. How would she explain her ease with machines? Henry's father owned a machine shop! But then, why wouldn't Henry work there? A family feud? A tragic death? Yes, Henry would be an orphan. A plausible and sympathetic story.

Henry was hired on the spot. On the shop floor, no one questioned his background. Rusty did her part to keep up appearances. *I tried to go to the bathroom as infrequently as possible.* Soon, she was accepted as one of the guys. The men invited Henry, and the Rusty underneath the Henry suit, out for drinks and offered their advice about women. *"Listen, kid, make hay while the sun shines. Don't let yourself get hooked by any one woman. You have plenty of time before you get married."*

She couldn't keep it up forever. *A boy of eighteen or nineteen should begin to grow a beard. That was the one thing I was unable to do, so eventually I had to quit.* Rusty had to say goodbye to Henry, but perhaps this was the moment she said hello to stage impersonation.

Rusty met John, her future impersonation act partner, at a gay bar that primarily catered to men. When he learned that she could dance, John invited her to join his act down at Coney Island. She's heard of another girl, a welder at the Navy Yard, who puts on a suit and a bow tie to work as a glorified waitress at one of the Manhattan clubs, the Howdy Club, or Club 181, or maybe now it was called Club 82, ever

since the owners got busted. They rarely let her up on stage, which is reserved, mostly, for the queens. John promises Rusty it won't be like that. He promises she'll get her time in the spotlight.

"And do I get to wear pants?" John nods. Rusty stands from her bar stool to hug him. The other patrons must think the two are really putting on a good show in case the cops turn up. *If a cop walked in, what was he going to say?*

After her Fred and Ginger act with John, Rusty likes to stick around to watch the rest of the show. There's the woman—*oh, I can't remember—Ginza?*—who takes a bath in wine, and the shuffling stagehand who mops up after her. Rusty heads to the bar for another beer. She's parked back in the front row by the time the next performer comes out. May Devoe. *A very high-class stripper.*

Still in costume, her own dapper suit this time, Rusty waits at the stage door. When the stripper walks out, Rusty crams her two pointer fingers in her mouth for a high, sharp wolf whistle. The woman is practiced in the art of ignoring her suitors. She keeps her head down, walks right past the spot where Rusty stands, her shoulders squared in defense of the softness of her body. Rusty takes another sharp inhale, ready to whistle again.

Then she took another look and she started to laugh.

"*This beats everything,*" the stripper says, voice light as a feather boa. "*I'm used to guys being out here trying to proposition me after the show and I have to fight them off, but you're a first . . . What the hell, why not? Come on, let's go.*" She grabs Rusty's hand and breaks into a run, even though no one's chasing them. Three blocks from the club, she stops just as suddenly as she started. It startles her, how truly alone they are now, and she drops Rusty's hand.

"Hi," she says. She sticks out the hand that just held Rusty's. Rusty takes it. "Well hello, *May Devoe.*" The woman shakes her head. "*Cookie Castle?*" She shakes it again.

"You can't believe everything you hear. Tonight it's just Terry."

This chick, this chick has got to be straight, Rusty thinks. *Anybody that looks like that, you know, has got to be straight. Well, she must know, or does she just have a thing on sailors?*

"Pleased to meet you, Terry," is all she says. "You can call me Rusty." Or maybe she gave her real name, the one her parents gave her before she ran away, the one on her missing birth certificate and death certificate, on her missing civilian navy records and institutional records.

Rusty and Terry go to a dinner that lasts so long it becomes breakfast. The next night, it's Terry who waits for Rusty at the stage door. *It was a slow seduction. I was afraid of getting too involved with her.*

It took nearly a year for Rusty to find her moment. *We were exchanging Christmas presents and I asked if I could kiss her. I had dreamed of a million different ways of getting her into bed and then it just happened automatically. She took her time. She wanted to be sure of me— that I would be stable.*

From that first kiss, that first Christmas night together, things moved as quickly as they had for Mabel and Lillian, a postwar U-Haul. *Shortly after*, Rusty asks, *"How about taking a place together? I suppose that would be impossible; you go on the road a great deal more than I do."*

Terry doesn't hesitate in her answer. *"Well, I'm thinking of not going on the road anymore."* She was already forty when she met Rusty, but it wasn't just her age. The freedoms that women, particularly queer women, had enjoyed during the war and in its immediate aftermath— the freedom to take over a man's job, to share a clandestine meeting in the engine room onboard a naval ship, to wear a pair of slacks in the street—were now viewed as a threat to the democracy the nation had fought so hard to defend. Senator Joseph McCarthy was on a mission to root out communists and queers from every level of government, the military, and public entertainment, from the high hills of Hollywood on down to the freakshows that lined the streets of Coney Island. With McCarthy in office, it was easier for Terry to consider

Rusty's offer to settle down, maybe even leave the city. Terry was already *low on work because of the way things were shut down* in show business. *"Things are getting a little rough. The show is closing anyway."*

~~~~

My participation in the Pink Flamingo kick line is preserved in just one photo taken from the stands. My hair had already grown back to shoulder-length after my failure to live up to the office's expectations of womanhood. Elated from the performance, counts and kicks executed without a hitch, we smile for the camera in our bright swimsuits, caps, and tennis shoes. I look hopeful, expectant, as if I have finally kick-lined my way to femininity on the tile stage of the pool deck.

My own stage presence is dwarfed by the woman next to me, the synchronized swimming coach. *I want to look like her,* I think when I look back now. She sparkles. Her swimsuit has sequins she hand-sewed into the fabric. Even after her pool routine, her lipstick is immaculate. Next to her, I look like a dyke—leg hair and chin hair and messy bun hair—wedged between queens. *Just for a day, I want to look like her.* I want someone to make me up like Rusty before she was thrown into the men's jail for the night. I want to be a *female* female impersonator.

~~~~

While Senator McCarthy may have succeeded in closing down clubs and driving performers out of town, he failed to suppress a storied art form. The roots of male impersonation can be traced back to the first century AD, when Chinese women in the Tang dynasty dressed up as men onstage in operas such as *The Butterfly Lovers.* Women also performed "breeches roles" in Europe in the seventeenth and eighteenth centuries, the less famous counterpart to men who wore dresses to perform women's roles in Elizabethan England.

It wasn't until the nineteenth century that performers turned breeches roles into an act all their own. In 1868, British actress Annie Hindle arrived in the United States and brought along a popular new stage act in her trunk: male impersonation. Back home in England she had had competition in other male impersonators like Vesta Tilley and Hetty King, but in America Annie got top billing. Women who took on breeches roles in previous eras had dressed like men and taken to the stage within the script of a play, but now being a man created its own script. Male impersonators sang and danced and developed characters in one-woman (or one-man) acts. Hindle paved the way for other acts to succeed over the decades, from Johnstone Bennet in the late 1800s, whose performance was so stirring it inspired Mary Casal and Juno to meet her backstage; to her contemporary Ella Wesner, who insisted she be buried in her suit; to Mabel Hampton's Harlem Renaissance friend Gladys Bentley, who stole hearts on and off stage; to Stormé DeLarverie, whose name, printed on a flier for the Jewel Box Revue, billed as "25 Men and 1 Girl" with the caveat that no one could guess who the real girl was, catches my eye in Mabel's file at the Lesbian Herstory Archives.

Stormé defined the art of male impersonation in opposition to female impersonation. While female impersonators simply had to put on makeup, a dress, and a pair of high heels, the male impersonator faced the more difficult task of taking things off. To become credible, to fool audiences, there was much to remove: A layer of makeup. Stockings. Heels. Manners. A delicate touch. All the trappings of femininity I had always longed to understand. Everything shed in exchange for the simplicity of a suit and a strong stance.

Male impersonators had always performed their songs, their dance steps, and their acts as men, aiming for the kind of verisimilitude that British male impersonator Vesta Tilley knew she had achieved when tailors rushed from the theater to copy her suit designs for their lords.

These male impersonators were succeeded by a generation of performers who approached masculinity from a new angle: drag kings. These heirs to male impersonators like Rusty Brown would not settle for simply imitating masculinity. They sought to illuminate and highlight it. Scholar Jack Halberstam defines drag kings as "anyone (regardless of gender) who consciously makes a performance out of masculinity." They camp it up. They grab their belt buckles and thrust their hips. They choose as their characters the most macho of men. Not, as Halberstam notes, famous gentlemen like George Clooney, who might be the male equivalent of the female stars like Marilyn Monroe and Whitney Houston that queens so often imitate. They opt instead for "sexist pigs," the extremes that render the mundanity of masculinity legible onstage and, even after you leave the lurid dark of the bar, out on the street.

The modern drag king movement, according to one of its founding fathers, Mo B. Dick, began in 1995 in the East Village. The kings performed in New York City venues and parties, many of them now shuttered or defunct: Club Casanova and HerShe Bar, Meow Mix and the still-standing WOW Café. They performed under names that make me bite my knuckles in private glee, like Buster Hymen.

I'd expect Mo to be my favorite, with his high pompadour and a name inspired by Melville. B., short for Bodacious. Not only is Mo the cofounder of Club Cassanova, he is also a drag king archivist, the creator of the site Drag King History. Instead, I give the king's crown to Haitian American performer Dréd, who also got her start in the mid-1990s and often claimed the top prize at HerShe Bar's drag king competitions.

While at Mo's Club Casanova, hardly any of the audience members wore drag, at HerShe Bar, the boundary between stage and seats, between audience and performer, was porous. A king could be anywhere. Dréd competed against audience members who clawed their way up on stage for a night to parade their butchness in the spotlight

to the hoarse cheers and wolf whistles of the crowd, but they had no choreography.

Dréd knows how to move. Where Mildred Gerestant was shy and soft-spoken, Dréd, her drag king alter ego, was the kind of "ladies man" Mildred thinks she might have been in a past life. "I want to be a household name," she said in an interview. "It would be nice to be more well known. My dream one day is just to make a living off my creativity." She wanted to elevate drag kings to the same heights that RuPaul has uplifted queens. (Did her eyes ignite enviously with each new season of *Drag Race*, the launch of *All Stars*, the spread of the international editions? If she asked me why I thought queens were more popular than kings, I might share with her some of the reasons people offered in interviews—the flamboyance of queens is better suited to capturing an audience's attention; women in suits are just scary.) It would be nice, too, if Black lesbians got the credit they were due in the history of drag kings, performers like Stormé and Gladys Bentley and all the unnamed butches in the audience, the way whitewashed pop culture is only just beginning to reckon with the influence of Harlem drag balls on today's queen culture.

I watched Dréd perform in the 2002 documentary *Venus Boyz*, released nearly two decades before she passed away. She wore a pencil-thin chinstrap beard and a long leather coat with tails that flared when she spun. Her act often ended with a striptease that revealed her bra and breasts, the figure of a woman buried under the illusion of a man. I was drawn to how she mastered two gendered performances while I struggled to find my own.

Not every king performs to blur this line between masculinity and femininity. When the stage lights go down, anyone could emerge from the dressing room: a butch, a femme, a trans masc person, a bisexual woman, an enby, a human who cannot find the words to describe the singularity of their gender identity. "When I donned a Drag King persona," writes photographer and performer Del LaGrace

Volcano, "it didn't feel like much of an act. I was astounded by how natural it felt to be a guy and be free of the anxieties I had lived with for years around not passing as a 'real' woman." These days, Del LaGrace identifies as a "part-time gender terrorist" and intersex person who feels more comfortable onstage as a drag queen than a king.

I can spot Rusty's legacy in these onstage performances, and also in this expansion of possibilities for gendered expression in everyday life. The combination of the work opportunities that opened during World War II and the performance possibilities that opened on stage at clubs introduced new ways for people who traditionally would have been traded by men to engage with masculinity. If it was now easier to do a man's job and to wear a man's clothes, then it was also easier to imagine more options than woman or bad woman, aka inverted woman, aka lesbian.

Perhaps someone that I claimed as lesbian by the terms of her own era, like novelist Louisa May Alcott, who went by Lou and declared she was "half-persuaded that I am a man's soul put by some freak of nature into a woman's body," would have explained her identity differently had she been given the opportunity to try on masculinity for a night under the spotlight or during the day at her factory job. Or through every single moment of his life.

~~~~~

I rode my bike through the last of the late September sunshine, the summer smell of hot trash suddenly supplanted by fresh laundry and warm sugar, to find today's drag kings. They were competing in the finale of Takes the Cake, the 2021 drag king tournament hosted by the Cake Boys. A field of forty fresh kings had been winnowed down to twelve over the course of the season, and only one could take home the crown: five hundred dollars, a supply of makeup, and mentorship from the Cake Boys.

I was as smitten with the kings onstage as with the crowd gathered

at the bar. Some, like me in jeans and a button-down, had made only a modest attempt at looking cute. Others had brought it all: fishnets and combat boots and leather harnesses; shiny charro jackets; faces done up with shaky pencil mustaches and beards. They could have been easily mistaken for the real kings who paraded out for their lip-synch acts.

Lucky Pierre, dressed in a tree costume worthy of Broadway, warned of the coming climate apocalypse against the crash of a heavy metal song, interrupted every so often by a recording of a Greta Thunberg speech. With a magician's flourish, Willy Killigan and Hugh Mann Race both pulled rubber organs from beneath their costumes. I expected dildos, but instead they revealed a string of intestines, a body part relied on more often for horror scenes than gender expression. Smol Papi pulled back the sleeves of a boxer's robe to take an injection of testosterone from his coach.

When Bucket took the stage, I finally saw the kind of king I had imagined all along, one who had perhaps taken his inspiration from Dréd. He wore a dapper purple suit with a frilled shirt, and I could tell even from far away, my elbows perched against the sound booth in the back, that he was short. He sang an old Backstreet Boys song into a mop. I waited for him to take off the suit. The jacket went. Then, with the strum of an air guitar, the button at the top of his pants, unleashed. He shucked them off. They caught around his ankles, a kite stuck in some branches, until he emerged in a nude leotard, triumphant. He knelt down on the stage floor beside a bucket and began to scrub, keeping time to a metal cover of "WAP (Wet Ass Pussy)." *Bring a bucket and a mop for this wet ass pussy.* He dipped a beaker into the bucket and surfaced with red-tinged water. Pussies wet with blood. He drank to cheers from the crowd. Water dribbled down his face and onto his costume, where it left a red stain.

At intermission, I headed to the bar with a friend I had dragged along to the show.

"What would your drag king persona be?" I asked to pass the time in line. Her partner planned to be a sailor for Halloween, complete with mustache and striped shirt, like some kind of French mime stuck out at sea. We both daydreamed about this woman, fine-boned and an expert winker, in costume. Did she love the knowledge that there was a soft body beneath the trappings of masculinity?

My friend already had her drink in hand by the time she made up her mind. Perspiration beaded against the plastic cup and her freckled face. "Grumpy old man," she finally declared. "All wrinkly. Can never find his keys. What about you?"

The closest I had ever felt to being a king was when I wore a strap-on, a performance for an audience of one.

"Bike mechanic." I fantasized about having the know-how and the strength to fix my own bike. "Understated, but an expert."

~~~

Lesbian Herstory Archives cofounder Joan Nestle came of age during the 1950s, but she never saw Rusty Brown or the male impersonators of the Howdy Club and Club 181 perform their acts. She focused her attention instead on a different, more personal performance. She spent her time at lesbian bars, like the long-gone Sea Colony in the Village, where the only shows on offer were the music from the jukeboxes and the personal performances of butch and femme roles. Rusty was a butch. Joan was a femme. Both the bars and the clubs were owned by the mob, but while the clubs attracted a fair number of tourists, the bars were a spot for queers alone.

This was the one reward lesbians received for their participation in the war effort: a stronger shared culture. *It was after the war before there was any place for a woman to go, a women's bar.* Faderman traces the role World War II played in fostering a "significant lesbian sub-culture." In the wake of the war, it became acceptable for women to wear pants not just in the factories where they had worked, holding

down the jobs of men who were away at the front, but also out in public. Gone were the days when lesbians, perhaps on their way to a rent party in Harlem, had to carry their slacks in a suitcase. Now that it was permissible to wear pants in the street, Mabel and Lillian's 1930s dynamic of *stud* and *wifey* cemented into camps of butches and femmes that still shape many lesbian communities to this day. The war had brought lesbians—butches and femmes, those who fell in between and those who opted out—to big cities for work, where they chose to stay long after V-J Day and sought out spaces to meet one another. Lesbian bars could open and rely on a more steady stream of customers than ever before.

There are entire manila file folders in the Lesbian Herstory Archives devoted to the history of lesbian bars. I opened the first one, and a sheet of paper with the names of deceased bars typed out like grave markers fell out. Eve Adams' Tea Room. The Welcome Club. The Duchess. Pandora's Box. Clit Club. Rubyfruit Bar and Grill, named for Rita Mae Brown's novel.

I moved to a New York City with only three lesbian bars: Ginger's in Brooklyn, Cubbyhole in the Village, and, just around the corner, Henrietta Hudson. Every few months, someone writes a nostalgic eulogy to the lesbian bars across the nation, from NYC to D.C. to Kansas to California. This trend started so long ago that yellowed newspaper clippings of the earliest examples have made their way into the folder at the LHA. None of these articles have uncovered a definitive reason why these bars, a legacy left by women's work during World War II, can't stay open, but there are a few theories in circulation.

Lesbian bars no longer face the threat of closure by a capricious mob boss owner or a surprise police raid. Still, there are estimated to be just twenty-one left in the country. That's fewer than half the number of gay bars that cater to men in New York City alone, and a meager fraction of the two hundred lesbian bars estimated to have been open in the 1980s. Comedian Lea Delaria narrated and executive produced

The Lesbian Bar Project, a documentary that celebrates and fundraises for those remaining bars. She dubs the reason for their closure "the million-dollar question." Theories abound. Perhaps women, who to this day make eight-two cents for every dollar a man earns, still lack the economic power to keep a lesbian bar open, evidence that lesbians still have not broken free from the impact of the traffic in women. Perhaps we have simply found other places to meet: the internet, apps like Lex, sports leagues, rotating parties, the annual Dyke March.

Dr. Marcy Adelman had a different idea. Lesbians, she told me, only want to find a partner and settle down. These days, now that they can get married and have children, they've entirely lost interest in fostering community and sustaining bar culture. At first I was skeptical of her theory. I have more interest in community than in walking down the aisle, toward the altar or the maternity ward. There's supporting evidence, though, dating all the way back to the days before marriage equality and increased access to adoption services and fertility treatments. Long before, there were homebodies like Mabel, who admitted she rarely went out after she met Lillian. And there's Rusty. *Sometimes we'd go to a gay bar. But somehow my girlfriend and I really never really cared for the bars itself so much.*

The burlesque dancer settled down with her sailor. Rusty found work at *a hotel in Brooklyn*, first as a bellhop running the elevator, then as a front desk clerk, then a room clerk, and finally a front office cashier. Each of these jobs allowed her to continue wearing slacks. She moved into a *small apartment* with Terry, a place to finally call home after a childhood spent in and out of institutions that couldn't even be bothered to hang on to her records. Like Mabel and Lillian, they developed an easy cover story to explain why two unmarried women lived together. *We didn't live as sisters or anything. We just lived as friends.*

Their *Italian land*lady, Della, *eighty-some odd years old*, didn't buy it.

"*How come* two nice girls like you don't have *no boyfriends?*" she asked.

Rusty, always quick on her feet and eager to put on a show, approached the *assistant manager* of the hotel, Angelo, *a gay fellow*, and *told* him *what was going on 'cause he was Italian.* "*Oh,*" he said, "*you got one of them kind of landladies.*" Together, they hatched a plan to throw her off their scent. *We put on an act that night in front of her,* kissing *right underneath the streetlamp.* Della came to the window. Rusty knew she was there because *the curtain was rubbing and shaking like hell . . . We gave her an eyeful . . . We really poured it on.*

The next time Della spotted Rusty, she cornered her with a barrage of questions.

"*Do you usually kiss boys like that that bring you home from work?*"

"*I happen to like Angelo.*"

"*Oh, he's Italian?*"

"*Yes, he's Italiano.*"

Della perked up. "*Italian boys make good husbands.*"

Rusty wasn't ready to quit her fun. "*Just because he's a good friend of mine doesn't mean I'm going to get married.*"

You should have seen the look on her puss . . . She didn't know what the hell to think.

It wasn't until scholar Judith Butler published their influential work in the 1980s that we all became familiar with the idea that gender is a performance. But some part of Rusty, it seems, intuited that from the start.

The performance didn't distract Della for long. Rusty and Terry *moved out of there because she was just getting . . . awfully nosy.* Eventually, they had to leave the city too. *When New York started to get so bad that you could get mugged going three blocks*, it was time to move on. The pair moved to the West Coast together in 1971—*to Oregon, Washington, and finally moved to Los Angeles.* Terry gave up show business to

become a nurse. They shared their happily-ever-after, alongside their *friction* and their *rages*, until 1979, when Terry died of a stroke.

From here, the trail goes cold. Len Evans, who conducted one of the oral history interviews with Rusty, has also passed away. There's no trace of the San Francisco social club Rusty helped found, the Slightly Older Lesbians, either. This might be all I get of her, the male impersonator who worked a man's job.

The lesbian feminists of the next generation would come to revile drag, particularly the queens who embraced the very trappings of traditional femininity that feminists viewed as the tools of their own oppression. "Goodbye to the Halloween Balls, the drag shows and parties," wrote one. "It is time to stop mimicking the heterosexual society we've been trying to escape." Some accused heterosexual women of always wearing drag while others warned against the "'butch-femme' syndrome," a dangerous reproduction of stereotypical gender roles, with the butch as "a cheap imitation of a man." Their perspective, though, seems to miss the point entirely.

"Butch," explains one of the drag kings in *Venus Boyz,* "is masculinity as an identity in a woman." Rusty's life, and the era she lived through, marked a moment when women could play and experiment with masculinity, in the form of a costume or a uniform or even a job, and decide how much of it they wanted to incorporate into their everyday identity. Even as a woman who feels ashamed when strangers make remarks about my masculinity, I can still celebrate the opening of so many new possibilities for gendered expression.

But what was masculinity to begin with? When you take off the pants and the suit jacket, the tough-guy exterior and the easy privilege carried below the belt, what's left? What parts of masculinity can become a performance, for an audience of one or of hundreds? At what point did performance become lived reality? Was Rusty, when looked at through the lens of trans identity as we understand it today, a man?

Inspired by Rusty, I went to Sephora to buy a stick of concealer, a makeup staple I had never owned, to hide the acne scars that made me so self-conscious. I still held out hope that all I had learned about drag, the postures and colors and flair that had ensnared drag writer Elyssa Goodman, could help me find pleasure in the tricks of femininity.

I immediately felt exposed under the fluorescent lights and overwhelmed by shelves lined with products I didn't know how to use, let alone name. When a friendly greeter asked if I needed help finding anything today, I said I was fine, thank you, just browsing. Had he already clocked me as an impostor? I had expected to find an entire aisle of concealers, but I was startled to discover that the store was organized by brand. To my left, there was a display of shampoos. To my right, perfumes launched by a celebrity. I backed away, ready to head for the exit, when I bumped into a display of flesh-toned tubes. I could stick it out a little longer. I had seen women, real women by every measure, test out concealer on their hands to determine whether it matched their skin tone. I picked a color at random, all of them named for foods—honey and oatmeal and berry—and unscrewed the lid until I could pull out the applicator with a vicious suction. I dabbed and rubbed until my hand turned greasy and mottled. None of them matched my skin, which has always looked somehow both pale and olive. Desperate to get out of there but also to triumph over my own shame, I picked one out at random, along with a brush to blend it into my skin, and marched to the checkout.

"That'll be fifty dollars," said the cashier. Undeterred, I forked over my credit card with quiet outrage. At least my failure at femininity has saved me a lot of money over the years.

I never used that concealer. It sits powerless in my medicine cabinet. As I go through my morning routine, I look at it and I remember that objects alone cannot bring us shame. The clack of a high heel or the kiss of lipstick cannot tease me. Objects hold only the power that

we give them. It takes people, cops and lurid headline-writers and mean girls, to police their use.

Alone in my bathroom, I feel at home with the pieces of masculinity and femininity that I have borrowed and stitched together. I am not butch or femme. I am not even kiki, a term Joan Nestle introduced me to, a label for a lesbian in the bar scene who did not conform to butch or femme. I am a lady jock. I am a disheveled professional. I love wearing colorful clothes and growing my hair long. I stick to the same hoop earrings every day. I don't have to put on makeup to become a woman.

The archive might be able to help me define womanhood on my own terms, but it cannot define Rusty's identity by today's terms. I am not here to solve the question of Rusty's identity as if it were a mystery but to thank her (him?) for the way she helped expand the possibilities.

Extracts | A SELECTION OF DRAG KING
STAGE NAMES

Backdoor Boys
Bucket
Buster Hymen
Cake Boys
Danny King
Dom Quixote
Dréd
Elvis Herselvis
Elvis Emulator
Justin Kase
Hugh Mann Race
Klon Dyke
Lucky Pierre
Maxxx Pleasure
Mo B. (Bodacious) Dick
Murray Hill
Oliver Face
Pencil Kase
Shon
Smol Papi
Willy Killigan

6.

The Lesbian-Ruled World: Gloria Anzaldúa, Cherríe Moraga, and Lesbian Community

(1977–1981)

GLORIA ANZALDÚA ALMOST DROWNED AT PADRE ISLAND. Just *about ten years old*, and this was already her second near-death experience. The first had been when she was three months old, and her spirit left her body. In that brief moment, another spirit entered, perhaps a more masculine one, certainly one that never felt at home in the body where it landed. This new *extraterrestrial spirit* pushed her body to menstruate early. Her mother, Amalia, found blood in Gloria's diapers. The doctor said it was because she was *a throwback to the Eskimo*, a dismissive comment that Gloria reclaimed because it deepened her connection to her Indigenous roots. The family couldn't afford any brand-name sanitary products, so her mother stuffed the little girl's underwear with cloth in the hopes that the other kids would never guess. Amalia filled her daughter with shame. Gloria came to the spiritual truth of her hormone imbalance, one that would bring her painful periods for her entire life, like *a vulture picking at my insides*, only through visits with psychics and psychedelic mushrooms,

or niñitos, as the Aztecs called them, which revealed the presence of this new spirit.

Her second visit with death was on a Sunday. The whole Anzaldúa family—*an* meaning heaven in Basque, *zal* for hell, and *dua* for *the fusion of the two*—piled into their red truck and drove to the beach. Spanish ships bound for Mexico used to stop there, and legend had it they had left behind buried treasure. No one in the family knew how to swim. That didn't stop little Gloria. *People thought I was water crazy.* She always went in deep enough to feel the waves crash over her, from head to toe. Amalia was *scandalized* that her daughter was the *only one in the extended family to wear shorts or a bathing suit and she'd say, "Oh, but your pubic hair is showing through the suit."* Once again, Gloria was taught to be ashamed of her body.

That Sunday, a current carried Gloria out to sea. She swallowed water in big gulps. *I had the feeling that the ocean inside me had joined the ocean outside me.*

She was saved by a sandbar. For three hours, she hopped up and down, just high enough to bring her mouth above the water line so she could breathe. When the tide came in, she *paddled* back to shore.

Gloria survived, for the time being. This wasn't the Gloria I was introduced to in my college linguistics class, though. That woman wasn't called Gloria at all. She was Anzaldúa, the use of her last name a reminder that we were there to study the Chicana feminist works she had produced and not her biography. We studied her politics, how she drew from her Mexican and American and Indigenous roots, how she wrote in English and Spanish, *Tex-Mex* and Nahuatl, with no need to reconcile this plurality of identities. My professor neglected to mention that one of those many identities was lesbian.

When Gloria's writing is taken separately from her life, it is easy to miss the heartbeat of her work. She lived at a time when lesbian was no longer just a sexual identity but also a political one. Lesbians used the word to invite romantic connection, and also to build community

with one another in the hopes of using their combined force to change the world. Lesbians built their own communes, published their own newspapers, and held their own dances. Long gone were the days of Mary Casal's believed isolation.

In case it isn't obvious yet, I am an *unforgivable romantic*. I love love. Not as a means to an end, a stepping stone on the path to marriage and children, but as a surrender to passion, even when it's surely doomed. Obsessive, selfish love that feasts on its own ruin. Love that can be enjoyed alone in the quiet hours of the morning, remembering the smell of someone else's laundry detergent, the pop of their jaw, the shape of their ears. When it comes to Gloria's archive, the extensive writings and interviews she left behind, I am frustrated in my search for this kind of traditional romance. Gloria's life, or at least the record she left of it, was marked by a love of community, and she poured that love into her writing. Her love story embraces a multitude of people over any one particular partner. Lesbians and feminists and lesbian feminists and Chicanas and women of color. People she fought with and people she fought beside. She is at the center of this story because her expansive, liberatory view of community, at odds with other lesbians of her time, remains an inspiration and still creates community today, even now that she is gone.

Community love is perhaps best described by Audre Lorde— *Black, lesbian, mother, warrior, poet*—in a paper she presented in 1978 at a women's conference hosted at Mount Holyoke College, "Uses of the Erotic: The Erotic as Power." *The erotic functions for me in several ways*, I read in the printed transcript. *The first is in providing the power which comes from sharing deeply any pursuit with another person. Eros*, an ancient Greek word that would have been cherished by Sappho, is not just the stuff of lyric poetry and pornography. It has the potential, when reclaimed, to animate our work. By work, she means the labor we do outside of our jobs, the labor we would continue to do even if we weren't paid for it, the labor we probably aren't paid for, the labor

that grows out of our fierce love for one another, the labor on behalf of the planet, on behalf of our chosen families, on behalf of our neighbors, on behalf of the people we don't know and will never meet. When people come together around a shared pursuit, they are bound as a community by the power of the erotic.

Within the celebration of the erotic in all our endeavors, my work becomes a conscious decision—a longed-for bed which I enter gratefully and from which I rise up empowered.

~~~~

For Gloria Anzaldúa, a love of the written word ignited in the place where most romances begin: the bedroom. As a kid in Hargill, Texas, a *one-grocery-store, two-service-stations town*, she *used books as my refuge, a little cave I could enter—a cave with a door through which I could go into other worlds. There was so much work to do on the farm that I didn't have time during the day. I would read in bed with a flashlight under the covers . . . working with images and writing became connected to night.* When her sister threatened to rat her out to their mother, Gloria brought her into the fold. She told her sister *fantastic stories about the coyotes, this little girl named Prietita which was my nickname, dogs, and horses.*

Gloria was *a seventh generation American, a poor Chicanita from the sticks*, the daughter of ranchers, migrant workers in their native land. *I stooped over the tomato fields bending, bending under the hot sun, hands broadened and callused, not fit to hold the quill, numbed into an animal stupor by the heat.* Gloria's mother, Amalia, had given birth to her at age sixteen. When Gloria became a teenager, her father traveled to find work without his family so the children could stay in one place long enough to attend school.

The words always leaped to life at night, even when Gloria moved to San Francisco in 1977, already in her mid-thirties, with a master's degree under her belt. *No one in my family had ever been to high school*

*much less college.* She often worked at night, hardly resting, *fifteen to seventeen hours in one sitting and I don't want to leave it,* only *the peck peck of my keyboard* to keep her company. Someone from her publisher would bring Gloria meals during the day. Gloria's relationship to writing, an act of community love-making that could happen in even the most quotidian spaces, stood in defiance of Virginia Woolf's solitary vision of a woman with "a room of one's own" in which she can write. (Woolf had a husband but still preserved her twentieth-century romantic relationship with Vita Sackville-West in her letters.)

*Forget the room of one's own—write in the kitchen, lock yourself up in the bathroom.*

~~~~~

The 1970s was an era of a new lesbian consciousness. It produced an explosion of lesbian magazines, newspapers, anthologies, bar fliers, and oral histories. It's no coincidence that this was the era when Joan Nestle cofounded the Lesbian Herstory Archives to hold on to all these documents. Inspired by the movements of the 1960s and early '70s—civil rights, the antiwar movement, environmentalism, the Chicano movement, and second-wave feminism—lesbians wanted to build their own communities outside the bars that Joan Nestle, Rusty Brown, and Audre Lorde visited, to use that shared energy to fight for their own rights. No one was in agreement about how precisely to achieve that vision, though, and many white-led projects were unwelcoming to Gloria and other women of color.

Del Martin and Phyllis Lyon had been two of the first to embark on the project of creating a space just for lesbians when they founded Daughters of Bilitis in San Francisco in the 1950s. While it began primarily as a social club, DOB became increasingly political over time in response to the twinned pressures of policing and McCarthyism. The first DOB national convention, held in 1960, was raided by police, as was their New Year's Eve fundraiser later that decade. Still, the

group asked their membership to remain conservative in both their dress and their political actions. The founders' vision of an assimilationist path to mainstream acceptance of lesbians is perhaps most apparent in their 1969 article for *Motive Magazine*, "Realities of Lesbians." They insisted that, sexual preference aside, lesbians are at once a diverse group and just like everyone else. While DOB never truly took off, Faderman notes that the organization was significant simply for existing in an era of vigilant witch hunts.

Both the Stonewall Riots of 1969 and the feminist rejection of lesbians ignited an anger that gave rise to a more radical wave of lesbian communities. My favorite among them is aptly called the Radicalesbians. The group formed, in part, in response to the infamous words of Betty Friedan, author of *The Feminist Mistique* and founder of the National Organization for Women, who called lesbians a "lavender menace" that distracted and detracted from the larger feminist project. At the next NOW Congress on May 1, 1970, a group of twenty women with those same words, LAVENDER MENACE, emblazoned on their purple shirts took over the mic to address the very issue of lesbians within the women's movement. These newly minted members of Radicalesbians laid out their manifesto in a paper passed out at the conference, "The Woman Identified Woman." It opens with an incendiary summary of how attitudes toward lesbians are shaped by a system of patriarchy and encourages women to imagine new, alternative ways of relating to one another.

I asked Flavia Rando, a former member of Radicalesbians who later inaugurated the Lesbian Studies Institute at the Lesbian Herstory Archives, what the collective aimed to achieve. "Our goal was to understand how we were oppressed, the specificity of it, and to do something about it." They paired this political agenda with a purely social one: planning dances. The group had grown out of the Gay Liberation Front. While the GLF meetings had a fairly even split of men and women, the dances, much like my swim team, were heavily

weighted toward men. "What would a dance look like with only women?" Flavia remembered wanting to know. She used to buy bouquets of flowers down in the Garment District to bring along to the dances she helped plan, as many as five hundred women filling up a SoHo loft, with support from the Daughters of Bilitis. Her face lit up to remember it. "Lesbians should have something beautiful."

Flavia also remembered that the group lacked the diversity and the radical agenda of the Gay Liberation Front. "We had a pretty narrow view of who our sisters were." Many women of color had joined Salsa Soul Sisters, a collective of lesbians of color, instead. Gloria spent a short time living in New York, but she never, to my knowledge, attended a Radicalesbians meeting. Had she gone, she might have confronted the same racism and classism that she later met in other predominantly white lesbian and feminist communities, an exclusion that would come to inspire her own vision of a community forged through writing.

When Radicalesbians slowly disintegrated, perhaps due to its lack of a hierarchical structure—Flavia reminded me that history rarely has the kind of critical turning points that narratives so often demand—a new offshoot formed with the remains of the Radicalesbians' budget: the Lesbian Food Conspiracy, "a once-a-week coop." They used the money for gas to drive up to Hunts Point Market in the Bronx with their broken-down cars to buy cheap food to resell to the residents of Chelsea. This new iteration of the group was still made up entirely of lesbians, but their mutual aid project was a more expansive one. The food was for everyone.

In their search for community, some lesbians wanted to create spaces, physical and intellectual, for lesbians only. Among them, the Collective Lesbian International Terrors, or C.L.I.T. for short, catches my eye because their provocative name demands my attention. When I read their manifesto at my desk, I worried that if someone were to drop in on me, they might think I was looking at porn. Their mission,

though, had nothing to do with sex. "Right now the Media State is involved in the most important war game plan of the century—they are defining what a lesbian is to the people of America as if lesbian was a new word." C.L.I.T. called for a boycott of the mainstream press that had so slandered the image of lesbians with their *Media Mindfuck* and phrases like *lavender menace*, and for the formation of an alternative lesbian press. "We do not believe that ideas should be bought and sold in capitalist competition style." Instead they published with a women's news journal run out of Washington, D.C.: *Off Our Backs*, "a paper for all women who are fighting for the liberation of their lives," which ran from 1970 to 2008. True to their word, C.L.I.T. published the first collection of original writing in the same issue, pieces written under pseudonyms reminiscent of drag names like Killa Man and Oedipussy Tuddé.

I quickly realized that these writings were meant to exclude. "Bi-sexuality," a member writes from the safety of an anonymous collective, "is a Media plot which keeps women in economic, emotional, intellectual and consciousness bondage to men while sexually the girls are allowed to play." This vision of community left no room for some of the original lesbians, like Sappho and Myra, who both had men in their lives that *complicate the case history*. It left no room for Gloria either, who identified as a lesbian but also had *a man lover* she felt no need to explain away.

Lesbian separatists carried this vision of a space "for lesbians only" to the extreme. In previous eras, lesbians had always found ways to carve out space inside the institutions to which they had been pushed, from women's colleges to women's prisons to the navy to mob-owned bars. Now, though, they planned to intentionally create a world without men, a community of women-born women who did not even speak to men. It was Flavia who gave one of the best definitions of lesbian separatism I have ever heard, though she does not consider herself one. Lesbian separatists, she told me, "refuse, to the best of

their ability, to have any connection to the heterosexual world. That is a very difficult undertaking."

Lesbian communes and colonies sprang up across the United States, but like so many utopian projects before them, they could not last. Not only did their purist vision lead to infighting, but they also, as Lillian Faderman notes, lacked "even the basic country survival skills such as splitting wood, plumbing, or planting." Before Heather Elizabeth became one of the founding Van Dykes, a band of wandering separatists who lived out of the van that gave them each their name, she bought a farm in Toronto with her girlfriend and another lesbian couple. The snow fell in piles around their poorly insulated house, a bitter reality none of them had prepared for.

The lesbian separatist utopia? wrote Cherríe Moraga, who would become Gloria's collaborator in her effort to dream up a community where women of color were at home. *No thank you, sister.* Neither she nor Gloria could join up with a group that was so narrow in its definition of lesbian and that failed to see *gender is not the only oppression.* Lesbians who were part of other movements, like the Black Panthers and the Chicano movement, needed to speak with men to organize against the other oppressions they faced.

When Gloria attended the Michigan Womyn's Music Festival in 1981, she found it to be yet another failed vision of lesbian community. *For the most part all the performers . . . were white.* None of the music was in Spanish.

Michigan Womyn's Music Festival is perhaps the "largest and best-known" of the more than twenty women's music festivals that have sprung up across the United States. They got their start in the mid-1970s as venues to showcase artists in the growing women's music scene, like those who recorded with Olivia Records, which was founded in D.C. in 1973 as the "first women's recording and distribution company." Bonnie J. Morris archived this history of women's music festivals and the ardent group of "festigoers" that they attracted

in her book *Eden Built by Eves*. "Although certainly open to *all* women
(and occasionally to men), the women's music festivals are produced,
organized, and attended by a lesbian majority." They were also a space
for, as Morris explained to her own father, "women to go off in the
woods and feel good about themselves for a few days," and to create
temporary lesbian feminist utopias over the summer.

Not only was the Michigan Womyn's Music Festival a predomi-
nantly white space, as Gloria noted, but it excluded attendees on the
basis of gender. Not only did they remove *men* from their name by
replacing the *e* with a *y*—a common reclamation of lesbian feminists,
alongside *wimmin*—they also limited festival attendance to "women-
born women." This policy excluded trans people from the space, both
the trans women who wanted to join in the celebration with other
women and the trans men who had come of age within lesbian and
feminist culture. In 1994 protesters built Camp Trans outside the fes-
tival gates as a reminder that this supposed utopia was built on a foun-
dation of exclusion. Morris writes in its defense, "Is it not possible for
there to be *one* event, *one* annual festival, intended for women born
female?"

Charlotte Bunch, one of the founders of the lesbian newspaper
The Furies, reflected on the successes and failures of the era's collectives
and colonies and what could still be learned from this great lesbian
experiment. "Separatism is a dynamic strategy to be moved in and out
of whenever a minority feels that its interests are being overlooked by
the majority," she writes.

Yet when lesbians adopted this "dynamic strategy," what other mi-
norities did they end up overlooking? What about the bisexual, pan-
sexual, and trans women of the world? Lesbian separatist rules about
who was allowed entry into women's spaces and who would benefit
from the revolution they sought to bring about are the roots of today's
TERFs, trans-exclusionary radical feminists, who deny that trans
women are, in fact, women. Several prominent separatists, concert

organizers, and women's music festival performers were among the earliest TERFs. I see no reason to record their names, or any more about their ideology, here.

Separatists, as Gloria and Cherríe witnessed firsthand, also created a community that did not address the needs of women and lesbians of color, who wanted to engage with the heterosexual world to fight the other oppressions they faced and wanted to see themselves reflected onstage. If Gloria and Cherríe wanted a new kind of community, they would have to build it themselves.

~~~~

Cherríe and Gloria met in San Francisco in 1977. By that point, Gloria was sick of academics, sick of the *disembodied language of academic discourse pushed on graduate students.* She had been the first in her family to go to college, Texas Women's University, but she did not find the women's college environment to be the haven her white, middle-class lesbian predecessors had created at places like Smith and Mount Holyoke, complete with women's dances, professors who lived in Boston marriages, and campus newspapers that reported the latest smashes and spoons. Gloria did meet her first lesbians there (*I was so horrified—you know, when you're afraid of something, you fight it?*), but all her teachers were white, and so were most of the students, aside from a relative who became her roommate. Gloria had to drop out after two years because she ran out of tuition money.

She finished her studies at Pan-American, and, after a short stint as a teacher, she began a PhD program at the University of Texas in Austin. *I always asked the professors, "Can I try to do this in a fictive mode?" I got away with it twice.* She quit after she had completed everything except her dissertation because the institution offered few opportunities for her to study Chicana literature or the women's movement. Still, she wanted to write, that late-night ritual that had carried her through her Hargill childhood, had carried her all the

way to California, the first of her family to leave Texas. She joined
the Feminist Writers Guild, a space filled almost entirely by white
women. *Somehow these women were great,* she remembered years later
in an interview. *They were white and a lot of them were dykes and very
supportive. But they were also blacked out and blinded out about our
multiple oppressions.* Cherríe was the only other nonwhite woman to
join the group at *Old Wives, one of my favorite bookstores.*

When Cherríe spoke on a panel about racism in the community,
Gloria—short, to the surprise of one of her editors, who expected to
meet someone whose height matched the power of her words—sat in
the front row, alongside four other Chicana feminists. It was a moment
of relief and recognition for Cherríe, who had also grown accustomed
to the sea of white faces that took up the most space in the women's
movement. *After the forum, the six of us walk down Valencia Street singing
songs in Spanish. We buy burritos y cerveza from "La Cumbre" and talk our
heads off into the night, crying from the impact of such a reunion.*

It would make for a nice fairy tale if the idea for *This Bridge Called
My Back,* the anthology put together by both lesbians that united non-
white writers around the possibility of liberation across many oppres-
sions, was born from that evening. If the mixture of beer and song
provided fertile soil for a shared eros to take root and rise tall. Truth be
told, the seed of this book had been planted much earlier for Gloria, as
a graduate student, when she was assigned to teach a course called La
Mujer Chicana and had to search *the long Vaticans and street-stalls of
the earth* to find the texts she wanted to share with her students. Texts
about Chicanas, yes, but also about homosexuality and Black femi-
nism, *which I wasn't supposed to do.* Gloria had sought her place in the
movements of the 1970s. The Chicano movement—which celebrated
Mexican American culture, honored the history of the United States'
theft of Mexico and Mexican people, and fought for their rights to
speak Spanish in schools and be treated as full citizens—was full of
men who didn't want her. *The Chicano community does not accept its*

*queers*. There wasn't much room for her in the predominantly white feminist movement either. *I've never been a separatist.* Gloria wanted to create a space that could hold all her inextricable identities, and she thought she just might be able to do it through writing.

In San Francisco, Gloria lived in a *commune of fifteen people* and did whatever work she could find: *a technical writer for the University of California, UC Med Center, temporary jobs with Bell Telephone and insurance companies. I'd work three months, and then quit and write three months.* She sucked the marrow out of every writing opportunity she could find in the city, joining groups and giving public readings of her poetry and fiction.

In February 1978, she attended one workshop on *goddesses and heroines* led by Merlin Stone, *a working class, spirituality-practicing, goddess-loving "white" woman*, that ignited the kindling Gloria had collected for years. She had received one of two $150 *scholarships for working-class or women of color who couldn't afford this out-of-the-way nice, scenic middle-class inn*, Willow. In the end, she was the only scholarship recipient to attend. When the other women *found out I was not a paying member . . . they started treating me differently. Like I didn't deserve a room to myself and I didn't deserve to eat what they ate.* Fed up with the *subtle and blatant forms of racism and classism from the white participants*, she knew it was time to open a new space.

By the time she left the workshop's toxic environment, *Bridge* had crystalized in her mind, and, with Merlin's support, she began to solicit contributions to what would become this radical anthology. She wrote letters to women's studies programs and women's organizations and friends of friends. She placed an ad in *Conditions*, "a magazine of writing by women with an emphasis on writing by lesbians," yet another new community for lesbians.

I searched for that ad in the back matter of several digitized issues, but I could not find it. In issue six, there's a section of a poem by Gloria, "Holy Relics," that will later become part of her solo book

*Borderlands*, a celebrated memoir of hybridity told in prose and poetry, in English and Spanish and *Tex-Mex* and Nahuatl. In number five, I bounced in my seat at the sight of her name again, this time next to "Cher'rie Moraga-Lawrence" under the headline "THIRD WORLD WOMEN." It was a call for women of color to submit their bios and become part of a directory for conference coordinators, reading directors, and women's studies programs. Gloria and Merlin would later call this project Dial-A-Token. By issue eight of *Conditions*, there's already a review of the completed anthology and an ad in the back with an accompanying jacket image, a line drawing of a woman on her hands and knees.

Gloria couldn't stoke the flames and produce a book so quickly all on her own. Even if she hadn't joined forces with Cherríe at La Cumbre, perhaps that night she had seen the potential for the erotic to provide *the power which comes from sharing deeply any pursuit with another person*. She would need power to read through all the submissions that would come in, to assemble them into thematic sections, and to find a publisher for this collected work.

*About six months after I started,* she dropped in on Cherríe at the restaurant where she worked and told her, *"Cherríe, this is your last chance."* Did she want Cherríe for all the things that set them apart? She had *a different kind of anger* than Gloria. Where Gloria's had simmered through an entire life spent with people who asked her to be someone else, from grade school teachers who hit her with a ruler when she spoke Spanish, to school administrators who wouldn't allow her to teach high school because she was a Mexican, Cherríe's was newer, quicker to boil over and shoot forth the hiss and steam of her words. When the two met among the shelves of the Old Wives Bookstore, Cherríe introduced herself as Cherríe Lawrence, the surname she had been given by her white father. Gloria prided herself on her ability to *spot a Chicana a mile away*. She recognized Cherríe's heritage, buried by a patriarchal naming convention, from the sound of her

voice. Between that moment and the printing of her name as Cher'rie Moraga-Lawrence in the seventh issue of *Conditions*, something had changed. *She had very recently begun to identify as third world.*

Cherríe grows impatient. She has tables waiting, food to serve. She has welcomed this woman into her life, and here she is, always asking for more.

"*This book, if we do it,*" Gloria said, "*is going to change your life; it's going to change my life.*"

In the end, Cherríe said yes, a promise stronger than a marriage pact. Her name and address were added to the end of the solicitation letter. Gloria would need her help, the power of that shared thing between them that Lorde, who would come to publish her poetry in *Conditions* and contribute to *Bridge*, might call the erotic. Gloria would need Cherríe's help because she *got very very ill and almost died.*

Anzaldúa's texts were taught to me in college as if they had sprung forth, fully formed, from the library, an Athena born from the head of academia. My professors encouraged me to believe she was all intellect and ideas, a thinker, a mind always at work. While the pages of her books are the only place to meet her now that she is dead, Gloria, or Gaudi, as she was *called at home all the time,* was, once upon a time, a body. A short body. A body that bleeds. A body that cannot produce its own insulin. A body that is now buried in Texas. *People don't deal with the body.* Let me look at you for a moment, Gloria. Let me sit beside your body.

Her infant body left red stains on her diapers at just three months old. By age six, she had her true period, breasts, and a hormonal imbalance. The only support her mother offered was a rag to put between her legs and a tight cloth to hide her chest. In spite of the shame her mother tried to instill in her, Gloria firmly believed *my body wasn't dirty.*

As an adult, menstruation brought her great pain—fever, nausea, genital aches—that alienated her from her own body and her sexuality. (My own period betrayed me in my early thirties, when it

would disappear for a few months and then return for weeks on end. It brought on bouts of depression that left me crying for hours on the bathroom floor.) Her own monthly cycle had none of the spiritual potency she imagined for her semiautobiographical character, Andrea, in her never-completed novel *El Paisano Is a Bird of Good Omen*: "During her menses she feels fragile, expansive, the limits of her body stretched beyond her skin, she flows out like a sheet, encompassing, covering chairs, people, everything around her."

Gloria found spirituality elsewhere. It gave meaning to her physical agony and her emotional pain. (With Gloria beside me, I wonder if my blood and my tears might be trying to tell me something I have overlooked, if my body might be trying to help me after all.) Gloria's spirituality wasn't the Catholicism of the colonizers. She found solace beyond La Virgen de Guadalupe. She drew strength from pre-Columbian goddesses and Aztec gods, gave tarot readings and often referenced her own astrological sign—Libra, one of seven air signs in her chart that she said made her *always want to control everything*. (*I have these Libra parties . . . This time I'm going to ask not only Libra suns but Libra risings and Libra moons*.) After she *drowned for a little while at Padre Island*, Gloria had two more *bouts with death*, which brought her even closer to the world of the spirits. At age sixteen, a high fever shocked her hair white. She would dye it with henna for the rest of her days.

Later in life, Gloria would name the state of spiritual awakening Nepantla, *which is a Nahuatl word for the space between two bodies of water*. The ocean inside joining the ocean outside. Gloria always occupied this space between—between life and death, between our world and the spirit world, between English and Spanish, between the Chicano movement and white feminism, between the *An* (heaven) and the *zal* (hell) of her last name—and built her home there. These roaming interests were simply *spokes of the wheel*, and *writing was the hub*. She was forever seeking new understanding: understanding of

her body, understanding of her Indigenous roots and the ancient pan-
theon of deities from which they grew, understanding of the world
around her and the world beyond. The spiritual became one of her
*longed-for beds* from which she could *rise up empowered.*

~~~~

I want to, for the most part, step aside here. I've taken up so much
space already. There is no need for my inventions when the truths
these lesbians left us have gone unheeded. I am startled by the way the
essays and poems Cherríe and Gloria have selected for their political
archive still resonate in my world, forty years later. The contributors
to *This Bridge Called My Back* organize against the powerful struc-
tures of capitalism, imperialism, and racism, and aim their efforts at
the places where these forces intersect. "We need political memory,"
writes Cherríe in an introduction to the 2015 edition, "so that we are
not always imagining ourselves the ever-inventors of our revolution."

You are angered by the arrogance of some articles
that would tell you that Virginia Woolf is your spir-
itual mother.
 —Nellie Wong, "In Search of the Self as Hero"

It is as if we think liberation a fixed quantity, that
there is only so much to go around.
 —Andrea Canaan, "Brownness"

Our situation as Black people necessitates that we
have solidarity around the fact of race . . . We strug-
gle together with Black men against racism, while
we also struggle with Black men about sexism.
 —Combahee River Collective

~~~~~

The power of the erotic fueled the idea for *Bridge,* and also its eventual publication.

In the summer of 1980, Cherríe Moraga traveled east to Boston in search of a publisher for the book she and Gloria had put together. She stayed with contributor Barbara Smith, founder of the Combahee River Collective, in Roxbury. On her train journey from predominantly white neighborhoods to the predominantly Black community of Roxbury, she reflected on the place of the anthology—I imagine she carried a mimeographed copy in her luggage and felt the weight of it tug at her as the train rattled underground—within the women's movement and also within the larger struggle for liberation. *What drew me to politics was my love of women.* As for so many other women of the era, from Flavia and the other members of the Radicalesbians to the writers that put together *The Furies,* lesbianism was a root that connected Cherríe to a deep underground well of power and community. *I hear there are some women in this town plotting a* lesbian *revolution.* Such a narrow revolution didn't speak to the concerns of the community, which had just the day before lost a Black boy to a white cop entrusted with a gun. *What does this mean about the boy shot in the head is what I want to know.*

Without an agent, Cherríe went alone to meetings with the women and lesbians of publishing. *We couldn't afford the costs that it takes when you're putting a book together—not only making copies but phone calls and postage and time.* No publisher wanted to print *Smashing the Myth!,* as it was then called, named for a subtitle within one of the essays. Every evening, Cherríe came home to Barbara, who greeted her like a sister. A Black woman embracing a Chicana who *used to feel more white.* The presses that rejected the manuscript remain unnamed, but I guess them to be the very same ones whose logos decorate the spines of the books on my shelves, presses that were founded to print the sudden proliferation of feminist and lesbian material, like

Alyson Publications out of Boston, Seal Press in New York City, and Naiad Press in Florida.

Cherríe wished Gloria was there to fight alongside her.

She returned home to San Francisco, to the embrace of her community and to her graduate work in feminist writings at San Francisco State University. Women's studies had not yet been accepted as a discipline by academia, so Cherríe had designed her own program with the support of her advisors, Sally Miller Gearhart, the first out lesbian to hold a tenure-track position, and her partner at the time, Jane Gurko. The racist rejections of the white women who held the keys to publishing had altered something in Cherríe, and she needed to change her life to accommodate this shift. How could she complete a traditional thesis addressed only to those inside the ivory tower of academia when she had more urgent work to share, work that held the power to reshape the world? *This Bridge Called My Back* became Cherríe's thesis, and Sally helped the book find a publisher in Persephone Press, which had published her own novel just the year before.

Had Persephone been one of the presses to reject *Bridge* before Sally threw in her support? The feminist press was once based in Watertown, Massachusetts, the starting point of Cherríe's train journey to Roxbury. This is not the story of the failings of one press or of the heroic actions of another. In her afterword to the book, Cherríe refuses the reading of Sally, or even of Persephone, as a savior figure in the story of *Bridge*'s success. If no traditional publisher had wanted to take it, she insists, she and Gloria simply would have mimeographed the entire thing and handed it out on street corners. I am reminded of the words of C.L.I.T.: "We do not believe that ideas should be bought and sold in capitalist competition style." Cherríe, Gloria, and all the writers they folded into *Bridge* had a message to get out, and they weren't in it just for the profit.

Persephone folded in 1982, and the writers were once again in search of a publisher. In response, Cherríe, her former East Coast host

Barbara Smith, hattie gossett, and Audre Lorde founded Kitchen Table Press to reprint the book. Since then, the book has gone in and out of print and been taken up by two more publishers. This book that no traditional publisher wanted, born out of necessity and anger and connection and eros, went on to sell more than one hundred thousand copies. That's not counting the copies that are lent out, like that of an old beloved that still sits on their ex's shelf, or taken out of the library, like my own, or resold after an undergraduate course on intersectional feminism ends, the torch kept alive by each pair of hands that passes it along. A community of hands passing a book.

Cherríe writes a special thank-you to yet another member of her lesbian community, Audre, who had already presented her paper on "The Uses of the Erotic" at Mount Holyoke College but who had not yet published her biomythography *Zami: A New Spelling of My Name*, whose fame as a poet, Cherríe believed, helped bring attention to *Bridge*. I look up to Audre, like so many of the lesbians of the 1970s, in awe. She has entered the historical record as a lesbian, one I had heard about before I sought everything that had been *said, thought, fancied, and sung of* lesbians. There is an entire biography dedicated to her, and T-shirts, too, some with her name printed alongside Gloria's in big block letters. Her life, cut short by breast cancer, is yet another strand of this lesbian love story. I have archived her words in my own diary: *Any world which did not have a place for me loving women was not a world in which I wanted to live, nor one which I could fight for.* In this moment, I honor her for how love and fight, lesbian and liberation, always went hand in hand.

This new community Gloria and Cherríe and Audre opened through their writing made room for a multitude of lesbians, and also the multitude that existed within Gloria. My college linguistics professor shared only one part of the woman when she handed out xeroxed PDFs that described how Gloria was punished in grade school every time she spoke Spanish—*three licks on the knuckles with a sharp ruler,*

like what the nuns would give my father when he spoke out of turn. We analyzed how Anzaldúa mixed languages, one of the first to capture the way her community spoke, without ever translating for her audience. The professor chose which parts of her to share and excised the rest.

To this day I'm not sure how my professors kept up this convenient fiction when Gloria, unlike the lesbians before her, left behind volumes of material about her identity, sexual and otherwise, more than I could possibly know what to do with. *Borderlands.* Her contributions to *Bridge.* Countless unfinished works she references in interviews. Her personal letters and papers, held at the University of Austin. Interviews. *In academia*, Gloria wrote, *I find that my lesbianism gets hidden behind the overt race stuff.*

Her lesbian identity was so important to her that she claimed it in spite of the fact that she could not live up to the standard of purity that the separatists demanded of those who set foot on their lands. *I have yet to have a full sexual relationship, a live-in relationship with a woman.* She mentions *a man lover* without dismissing or qualifying their relationship. She embraces her contradictions and makes no effort to resolve them just to make others comfortable. She lays bare how the pain caused by her hormonal imbalance complicated her relationship to sex and delayed her interest in physical intimacy. For a while, *I just didn't have a sexuality. Do you think I'm a lesbian when I'm celibate?* Then, in spite of her Catholic upbringing and in spite of the heterosexuality that surrounded her, she *made the choice to be queer.* Lesbianism was yet another marker of the duality, the plurality, that lived within her. *I, like other queer people, am two in one body, both male and female.*

Even though Gloria chose *lesbian*, she did not want to be pigeonholed as a lesbian writer. *Middle-class, white, heterosexual people* had the privilege of being simply a writer, no pesky *little adjective* out front to qualify their work. To call Gloria a lesbian writer would deny the other aspects of her identity, the other parts of her self. *One's own*

*body is not one entity.* She did not limit *Bridge* to contributions from lesbians. In place of separatism, which would ask her to deny not only the male within but also the men who joined her in the fight for liberation, she believed in El Mundo Zurdo, the Left-Handed World, a world where *the colored, the queer, the poor, the female, the physically challenged* would be empowered.

*I'm married to the writing. The writing is my lover. I call her la Musa Bruja.*

Before Gloria and others of her era, *lesbian* was rarely more than a sexual identity. Sometimes, it was the passcode to a private party or an invitation backstage at the end of the show. Just recently, it had grown into a nighttime culture at the bars where butches met femmes, and at the clubs where male impersonators performed. Now—no matter whether you were the founder of a lesbian newspaper, a member of a lesbian commune, a contributor to *This Bridge Called My Back*, or just another festigoer who swayed to women's music on blankets in the woods—it could be a political identity too. What this generation of political lesbians couldn't agree on was where to channel the energy, the erotic power, they had uncovered with the reclamation of a previously pathologized identity.

Sappho and Lorde, two great lesbian poets, both grappled with the longing that sprang forth from their beds. For Sappho, her *soft bed* was the place where she pursued her desire, a *longing* satisfied. There was no lesbian (little *l*) identity to unite her with the women she brought there, so she could do little with her love save slip into it for a moment to forget her fate, sing of it in song. Lorde, a Black lesbian who battled with cancer, *longed for bed* itself. Not a bed of spring coils and goose feather but the bedrock of her work, *which I enter gratefully and from which I rise up empowered.* Through some alchemy that unfolded across the centuries, what took place between the sheets became political.

Gloria's bed was a site of private discovery, the place where she

found the written word and her voice as storyteller, desperate for her sister to keep her secret. It was also a place to retreat from the world and regain her strength. In her untamed book *Borderlands/La Frontera*, she reclaimed *Coatlicue*, the early Mesoamerican serpent goddess who was pushed into the margins by the Aztecs and then subsumed into Christianity by the Spanish. *Coatlicue* is the one who encourages rest, a shedding. *I locked the door, kept the world out; I vegetated, hibernated, remained in stasis, idled. No telephone, no television, no radio.* Gloria cut off the world to heal from the wounds of the world, the pain at home in her body. She lays down, despite a lifetime of being *told that Mexicans are lazy,* to rise up again, to write again, to be born again. *Coatl* means skirt, but it also means twin, the twin sister of Lorde's idea of *self-care,* a phrase which, before it was commodified, once meant the radical possibilities that opened up when those that society did not care for stopped to take care of themselves.

When Gloria emerged, she sought others to join her in her work. She called on Cherríe to edit the book alongside her, to find a publisher in Boston. She called on writers she had never met to contribute to the book. When the time came for her to write her own book, Gloria called on her publisher to bring her food, to keep her writing through the night.

Now, I feel, Gloria calls on me. She asks me to share *deeply* in this work that is not yet done. The work of research and of writing, but also the tangible work of protest, of organizing, of mutual aid. A *rosy-fingered* tendril of the erotic reaches out and grabs hold of my wrist when I crack the spine of *This Bridge Called My Back.* I read passages aloud to a beloved, whose head rested, for the moment, in my lap on the couch.

*Touching is an act of making love,* I read as I ran my fingers through close-cropped hair, *and if political touching is not made with love no connections, no linkings happen.*

"Come on," I said. "Let's get to bed."

## *Extracts* | LESBIAN LANDS AND COLLECTIVES

Adobeland

Cabbage Lane

C.L.I.T. (Collective Lesbian International Terrors)

Daughters of the Earth Farm

Dykes & Gorgons

Fly Away Home

The Furies

Gutter Dykes

Huntington Open Women's Land (HOWL)

Outland

OWL Farm

Ozark Wimmin on the Land

Radicalesbians

Rootworks

Sassafras

Seattle Collective

Spiral Wimmin's Land Collective

The Van Dykes

We'Moon Land

Whippoorwillow

WomanShare

Yellowhammer

# 7.

## A Lesbian's Best Friend:
## Amy Hoffman and Mike Riegle

~~~~~

(1980–1992)

CONEY ISLAND HAS ALWAYS BELONGED TO THE QUEERS. THE beach was the dominion of poet Walt Whitman, my father's favorite, who ran along its shores shouting lines from *The Odyssey* into the wind. It belongs to the sideshows and freakshows, the male impersonators and the strippers. Its sands hold the promise of a vacation for just the cost of subway fare. It must have been a lesbian beach at one point too. Mabel mentions that she hung out there, long after she retired as a dancer, even though she never learned how to swim. Lorde writes, *On summer Sunday afternoons, Muriel and I would split from the gay beach at Coney Island.* It is the home of the Mermaid Parade, that annual summer boardwalk celebration of sailors and their bare-breasted seducers, of the misfits of the sea. We share its waters with the creatures who were also once deemed unlovable: moon jellies and sea lice and schools of blade-thin fish.

Coney Island also belongs to me and my best friend John.

I don't remember the day John and I first met, though it must

have been at the pool where we swam together in Brooklyn, or even
how we became friends, though it must have happened a bit like get-
ting into shape: building up slowly over our shared time in the lane,
without either of us realizing. He was quiet during workouts, up until
the very end, when he would haul his body up onto the deck and call
back to me, "Peace out, girl scout." Sometimes, we'd have breakfast
together after our workouts at the overpriced diner across the street. I
memorized the rhythm of his order. "He'll have two eggs over easy,"
I'd tell the waiter. "Bacon—extra crispy—and wheat toast." John
couldn't start eating his eggs until the toast came, breaking the yolks
and spreading them across the bread.

There are pictures of us in those early days, when his hair was
shorter, beard scruffier, frame lankier, the days when I could beat him
in a race, photo evidence that we already knew each other, standing
side by side in our swimsuits, jaws gone slack from exertion. In my
mind, though, I will always see him as he was one day on the beach:
Just past thirty, sun-streaked curls reaching his shoulders, beard so
thick it almost hides the mole on his upper lip, white skin tanned and
stretched taut over muscles so toned by CrossFit I can see the defini-
tion of ones I don't even know how to name. Most people joke that he
looks like Jesus, but I'd say he's a Greek statue, one of the homoerotic
ones, or maybe Poseidon, wielding a trident.

John is the kind of person I never thought would become my friend.

I had spent my youth constructing a taxonomy of friendship. Each
pair I saw on the playground or the TV screen could be sorted into
a neat little box and placed along a timeline. In elementary school,
everyone had a best friend. I stood with mine on the front lawn, both
of us in matching Fourth of July swimsuits. We had dredged up giant
purple storage bins from the basement, filled them with the garden
hose, and jumped in. The photos my mother took on film are too
grainy for me to make out what we're wearing around our necks, but I
know what's there: friendship necklaces, half a heart each that we had

bought from Claire's with our allowances. They were so cheap that the clasps broke long before she moved away and we lost touch.

By middle school, our former best friends became our competition. We fought for valedictorian, for first place at a swim meet, for the top spot in some boy's heart. We found new friends. Together, we showed up, lent an ear, remembered birthdays, brought ice cream to a breakup. *Girlfriends*, my coworkers call them. Grown women who gab on the phone and attend each other's bachelorette parties, who all marry men but maybe kissed a girl in college, the women we readily recognize on screen in characters like Monica and Rachel of *Friends*. Girls who had played house with tea sets and stuffed animals were now women who rehearsed the emotional intimacy they might one day share with a partner. Monica and Rachel move in together, practicing until they can move in with boyfriends and husbands. Practicing, the perfect cover for the students who fell in love at women's colleges. I had, and still have, these friends. I just refuse to call them anything as romantic as girlfriends.

Then there are the bromances, like Chandler and Joey. Homophobic men who reject emotional intimacy as "gay" and yet still forge deep, loving connections. Nothing captures this better than the episode of *Friends* when Joey gifts Chandler—not just his longtime roommate but also his coconspirator in watching TV, playing foosball, and raising pets ill-suited for the city—a gold friendship bracelet that matches one he bought for himself, the upmarket, adult version of those friendship necklaces. Chandler is torn. He wants to make his best friend happy, but he doesn't want to get caught doing something as effeminate as wearing a bracelet. He doesn't wear it. Joey asks him where it is. Chandler wears it, buried beneath long sleeves. It slips out and someone teases him. The friendship carries on. Men, we are led to believe, don't need to participate in any rehearsals for marriage, but they long to anyway, and must bury their longing.

I wanted to be friends with men too. Or the boys, at least. Like

Mary and Rusty before me, I fell in with the boys naturally. I joined them for games of soccer during recess and weekend pillow fights that broke my glasses more times than my parents could bear. These were always tacit friendships, feral, shrouded in a cloud of body odor—pine and buttermilk and vinegar funk—devoid of grand gestures or emotional conversation. The boys were reliable, though, always there when I reached for them.

High school brought its own sea change. The boys and I now had to face the specter of romance in our once uncomplicated friendships. One of them, now a filmmaker, suggested we watch *When Harry Met Sally* one Friday night. I suspect he picked the movie in the hopes that the characters' endless conversations about whether men and women can ever truly be friends would convert our own friendship into a romantic relationship. "What I'm saying is—and this is not a come-on in any way, shape, or form—is that men and women can't be friends because the sex part always gets in the way," says Harry, played by Billy Crystal. In the end, the script proves Harry right, at least when it comes to him and Sally, but we forget to be mad at him for being such a know-it-all because it feels more like love won that argument. The line worked for my friend, too, who eventually won the campaign for me to become his girlfriend.

If straight women befriended gay men, would that ensure romance was out of the question? *Friends* is too homophobic to feature any recurring gay characters, but *Sex and the City* offers up the first "fag hag" trope I ever watched with heroine Carrie Bradshaw and her best friend, Stanford Blatch. He's just as necessary an accessory as the latest designer handbag or pair of heels she can't afford. Together, they can go out to the theater, obsess over why some man hasn't called them back, or indulge in a little pick-me-up shopping. They'll never have to risk falling for the same man, or falling for each other. Instead, they can invest in perfecting a performance that will attract men.

After exhausting all possible pairings, I thought I had solved it:

friendship is tethered to the ideal of heterosexual love. We forge friendships through shared romantic interest in a particular gender as a way to perfect our own gendered performance, and we use these friendships to learn from each other how best to lure in a romantic partner, to practice the emotional intimacy of being with that partner. We all have roles to play as friends, roles dictated by gender. Even friendship helped promote the traffic in women.

If I followed my own logic to its bitter end and used it to make new friends as an out lesbian, then my natural ally would never be John. We would quickly tire of each other after I failed to feign interest in men and clothes, and he'd become increasingly embarrassed by my attempts to braid his hair and strike up emotionally intimate conversations. Instead, I should cozy up to a straight man who could sit outside a pub with me on summer nights and help objectify the women who walked by in daisy dukes and short skirts.

In my study of the lesbian archive, I have been so obsessed with romantic love, the love between lesbians, that I overlooked something crucial. Rusty tries to tell me about her gay friend, also named John, who got her into show business, and the countless unnamed gay men who shared space at bars with her to create a convincing cover in case the cops showed up. Gloria tries to tell me about *this fairy faggot named Randy. He and I became best friends.* Once I open my eyes, I notice more and more of these pairings. Writers Carson McCullers and Tennessee Williams, or "Tenn," as she called him. The Harry Ransom Center has an old photo of her standing with a group of gay men in Speedos, though Tenn isn't among them. I've heard of Jack Hock and Lee Israel, alcoholics who almost pulled off one of the greatest literary letter forgery businesses of all time. They betrayed each other, in the end, and Jack died of AIDS.

I need to fill this section of the archive, too, with stories of solidarity between gay men and lesbians and with the story of John and me, set to a soundtrack of Taylor Swift songs.

My search for more lesbians allied with gay men led me to Amy Hoffman and her slim memoir *Hospital Time*, about the days she spent caring for her friend Mike Riegle when he was dying from AIDS.

"Most of my friends are gay men," I told her over coffee on a Saturday morning. My hands threatened to knock over our drinks with their over-eager gestures in the air. "It's nice to know I'm not the only lesbian out there with a gay best friend."

"Well," she said, her voice high and strained but still certain, entirely unlike the one I had imagined narrating the book in my head. She looked nothing like the author photo I had imagined on fast forward either. Her curls still stood strong and dark over her white face. "I don't know how far you've gotten in my book, but Mike was a very difficult person."

I don't miss him, she writes in the opening pages. *He was such an asshole.* A portrait of Michael, mostly unflattering, quickly emerges. The two met when they worked together in the 1970s at the *Gay Community News* in Boston, since shuttered, where Amy found an unusually mixed community of gays and lesbians in the office. Mike was marked by his passions, and his smell. *Cleanliness, sanitation—he believed these were bourgeois affectations. It was a political position.* Even before he got sick, he rarely bathed or washed his patched clothes. *Michael was brilliant, no question, spoke three or four languages, played the piano by ear.* He devoted his time outside work to corresponding with prisoners and sending them books. He was a mooch, bingeing an entire pint of someone else's ice cream or box of cookies and then abstaining entirely from the bodily pleasure of eating. He had a *deep voice* to match the depth of his convictions. *Desire and fury. Furious: he never lost the energy for that.* There is a before: and there is an after. Sickness was the impenetrable demarcation between them, impossibly contained by a colon. He didn't thank anyone for their caretaking, before or after.

Amy reveals herself on the page too. She first offered to help Mike

in the offices of the *Gay Community News,* twelve years after the friends first met, long after Amy had quit working there. *It was an impulse,* she writes of the offering, a split-second decision made without premeditation but no less earnest for its sudden onset. That initial offer of help became a legally defined role when Amy was named Mike's *healthcare proxy.* Still, this designation brought Amy little peace. She both resented Mike for needing so much and judged herself for failing to meet those needs. *I hated myself in the era of Michael's sickness,* she writes. *I also became jealous* of Mike's other caretakers. *I wanted to be better than all of them.* The other patients at the hospital, many of whom I imagine had taken to bed with more routine maladies— stents in the heart or appendectomies—saw Amy and Mike bickering together, two white bodies holding each other once or twice, and mistook them for a pair with a different legally sanctioned relationship, one they knew how to name: husband and wife.

~~~~~

I take some small pride when strangers mistake me and John for a couple in the darkened movie theater or at a crowded restaurant. They lean across the table to whisper conspiratorially that we should enjoy this time before the kids come and then gesture at their own brood busy draping noodles across the table and chairs. John is, by all measures, a good catch. A Stanford man who competed on the triathlon team, sang in an a cappella group, and danced with the step team. A triple threat. These days he works as a consultant, surfs in the mornings before getting down to business. Wants to save up enough to get a dog and his own place. Does the Sunday crossword. Enjoys old Cary Grant movies for their sarcastic banter and escapist locales, or a good mystery novel. Did I already mention his muscles?

John is the friend who often takes care of me. After I had my appendix out, he was the one who showed up at my door to crack jokes.

"Hello, friend." His voice filled up my first New York City

apartment and woke my roommates. He spread his arms as if to go in for a hug, then pointed at my abdomen. "Anything else in there you need me to take out?"

I had gone to the doctor's office on a Wednesday afternoon complaining of a stomachache and ended up in the ER with a radiologist's description of my insides in hand: "Ovaries: Unremarkable. Appendix: Inflamed." I spent the night in the hospital alone. I was between girlfriends. My family was in Pittsburgh. My roommate was in India. The woman in the bed next to me kept me company with her moans and cries. *She's going to die tonight*, I thought with a flair for the dramatic. *I'm never going to wake up from surgery, and the last person I will have spent the night with is this old Russian lady.* When I awoke from the anesthesia, the other patients began to check in on me. "Is there anyone here with you?" they asked. I shook my head as if to say "Just me." Two days later, John showed up at my door with strawberries from the farmers market and board games to pass the time.

It was John I called when I needed help installing my AC a year later.

"What's going on?" he asked on the phone.

"I bought an AC, opened it up, and it's already broken." I tried not to cry, because John would see it as a weakness. I had seen him give in to tears only once, after we watched an animated movie. "Maybe I broke it. It's my fault. It's so heavy."

"Okay?" He wanted me to ask outright.

"Can you help me?"

He sighed. "Give me a minute to get ready."

John and I shared a certain stubbornness. We both bragged about the fact that we had lived in the city for years without air conditioning. The threat of ten consecutive days with temperatures above ninety had us, along with the rest of Brooklyn, reconsidering. I would never admit it to him, but my change of heart had been caused by a girl. She lived in Manhattan with the luxury of central AC. Determined to prove to her it was possible to live without, the previous night I had tucked myself

into bed with a Ziploc full of ice cubes and listened to the pitiful gasps of a fan I couldn't feel. By midnight, I was out on the train platform, Manhattan bound. The air inside the subway car was already a relief, and I spent the ride to her apartment with my head lolling, teetering on the edge of sleep. When she opened the door, she announced, "I'm not spending another night at your place until you get an AC."

Thirty minutes later, John arrived in khaki shorts and a white T-shirt with the sleeves cut off, showing off the arms that were the very reason I had called him. But his strength isn't just physical; it's also practical. He called a car to take us the three short blocks, made long by the weight of the machine, back to the neighborhood discount store to return the thing, and then on to downtown, where we bought the last unit on the shelf, perhaps in all of Brooklyn. We installed it together: John, sweating by the window; me, standing in the doorway of that boxy little room, holding the instruction manual upside down.

"You know," he said on his way out the door, "I'm always happy to help you, but I think you're more than capable of doing some of these things on your own." From that moment, I became determined to be the one to help him, or at the very least, prove that I could take care of myself.

~~~~~

I cannot imagine AIDS. Not in numbers, not in stories. As of 2018, 675,000 people have died of the disease in the United States, and 69 percent of new cases that year were diagnosed in men who have sex with men. Well over half of those people had already died by the time Amy's book came out in 1997, just fifteen years into the crisis. I can't imagine the days when it was called GRID, Gay-Related Immune Deficiency; I can't imagine when doctors did not touch their patients, when families did not visit, when Charlie Carson and the other old-timers on my swim team went to a funeral every week. I can't imagine carrying around so much grief mixed with rage at the people in charge, who

weren't doing anything because it wasn't happening to their people. An era when sex could be scary, even protected sex, and the wait for test results excruciating. Charlie didn't come out until a year and a half after he moved to New York City, and he swore "it helped keep me alive."

So far, I've been spared from death. All my friends are alive, vibrant and healthy. I have yet to lose a single one. I can only listen and take notes for when the survivors are no longer with us. I can try to see things through Amy's eyes.

Amy wasn't the only lesbian to care for a man dying of AIDS. She wasn't even the only lesbian to care for Mike. *He surrounded himself with women like me.* At the hospital, friends left *photographs of their children (these from the lesbians),* and when friends were finally allowed to visit him at home, *a brigade of lesbians came over and painted and moved the furniture around.*

Lesbians, Amy explains, already *had considerable expertise in community-led health initiatives from years of being involved in the women's health movement.* Little did they know that the social movements of the 1970s, the collectives and communes, the meetings and the protests, had been a training ground for this crisis.

Amy was the only lesbian, though, to clean up Mike's shit when he collapsed on the floor of his apartment in the middle of the night, unable to make it to the bathroom. And when he collapsed again, this time in the Memphis airport en route to Austin to visit a friend, Amy was the one who flew down on borrowed airline miles to be with him in the ICU.

December. The Memphis Methodist Hospital decorated for Christmas with *red and green bunting, more blinking lights, candy canes,* and *little fake trees.* Mike's *amaze*ment to see Amy appear at his bedside, shining like an angel of the lord, was only matched by the relief of the staff, who had never seen an AIDS patient on their wards. Now, at least, this one belonged to someone, though her precise role in this sickbed nativity scene—mother, wife, sister—remained unclear.

Taking Mike to be a lost cause, the doctor called Amy into a generic, soulless little room, where I'm almost certain the fluorescent lights hummed, and asked her to sign a DNR so there would be a clear plan, so the question of his body wouldn't be an added burden on their hands. Here Amy let all her anger and pain and frustration flare, not at Mike, but in defense of him. She would have to talk to him before signing anything. *I want to live,* he wrote, still on a respirator and unable to speak, in defiance of the nurses and the doctor, of the tubes and the monitors, of the disease that was almost certainly a death sentence. There was only one way this story was going to end, but he still, maybe, had some time left.

In addition to serving as Mike's legal healthcare proxy, Amy also took on another crucial, but less official, role during the days and weeks and months he spent dying: Custodian of Mike's Things. It was something she did in his home back in Boston, rearranging the objects that made up his life when he was too tired to do it himself. *I'd clear off his night table or move boxes from one closet to another. I tucked certain items into his shirt pocket and arranged others on the rollaway table beside the bed: pen, memo pad, and checkbook in his shirt pocket; glasses; acyclovir, swabs, clipboard, bouquet of pink freesias (from me), and book beside the bed.*

If Mike was going to live, if he was ever going to walk out of this hospital and go back home, he would need something to wear. He had shat in the clothes he arrived in when he had collapsed in the Memphis airport, and now they sat festering in a plastic bag in his hospital room. For some inexplicable Mike reason, he wanted to wear those clothes, not the ones he had packed for Austin. And Amy would be the one to wash them, to carry them into the laundromat, to shake them into the machine without touching them, to sniff them when they came out, hot from the dryer, to gingerly fold them. *Still,* she writes, in spite of her doubts and her anger and her resentment, *I think I helped him.*

As I read, I take a mental inventory of Mike's symptoms, how

AIDS stripped him of his dignity in ways I have never witnessed in my adult life: diarrhea, night sweats, neuropathy, excessive weight loss, shitting out the lining of his own stomach. Living on his own, without a nurse or a health aide or a hospice worker or even a friend, just a freeloading roommate who refused to pay rent, Mike suffered even greater indignities than most. One night, he fell in the bathroom, hit his head on the radiator, and came to, covered in his own shit, immobilized. All he could do was close his eyes and go back to sleep.

In the face of this incomprehensible disease and the even more incomprehensible response, there has long been the impulse to take stock, to collect, perhaps to see if, with enough stuff, a comprehensible picture could emerge, or perhaps simply to remember, to hang on to both the wasting bodies and the people they carried, to memorialize those who were often denied funerals because families refused to arrange them or because funeral homes refused to handle the remains. Mike's death, multiplied by a hundred thousand, by seven hundred thousand. There is the AIDS Memorial Quilt, created by Cleve Jones, made up of forty-eight thousand three-feet-by-six-feet panels, together commemorating over ninety-four thousand individual lives. Amy writes of the more intimate practice of the Calling of the Names at gay gatherings, people speaking the names of their own loved ones when they feel so moved, as if at a Quaker meeting. Mike Riegle. Mike Riegle. Mike Riegle.

I am building my own collection of names. Queer women who sat by bedsides, who held dying bodies, who cooked and cleaned, who remember. Rebecca Brown devoted herself to caring for people living with AIDS and dying of AIDS-related causes. She was a home care worker, offering the kind of at home help that Mike always refused, or rather relied on friends to provide. The unnamed narrator of her gutting novel-in-stories *The Gifts of the Body* reads as a stand-in for Rebecca herself, whether she's bringing one man his favorite cinnamon rolls or cooking for a grandmother who contracted the virus through

a blood transfusion. The novel is its own kind of collection, and not just in the literary sense. Each chapter is named for some small, over-looked miracle the body can perform, functions that are noticed and longed for only when they are taken away by disease: "The Gift of Sweat," "The Gift of Sight," "The Gift of Mobility." It is an archive not of names or remembrances but of the body, what it can do and what can be taken away, even by its own systems.

Rebecca's wife, Chris, was a nurse practitioner who also worked with patients struggling to live with AIDS. A third name for my list.

Because I am busy noticing Mike's body and the people who sur-round it—Amy, *all of us lesbians in his life*—it takes me a moment to realize who isn't there. His mother or father, who *stopped writing to him after he came out to them.* Any blood relations. His close friend Charlie. A lover. Amy doesn't name the shameful reasons these people stay away, but it's easy to read the silences. The stigma of AIDS kept away those outside the community, while those within it couldn't bear to think what the disease might take from their own bodies. That left Amy, who wasn't even his best friend. She pauses for a moment to wonder who they would be to each other if Mike had never gotten sick. *Mike would merely be my friend, my old, difficult friend. I wouldn't think of him every day, as I do now, still. I wouldn't carry him around like a flame I dare not let gutter . . . Oh, why couldn't I simply love Mike and be generous!*

~~~

"Do you want to swim the 10K at Lake George this year?" I asked John at the pool one morning. It was deep enough into spring that sunlight streamed through the windows. He had already laid his hands flat on the gutter of the pool, triceps twitching in preparation to lift the rest of his body out of the water.

"Sure," he said.

"Sure enough to sign up today?"

He lowered his body back down and turned toward me. We were separated by the metal cord and plastic buoys of the lane rope, evidence that he had grown faster than me over the past few years.

"We would have to train for it," he said. I nodded. "And we'd have to start, like, now." I nodded again.

"I'll go to the beach with you," I promised. "Every weekend."

He stretched his hand out across the divide between our lanes. We shook on it. Could this be my chance to do him a favor, after he had done so many for me?

"Peace out, girl scout."

That summer, I came to know John's body as intimately as that of a lover. I spread sunscreen across the mole-flecked expanse of his back, so broad I had to stand up on my tiptoes to get at its farthest reaches. I waited for him as he put Vaseline on his groin and behind his armpits so his widening lat muscles wouldn't chafe against his triceps, and as he drifted away from me in the middle of the ocean to pee. In the water, when I lifted my head forward to breathe, I sought out his head on the horizon line, like a neon bird bobbing in the waves, separating the ocean's seven shades of blue from the sky. Certain he was safe, I let my head drop back down into the slurry of salt and algae, skeins of seaweed wound around islands of trash. There were rare moments when we swam side by side and turned our faces toward one another to exhale with a synchronicity that's something like dancing or the shared hush of a high school make-out in a darkened basement.

We worked our way up. First, just two miles, from Brighton Beach to the Coney Island pier and back. Then, a three-mile loop, tacking a jaunt to the white building—recently painted red but now and forevermore referred to by the name open-water swimmers had given it years ago—onto the end of our pier loop. Pushing ourselves farther still, we passed under the pier, dodging fishing lines as we went, and swam the two miles to Seagate and back.

Finally, the day came for our five-mile swim, the longest one we

would attempt before the race. I stepped off the train, and there was John, waiting on the platform. He carried his umbrella over his shoulder as if it were no heavier than something made of toothpick and paper, something he could glide into the ground as if slipping it into a tiki drink. The sun had already decided on heat, and sweat stains pooled on the fabric of his tank beneath the creases where his arms met his body. As we walked past the tables piled high with Russian pastries, the conversation inevitably turned to our plan for the race, now just two weeks away.

"What are you bringing for your feedings?" I asked.

"Probably just some gels from the running store," he said. "That reminds me, I still need to go. Want me to pick you up anything?"

"Nah, I can take care of it. And what's your plan? Are you going to eat after every lap?" I had packed an orange safety buoy with a drybag inside so we could carry along snacks and practice our feeding schedule.

"At first I wasn't planning on it, but then someone told me that if you're feeling hungry, it's already too late. So probably. Yeah."

We turned a corner, and the boardwalk opened in front of us, already teeming with joggers and bikers at 8:30 a.m., the kind of land people I couldn't understand. The sights had become familiar over the years—the pavilion where men slept on benches and woke up still drunk, the roofed bathrooms decorated with plastic flowers, the open-air showers, the Mister Softee truck just pulling in for the day.

"And what about when I have to pee!" I threw my hands out beside my hips to gesture at expelling something from the body.

"Just pee in the water."

"I can't swim and pee! I'm using my abs too much."

"When I did triathlons," he began, and somehow out of his mouth it wasn't a brag, "we would just tuck our penises into our shorts legs and pee off the side of our bikes. I love penises." That deep giggle again. "My penis. Other people's penises. I've seen so many in my life. Some have pretty dramatic curves."

"Does an angled penis make it easier to pee off a bike?" I asked.

"You know, I hadn't considered that."

As much as John loves penises, he hates vaginas. "They're all twists and turns!" Perhaps, never having seen the genuine article, he has envisioned something built as the complement to the penises he has seen, an equal but opposite force. When we went to the Georgia O'Keeffe exhibit at the Brooklyn Museum, I had to explain to him what those yawning flowers are thought to look like, in spite of the artist's protests. To me, this is John's flaw. Not just the disgust that makes me feel ashamed of my own body, the bumps and curves he could never find beautiful, but also his disinterest, his lack of knowledge about where he came from, about the fact that not all men have penises and not all women have vaginas. The privilege of not knowing.

Social psychologist Sarah DiMuccio discovered something surprising about masculinity: its definition varies culturally, and it's perhaps most easily defined by its opposite. "Comparing the Danish idea of masculinity with the American one, she found that the major difference between them was that in Denmark, men said to 'be a man' meant not being a boy. American men said that to 'be a man' was to not be a woman." Her findings hold a clue as to why cis white gay men often show such disdain for women, whether through outright insult or a more casual disinterest. If you are a man who embraces clothes and gestures and even vocal qualities traditionally categorized as feminine, and perhaps are even teased and bullied for that embrace, then it becomes more important to establish that you are not, in fact, a woman. You want to prove that you are still entitled to all the privileges masculinity holds. In the era of *Friends*, it was urgent for men to prove that, in spite of feminine habits like wearing a bracelet, they still weren't gay. Now that homosexuality has won some mainstream support, along with pop culture cachet, it has become urgent for a certain class of gay men to prove that they aren't women.

John has other flaws, too, believe me. For one, he hates receiving

gifts. One summer when we gave him a thank-you basket after he arranged a group vacation, he walked out of the room. He is overcome by the same bashfulness when given the words *I love you*. (He will hate that I am writing him this extended love letter.) There aren't many people left who say it to him. It's been a long time since he has had a boyfriend. I doubt his circle of gay boys—sarcastic, posturing, sometimes catty—say it with the ease my friends do. His mother, an airline stewardess for TWA, died when he was twelve, after years of deteriorating from Alzheimer's. He hardly remembers a time when she wasn't sick. "I hate being sad. There's so much further for me to fall. Losing her carved out a new bottom." This could be the source of his practicality, his generosity, his insistence that he needs nothing from anyone, not words, not things, but there is always more of him, unspooling before me.

"I'm always available as a fallback plan," I remind him often.

"Thank you," is his refrain, "but you don't have a penis."

We arrived at the beach and prepared for our swim. I set down my bag among the other sports backpacks and duffels that had been hurriedly abandoned near the waterline by fellow early risers. A battered paperback spilled out: Tana French's *In the Woods*.

"Here," I said, holding it out to him. "Do you want to read this?" An ex-girlfriend had given it to me, and I had read it alone in my first New York City apartment, staying up all night in a terror tautened by every footstep on the stairs, every shout from the street below. If I pretended just to lend it to him, he might not notice it was a gift.

"Thanks." He began to unload his backpack to begin our morning routine—sunscreen, cap, goggles, water bottle—and to make room for the book.

John was the first in the water. He rolled over onto his back, as sleek and eager as a seal.

"Get in!" he shouted. I whined the whole way as I gave myself over, limb by limb, to the late-summer chill. We set out together for the pier, our one-mile marker. The ocean was blissfully flat, and my

sleep-stiffened muscles loosened to let the blood in. I turned my head toward the shore to breathe, toward a line of ocean-view apartment buildings so familiar I had long since stopped dreaming about renting one. The only thing missing from the horizon was John, the orb of his head and the flick of his arms.

I paused at a jetty dotted with seabirds to look for him. I treaded water, lifted my face to the sun to thaw. There was John behind me, getting buffeted out to sea.

"Are you okay?" I asked when he caught up.

"Yeah, I think the buoy is pulling me off course."

"Do you want me to take it for a little?"

"Nah."

"Maybe we could switch off halfway through."

"Maybe."

My arms spun around their sockets. I timed my breath to the one-two-three of a waltz. We dodged floating trash, ragged newspapers, and lost toys. Other swimmers passed us on their way back to the starting line. John pulled up alongside me. He must have found his gait. I dug my hands deeper into the ocean to find more purchase. I wanted to keep pace. With each breath, I lifted my head forward to check my progress, but every time I found that John had become a smaller scratch against the horizon. He reached the end of the beach before I did, and I clambered onto shore after him, legs shaky from our mermaid hour. We pulled our snacks out of the dry pocket. Their sweetness cracked the salt rind of my mouth.

Three miles to go. We ran back into the water, turtled green and brown by algae. The weight of the buoy lessened, John pulled even farther ahead. My arms had gone soggy and useless from trying to keep up with him, and the current was turning against us. It was an uphill climb. Water crashed against my face and blocked my view of anything that wasn't blue on blue. I focused on each stroke, the pull and churn of it. I told myself there was no destination.

I almost crashed into John, waiting for me beneath the pier. Relief rushed through me as we waded out onto the sand, toasted by the sun and filled with people, boombox tunes, and the sour smell of smuggled alcohol slurred with the metallic tang of sunscreen.

"How am I going to make it?" I asked.

"You will." He rushed into the water, and I staggered along behind.

The memory of that fourth mile is lost to me, but I must have gone arm over arm, stroke by stroke. I can summon the signposts: Coney Island's Cyclone, the new shark exhibit with its hundreds of scales shimmering as they turn and twist in the wind, the aluminum first aid trailer propped up on stilts like an alien spaceship that has lingered for too long.

"Can I take the buoy?" I asked when we paused at the very spot where we had gotten in. I spit salt water out through chapped lips.

"No," he said. I gave up on the daydream of cutting our swim short and returning to shore. I counted my strokes. My breath hollowed me out until there was nothing left but the thud of my heart and the lug of my arms. Every part of my body ached, but at least I knew it worked.

When we got to shore, a stranger handed out donuts like some kind of mirage. Completely spent, I forgot my manners and grabbed one right out of her hands. The sweet was my homecoming after hours of salt.

John texted me later in the week, while I was rummaging in my desk drawer for something to eat that might take away the hollow ache in my stomach. He sent a photo of the Tana French book held open at the halfway point. Tucked into the cracked spine was a tiny rectangle of paper with three words written on it in someone else's handwriting, punctuated by an exclamation point: "I love you!" I had no memory of ever seeing the note before, but it must have been left there by my ex. "I don't know if this was meant for me," he wrote, "but I love you too."

*Mike Riegle, gay liberationist, prison rights activist, and longtime resident
of the Fenway, died on Friday evening, January 10, 1992, at Beth Israel
Hospital in Boston after a long struggle with AIDS. He was surrounded
by friends.*

Amy wasn't among them. Following a long afternoon at the hospi-
tal, she had been on her way out the door, off to dinner with her lover,
when the phone call came. For weeks, she had tied up the line acting
as Mike's designated caller, yet another unofficial role. She dialed the
hospital once in the morning and once before bed to ask the nurses for
the latest update, passing the time in between at Mike's bedside. *I was
either at the hospital or calling the hospital.* When there was news, she
changed the message on her answering machine to spread it faster: *Hi!
If you're calling about Mike, he's out of Intensive Care! He's been sleeping
a lot, but I'm sure he'd love visitors!*

Back home in Boston, Amy did sign a DNR, in defiance of Mike's
Memphis declaration that he wanted to live. The failings of his heart
had become too many to deny. He never moved to hospice. That
would have been the ultimate sign of giving up.

Mike experienced the kind of final bloom I've only ever seen hap-
pen to patients on TV medical dramas. Early one Sunday morning, he
awoke chatty. Amy rushed to the hospital to see him. They had taken
him out of the ICU because the treatments weren't helping, had only
started hurting him more. *He was full of excitement about* Leaves of
Grass *and Whitman*, which Barb (whose name alone conjures yet an-
other lesbian) had been reading to him the night before out of an old
Penguin edition that now perched at his bedside. After enthusiastically
telling Amy about the book and the time he went to Washington to
research Whitman's letters, he sent her back to his apartment for his
reading glasses and some medicine. That was their last conversation. By
the time she got back, he had fallen *into a kind of sleep, neither refresh-
ing nor dreamless, from which he awoke only to his death five days later.*

That Sunday was their last conversation, but it was not to be the last

of Amy's duties. It fell to her to pick up his ashes and carry them to the funeral, held outdoors one bitter winter day at Mike's old Fenway cruising grounds. His ashes: his final possession. Even when they were gone, scooped out of their white cardboard box with a clamshell and tossed onto the path where *intrepid gay men, ready for a tryst no matter what the season, would tread on them*, Amy found more ways to carry him, to labor for him. She inherited his deceased father's VA life insurance, about fifteen hundred dollars, which she split between the Prison Book Project and the defunct gay men's newspaper *Fag Rag*, per his wishes, organizations she had to practically beg to take the money. She began writing about Mike. First, his obituary for the *Gay Community News*, and then a whole book. She became known as *a Mike collector*, the one people turned to for simple facts, like his date of birth. *As I write, I create him, and he's mine, all mine, his deeds and effects.*

She was still carrying him that foggy winter morning at the coffee shop, where, between the hiss of the latte machine and the clatter of students banging out their term papers, her eyes danced with mischief when she spoke of him. If he were here today, he would have been energized to see that the prison abolition movement has grown, but he wouldn't be happy about it. He would still be pushing for more.

"And now," she said, "here we are. We just celebrated the fiftieth anniversary of Stonewall and Pride, with hardly a mention of AIDS."

Her comment reminded me of a moment in the book, the anger and frustration that bubbled to the surface in the aftermath of someone else's funeral.

"*Every AIDS funeral should be a massive protest march*," announced Kevin, a friend of the deceased, already mean with drink.

"*Protest march against whom? To where? It's a virus*," Amy shouted back in anger.

"*I hate gay people. Do we ever defend ourselves? Do we avenge our dead?*"

That funeral was before Mike's, when ACT UP—the AIDS Coalition to Unleash Power—was in its infancy. Founded in 1987, ACT

UP channeled the outrage and grief of the AIDS crisis into direct actions and mobilizations designed to attract media attention, secure better access to care and services for patients, and, ultimately, end the pandemic. The group was so effective that they provided subsequent generations with a model for organizing. A bit like Mike, they weren't nice. They took as their target not the virus—just matter evolved to replicate—but the societal structures that denied services to those who needed them most. Ambulances that refused to transport AIDS patients. Doctors and nurses who refused to touch them. A president who failed to even name the disease in public. Pharmaceutical companies who charged outrageous prices for life-extending drugs because they wanted to turn a profit.

March 24, 1987. As their first action, they marched down Wall Street to protest those greedy practices, chanting "Wall Street trades on people with AIDS!" and holding signs with slogans like "AIDS DRUGS Your Money or Your Life." Seventy-three people were arrested. Later, another group marched from the Capitol to the White House and threw the ashes of their loved ones on the lawn so they could no longer be ignored. They staged die-ins and kiss-ins and protest marches. Amy describes them *chaining themselves to the FDA and blockading the Brooklyn Bridge during rush hour.* The women's committee of ACT UP staged an action at Shea Stadium to push heterosexual men to take responsibility for wearing condoms. After three and a half months of planning, four hundred members of ACT UP filled the seats and held up six black banners covered in white letters that reflected the lurid stadium lighting and caught the attention of TV cameras. "Men! Use condoms." "Strike out AIDS." They would not be ignored.

I watched footage of the marches, of the practice sessions for their chants, unable to tell whether everyone wore faded clothes or if the negatives themselves had lost their luster. The frames filled with dated haircuts I wanted to try on like wigs, slogans written in Sharpie I had

to pause the video to write down. I tried to guess who among them were lesbians based on the length of their hair and the shape of their shirts alone, using the clues of my own era. There's no official count (and who is to say what number would be *enough*), but there were certainly lesbians and other queers who did not fit into the neat category of gay man among their ranks. Some were there because friends and loved ones had tested positive, others because they themselves had the virus, a living refutation of the doctors who had excluded them from clinical trials due to concerns that our fluctuating hormone levels would lead to false data.

Women and lesbians were caretakers, but they were also patients, and the legacy of that exclusion still lingers today. About a fifth of new HIV patients in the U.S. are women, and more than half of those diagnosed are Black women. Women make up about a quarter of people living with AIDS in this country, and yet we account for less than 5 percent of PrEP users. Globally, it's an even grimmer picture. Half of people living with HIV worldwide are women, and AIDS is the leading cause of death among women of childbearing age. Women's health issues, particularly those affecting communities of color, have long been invisible, yet another fissure where the virus found room to replicate. Always the caretaker but rarely cared for.

Prolific lesbian novelist and playwright Sarah Schulman was an early member of ACT UP, and she has taken care to document that time with the ACT Up Oral History Project, with her nonfiction tome *Let the Record Show*, and in her semiautobiographical novel *People in Trouble*, now out of print in the United States. Molly, a stand-in for Sarah herself, ignites an affair with a married woman the same *suffocating* summer that her friends begin to die of AIDS. *Passing acquaintances became friends. And when her friends did get sick there was a lot of shopping to do, picking up laundry and looking into each other's eyes. She had never held so many crying men before in her life.*

I add Sarah to my count. The fictional Molly too.

In the early days of the crisis, Larry Kramer, writer, activist, and a catalyst for the creation of ACT UP who was known for his consistent outrage, had a word for all these queer caretakers: *sissies*. He was mad at his own community because so many were focused on taking care of loved ones and grieving their loss rather than standing up to fight. (Charlie Carson told me that Larry once turned up unexpectedly at his apartment for dinner and asked him why he was involved with some gay swim team rather than ACT UP. "We were feeding Larry Kramer, and he was fussing at the hosts.") It was an argument similar to Kevin's, that angry drunk who confronted Amy at a funeral. If I had been there, I might have asked, "Isn't taking care of our friends the most radical thing we can do? Isn't it only seen as less than that because it's so often been the purview of women, the original sissies?"

As I collected the names of these sissy caretakers of the AIDS era, Amy and Rebecca and Sarah and Molly, I had also begun, unknowingly, to revise my theory of friendship. Whatever it was that tethered me to John, that bound Amy to Mike's bedside, it wasn't something less than heterosexual love. It wasn't a rehearsal. Queerness may be at its most visible when it defines romantic love, but it is also inscribed in our broader communities. Friendship is resistance to Gayle Rubin's traffic in women and the very structures that built this system of traffic.

Through the decades, one of the most common denouncements of queerness is that same-sex couples threaten to destabilize the traditional nuclear family. Critics argue that granting rights like marriage equality devalue the sacred bond that can exist only between a man and a woman. What they really mean, though, is that their own wealth and positions of power are threatened by the idea that one does not need a traditional family to access the basic right to healthcare, to inherit property, to live with a safety net, or to know that there will be someone to visit you in the hospital and install your AC. The traditional nuclear family is one of the last remaining vestiges of Rubin's

traffic in women, and as Pat Parker writes in *This Bridge Called My Back*, "in order for us to move to revolution it has to be destroyed."

*Actually*, Amy writes, in defiance of them all, *Mike* was *my family, and I have the paperwork to prove it.* When all of Mike's blood relations abandoned him, she was his healthcare proxy, the washer of his clothes, the one to sign his DNR, the custodian of his ashes, the inheritor of his father's life insurance policy, his archivist. Not because she was obligated to by custom or by blood or by birth but because she just wanted to give her caring freely, in spite of her doubt and frustrations. It is important to fight, to demand a safety net for those who have been left in the dust by the engines of capitalism, but while we push for change, what could be more radical, more threatening, than people giving their caretaking not because it is paid for or legally assigned or out of blood fidelity but freely, out of genuine love, a love flecked with annoyance and bitterness feebly expressed in words, out of a sense of community woven across the fractures?

"What relationships, through homosexuality, can be established, invented, multiplied, and modulated?" asked French philosopher Michel Foucault in a magazine interview he gave near the end of his life called "Friendship as a Way of Life." "The problem is not to discover in oneself the truth of one's sex, but, rather, to use one's sexuality henceforth to arrive at a multiplicity of relationships." He never mentions lesbians in the interview, but if he did, he might say something like: being a lesbian shapes not only how one relates to other lesbians but also how one relates to the world.

~~~

Decades after Amy wrote about Mike, decades spent caring for other friends with AIDS, and then her aging parents, and then her aging friends, Amy returned to writing about AIDS because yet another disease had reshaped the world around her and exposed more fractures in our social structures: COVID-19. I was struck by the title "Love One

Another or Die," after a poem by W. H. Auden (another of my father's favorite gay poets), and by a line buried halfway through: "A cliché about the AIDS crisis is that it finally brought gay men and lesbians back together after they parted ways after Stonewall, as lesbians cared for their dying gay brothers."

If that's the cliché, it's not one that made it down to me. As a teenager, I learned about AIDS from Broadway, memorizing the lyrics to Jonathan Larson's musical *Rent* and reading Tony Kushner's play *Angels in America*. Schulman alleges that the plot of my beloved musical was plagiarized from her novel *People in Trouble*. When folks— composers, librettists, directors, producers—approached her about adapting the work for the stage, they were all too often gay men who suggested taking out the central lesbian couple. She gave up. Then she saw *Rent* and realized they had moved on with a heterosexual white male playwright.

Reading the novel for the first time a decade and a half later, I found similarities that sent shivers down my spine. Broad themes and entire characters seem to have been lifted, but most chilling is a quiet moment at a meeting of people living with AIDS where everyone introduces themselves in a rush and tumble of prose, their names and interjections becoming one collectively spoken sentence, a sentence that almost exactly mirrors the lyrics in the song "Life Support." But Schulman's outrage comes not just from discovering what material was lifted but also from reckoning with why it was so successful. It reveals what work is considered commercially viable and valuable, as well as who gets to contribute to the cultural record.

"There still has yet to be a substantial corporate product that has accurately represented the AIDS crisis, even to date," Schulman writes. "That's why the old chestnuts keep getting revived." For her, these "old chestnuts" make the story of AIDS palatable for mainstream audiences by centering white, male, and often straight characters and pushing lesbians and people of color into the margins. They're

continually remaking *Rent*, with a live production on conservative *Fox* as its most recent iteration, but *People in Trouble* remains out of print in the United States.

There's a rumor that the *L* comes first in *LGBT* as a tribute to the lesbians who cared for people living with and dying of AIDS, but is it wrong to want more?

At the coffee shop, Amy told me of her own frustrations trying to publish *Hospital Time*. Her agent thought the book was so topical back in the early 1990s that it would be a slam dunk, with all the major publishers clamoring to get it out into the world. Instead, she got all kinds of evasive feedback. *We've already published enough AIDS books. It's hard to publish a book about the crisis by a woman.* Eventually, she published with an academic press. She bought a box of discounted copies from them, which now sits in her basement. No wonder these stories never made it down to me.

~~~

Even after nearly thirteen years of friendship, Amy discovered new facts about Mike after he was gone. At a dinner party, an old lover of Mike's told her about his dick, perhaps to him Mike's most memorable feature, something Amy had only seen when it was flaccid, in all the indignities of his illness. When it was hard, the old lover explained, Mike's dick *went at like a 45-degree angle.*

*He loved me,* Amy writes. *The idea is new and strange . . . From the very beginning I saw him, Michael, in all his Michaelness, and I never lost sight of that no matter what, and I think that is love . . . He never said that—love—and I didn't much either.*

~~~

I wish I could say that I learned something new about John from our 10K race early one August morning, or that it was finally a moment when I was able to help him. At the very least, I wish I could say that

I won. Instead, it was just another day in our lives together, and we fell into our usual rhythms. We swam side by side for the first half of the course, and then John took off into the distance, but not before he helped me open my snack at the feeding boat and sent me off with a few words of encouragement. As I crossed the finish line after three hours in the water, it was John who cheered me on. I had never been a swimmer for the races, and I had never truly felt at home on the team, but out in the open water, I had finally found my community.

The truth is, John will live. Our story isn't a retelling of Mike and Amy's. The global AIDS crisis isn't over, but it has ended for people with access to condoms and PrEP. People like John. We get to write a new chapter on friendship, on the love shared between lesbians and gay men. I have memorized his Poseidon face at thirty, but I will also get to see it at forty, and even fifty, when we will both likely have gone a bit soft and gray. He swears he will die by drowning. He has seen it in his dreams, but he's not afraid. It might even be nice, he thinks, to pass while doing something he loves. It's the most spiritual thing I've ever heard him, a man who hates astrology, say.

Besides, it was always John taking care of me.

I allowed myself to ask one more favor. (I am sure it will not be the last.) I asked John to drive me up to the Bronx, to visit Mabel Hampton's grave.

On my last visit to the Lesbian Herstory Archives, somewhere between Mabel Hampton's awards, recognitions, invitations to speaking engagements, and thank-yous for giving interviews, I found a box tied shut with a ribbon. There was no one around to tell me not to open it. Inside, I found a note in Mabel's rollicking blue cursive: "In case I pass away, see that Joan and [illegible] get this at once, Mabel. St. Raymond Cemetery. Call about where I am buried." There are also bills for Lillian's interment, $1821 for burial expenses, which Mabel tried to pay off in installments, an additional $320 for the flowers, and $644 for the monument. The last item in the box was an embossed

card from Lillian's service, held in August 1978, that listed the location of her grave: St. Raymond's, 05, Range 110, Grave 18.

On the way from Brooklyn to the Bronx, John and I picked up a dozen red roses at the corner bodega. Joan Nestle lives in Australia now, and I doubted there was anyone left to visit Mabel anymore.

The day was freezing, and I could feel John's impatience emanating from the car as I studied the cemetery map. Half the sections were labeled with religious names like St. John, St. Elizabeth, Holy Cross, and Our Savior, while the other half were numbered. There was no number five. I stomped my feet to warm up, and to just maybe shake loose an idea. *The dead take care of me, and so do the living.* It hit me. It wasn't zero five. It was *O.S.* Our Savior. I raced back to the heated car.

As we wound our way through the gravestones, John asked me why we were here. This would be easier than explaining Georgia O'Keeffe's paintings. I told him that I had grown up without any lesbian role models, and so I had gone out in search of them.

"I get that," he said. "I don't have any role models either. There's a whole missing generation. I feel like that's why so many gay men feel isolated and depressed, or get addicted to drugs. We're not afraid of AIDS anymore. We're just afraid of actually having a future."

I had lost my role models in the abyss of the archive. He had lost his to a pandemic.

John was the first to spot Mabel's headstone when we got out of the car. There were three names engraved on it: Mabel Hampton. Lillian Foster. Alma Love.

"Who's Alma?" he asked.

"I don't know."

"I like that. I like that you don't have to be buried with your blood family."

We laid our flowers down on her grave and stood in the wind as long as we could bear it before racing each other back to the car and blasting the heat until it brought life back into our fingers and toes.

Extracts | SELECTION OF BOXES AND FOLDERS IN
MIKE RIEGLE'S ARCHIVE, HELD BY THE HISTORY
PROJECT IN BOSTON

Box 1 Series 1: People
Subseries: Michel Foucault
Folder 1: Articles and Interviews 1979–1990, undated
Folder 2: Essays—Sexuality and Postmodernism
Folder 3: Reviews—The History of Sexuality

Series 2: Subject Files
Subseries: AIDS
Folder 1: AIDS

Subseries: Death
Folder 1: Articles

Subseries: Lesbian Sexuality
Folder 1: *Bad Attitude Magazine* 1984–1985
Folder 2: *Lesbian Contradiction* Winter 1989
Folder 3: Articles 1976–1979, undated
Folder 4: Articles 1980–1990

Box 3 Subseries: Rights vs. Liberation
Folder 1: Articles 1973–1983
Folder 2: Articles 1984–1990
Folder 3: Articles, undated
Folder 4: Essays
Folder 5: Newsletters 1975–1987
Folder 6: Notes, Excerpts, and Outlines
Folder 7: Organizations—Bylaws and Manifestos 1974–1987

Epilogue.

The Lesbian Future

~~~~~~

I T'S TIME FOR ME TO CONFESS. I'M NOT REALLY A LESBIAN.
At least, I'm not the kind of lesbian who would earn a gold star because
she has never slept with a man, or the kind who would be allowed on
lesbian land because she has agreed never to speak with men again.
I'm not the kind of lesbian who lives up to any definition that contains
the word *only*. I'm not the kind of lesbian my middle school classmates
would have recognized either. I wear my hair long and, on a hot day,
I've been known to put on a dress. Besides, I have had beloveds who, as
Campbell said of Sappho's husband, *complicate the case history*.

As I built my collection of lesbian love stories, I worried over what
makes a lesbian. Where lesbians had been and what they could be-
come. The whole time, I assumed I already had a solid definition of
love, built from the wisdom of friends and mentors and books.

My middle school English teacher:
*Romantic love is the thing that is felt for just one person.*

My high school best friend:
*Love isn't just making out with your best friend.*

Ovid:
*What did Sappho teach her girls, except how to love?*

243

The lesbians I met had something else to teach me. They are tied together by more than a shared sexuality, a shared identity, or even a shared vision of romantic love. They are also bound together by their ability to create safe havens in even the most hostile circumstances, projects now buried that were a direct response to the systems that tried to trap and trade women. I am in awe of what they have done.

Mary Casal, who abandoned her husband to start her own business and live with a woman, who set down her own story, now largely forgotten, so that others might know they are not alone. Mabel Hampton, who gave and received support in equal measure wherever she went, whether it was prison or a rent party, who reminds me that the dead take care of us, but so do the living. Babe Didrikson, the unwitting, unstoppable force who helped create a league where women could earn money and independence through sport. Rusty Brown, who found the space to play with masculinity as a male impersonator on the stage and as a butch at the bars. Gloria Anzaldúa, who opened even more space for lesbian community through her writing and who challenged the colonialism and racism that often excluded her from other feminist visions of the era. And Amy Hoffman, who freely gave her care to a man who wasn't her husband, wasn't her family, wasn't even her best friend.

I call myself a lesbian because I share their vision of love.

This constant making and remaking of these protective cocoons is just a temporary strategy though. It helps only the people who fall within the defined boundaries of an identity or space. A better solution would be nothing short of revolution.

I have used my own lived experience to imagine snatches of these lesbian stories. Could we also use their lived experiences to imagine our own future?

A future without prisons. A future where monogamy and the nuclear family is not idealized above all else. A future where housing

is not sold as a commodity. A future where our bodies are not scrutinized by the media, regulated by sports officials, or policed by the state. A future without the military. A future without borders or identity labels. A future where we know and support our neighbors. A future that embraces chosen family. A future where masculinity is not just toxic and femininity is not just weak, where everyone can freely borrow elements of both. A future where healthcare is not contingent on marriage or employment. A future that welcomes immigrants and refugees, that speaks many languages and honors many gods. A left-handed future. A liberated future. Can you see it?

I want to lay flowers at the graves of all these lesbians in thanks for their radical daring, for their pioneering experiments in love. Violets for Sappho. Violets for Mary, too, so she can be the one who is wooed, for once. I lay roses at Mabel's grave. *Roses*, Gloria writes, *are the Mexican's favorite flower. I think, how symbolic—thorns and all.* She is buried in Texas, just a few hours' drive from Babe, who would probably reject my gesture with a comment like, "Flowers are for sissies." Flowers for Rusty, if I could ever find her and the name that was engraved on her headstone. Flowers to decorate the dances held by the Radicalesbians, and to cheer up hospital rooms, not for the patients but for the lesbian caretakers. A flower for me, a flower for you.

I want anyone and everyone to claim the word *lesbian*, so we can usher in this world together.

～～～

After I had learned enough about lesbians to hold my own, I reached out to Joan Nestle for an interview. We made our own oral history video, one that I hope will live on in her archive as well as mine.

"Is this helping?" she asked early on in our conversation. "You have to put up with me because I'm eighty-one." I thought I would be intimidated by her, but I was charmed. She asked about my cat, asleep in

my video background. She brought her partner on screen, the woman who had led her to leave New York for Australia decades ago.

Because the Lesbian Herstory Archives was a project of the 1970s, I feared that Joan would share her contemporaries' narrow definition of lesbian. She dispelled my fear before I could even come up with the courage to ask. "To me, lesbian incorporates queer, it incorporates trans, it incorporates bi, it incorporates intersex, because lesbians occupied all those positions."

I had planned to just ask her about the details of Mabel's life. "The loss to me personally," she said, "is too huge to even talk about, even after all these years." Instead, we had a conversation full of digressions. She took us from Eleanor Roosevelt (lesbian) to sex workers (also lesbian) to her own reasons for becoming a lesbian archivist.

"The archives was created to break the concept of fame," she told me. "If you have the courage to touch another woman and to claim that touch . . . that, for us, was fame enough."

# Acknowledgments.

My thanks, first and foremost, to the queer historians who came before me, and to the archivists who helped me locate the records of the lesbians in this book: Isaac Fellman at the GLBT Archives in San Francisco; Frances Lyons at the United Methodist Church's General Commission on Archives and History, housed at Drew University in Madison, New Jersey; Saskia Scheffer at the Lesbian Herstory Archives; Shannon Doody at the USGA; and the unnamed librarians at the New York Public Library's Rose Reading Room, The New-York Historical Society, and the New York State Archives, who remained custodians of the archive even during a global pandemic.

This book would not exist without Cam Delaney, who appeared at the foot of my stairs in an unforgettable button down at the moment I began to think seriously about this project—two days, we would later realize, before the world shut down—and provided a theoretical framework to hang these stories on.

Gloria Anzaldúa called interviews a "community-making ritual." My gratitude to all those who took the time to share in community with me, including: Hugh Ryan, Joan Nestle, Amy Hoffman, Dr. Marcy Adelman, Cayleff, Carolyn Gage, Elyssa Goodman, Lisa E. Davis, Flavia Rando, and Charlie Carson.

Thanks to the wonderful dykes in my life who offered up their unwavering support throughout this process, especially Hannah O'Grady, who read early drafts with an editor's eye and a friend's heart, Bryn Clark, who never met an anxiety or a pimple she couldn't pop, and Becca Farsace, who gifted me a cast-off chair from Ginger's

Bar so I could write with old lesbian sweat to keep me company, and then took my author photo while I was sitting in the very same chair.

Tasha Lewis, Sam Goodman, and Dante Fuoco inspire me every day with their passion and creativity and disciplined art practices, and I am grateful to each of them for reading early chapters and talking me through obstacles over the phone. Eli Stevens, who helped me embrace the word *lesbian*, also provided invaluable feedback on early drafts.

Thanks to CB Money, who sparked joy in a dark time. I wish you were still around.

My incredible publishing team saw what this book could be before I did. My agent Sarah Levitt coached me through countless drafts of the proposal, and my editor Megha Majumdar buoyed me along during the largely solitary writing process with her kindness and insightful editorial comments. Alicia Kroell and Laura Gonzalez shepherded the book through the production and publication process with incredible care and enthusiasm. Sue Ducharme's tender copy edits both strengthened the text and gave me much-needed encouragement. Megan Fishmann, Alisha Gorder, Laura Berry, Rachel Fershleiser, Kira Weiner, Mikayla Butchart, and Summer Farah at Catapult all helped bring this book out into the world.

Tal, whose final edits arrived in the nick of time.

Thank you to my family of writers and storytellers and teachers, who raised me to be the aquatic lesbian archivist I am today. Even though as a child I refused to sit still during his ancient Greek lessons, my father, Dr. D. Mark Possanza, still patiently translated Sappho's lyrics with me for the book. My mom, Jennifer Kraar, gave me her sense of humor, a librarian's appreciation of organization and lists, and the room to always be myself. My sister Kyra instilled in me an early love of learning when we played school together as kids, and her work as a teacher today continues to inspire me. I'm proud of you!

Thank you also to my chosen family at Team New York Aquatics: Nathan Burstein, Lorenzo Di Silvio, Asya Graf, Jess Jiang, Jenn Leyva, Jay Pulitano, Pauline Shu, and John Thomas. It is always a pleasure to be in the water with you.

I wrote much of this book on the unceded lands of the Lenape people, many of whom were pushed out west by the arrival of colonial settlers and the ensuing genocide and forced migration. I send my gratitude to the generations of displaced peoples who have helped build this city now known as New York.

# Notes.

### Introduction: Collecting Lesbians

1    "**You look like anyone else**": Brown p. 174.
3    *appears to have gone through the long Vaticans*: Melville p. 8.
4    "**It is a truth universally acknowledged**": Austen p. 1.
4    "**It would be incorrect**": Wittig, *The Straight Mind* p. 32.
5    *best girl*: Casal p. 176.
5    *stud*: Mabel Hampton Undated, Tape 1.
5    *in the life*: Mabel Hampton, Tape 1.
5    *wifey*: Mabel Hampton Talks About Lillian.
6    *of isolation and frustration*: Anzaldúa, *Borderlands* p. 279.
6    *such an asshole*: Hoffman p. 121.

### 1. *The Names for Love*

11   **YWCA hotel**: The hotel where Casal stayed is not specified in her autobiography. Sherry A. Darling makes a convincing case that it was the Margaret Louisa Home, opened in 1890 by the New York City Young Women's Christian Association (YWCA), in her 2003 dissertation, p. 53.
11   **a skirt paired with a man's shirt and tie**: For the inspiration for Casal's outfit, see p. 139 of her autobiography.
12   *the most beautiful hands*: Casal p. 144.
12   *Please comfort that girl*: p. 144.
12   *fat . . . forty . . . unfair*: p. 143.
12   *expensively printed . . . framed*: p. 144.
12   *I wasn't looking for her; she just came into my life, and I knew*: p.146.
13   "**Among the rare early American books**": Carter p. 8.
14   *Does one often have the courage . . . two distinct lives all my life*: Casal p.8.
14   *Gemini*: p. 93.
15   *Rapturous period of wooing*: p. 151.
15   *a bunch of lovely violets*: p. 146.
15   *chance meetings . . . magnificently proportioned figure . . . white silk shirt*: p. 147.
15   *My personal appearance? . . . well-modulated*: pp. 150–151.

15    *I remember little of the play*: p. 147.

16    *hotel, where it was permissible*: p. 148.

16    *without a penny*: p. 149.

16    *deeply in love . . . those eyes so red*: p. 148.

17    *My heart was calling for her as a mate*: p. 151.

17    *patiently waiting . . . should be firmly established*: p. 152.

17    *very proper little kisses*: p. 151.

17    *that she not only loved me . . . yielded to mine*: p. 152.

17    *a great thrill*: p. 50.

20    *We spent many nights together*: p. 50.

22    **"I am more than half-persuaded"**: This quote originally comes from Louise Chandler Moulton's interview with Alcott for *Our Famous Women: An Authorized Record of the Lives and Deeds of Distinguished American Women of Our Times*. Here I am citing Wikipedia.

22    **Mount Holyoke Female Seminary**: This timeline of women's college openings is taken from Faderman p. 13.

23    *the last one of all that large family left*: Casal p. 73.

23    **"When a Vassar girl takes a shine"**: quoted in Faderman p. 19.

24    **"If you're not going to eat pussy"**: *Sex & the City*. Season 2, episode 6. 1998.

24    *My Ever Dear . . . You must know, dear*: quoted in Faderman p. 26.

25    *Ah, my Cleopatra*: quoted in Faderman p. 33.

26    *A word or a photo does all*: quoted in Faderman p. 31.

26    *The side of my nature which called for a female mate*: Casal p. 81.

27    *was mystified*: p. 152.

27    *Having at last concluded . . . to be sent to her regularly during my absence*: p. 153.

27    *Come, every bit of me wants you*: p. 154.

29    *affections were turning Flo-ward very rapidly*: p. 85.

29    *Little kisses and big kisses . . . I could hardly bear*: p. 86.

30    *protested* p. 87.

30    *attachment . . . the usual festivities*: p. 88.

30    *This fellow was good looking*: pp. 82–83.

31    *I felt that I was quite "in love" and had the proper feelings . . . begged*: p. 88.

31    *be married then and there . . . really marrying him*: p. 89.

31    *Peter probably thought he would be able to have . . . and I hating them both*: p. 90.

32    *All the new books had to be catalogued . . . grown to love me*: p. 79.

32    *I was going to leave the room . . . yielded . . . peace in the family*: p. 80.

32    *an unwilling piece of furniture*: p. 81.

32    *How I wished . . . I just didn't care much what happened*: p. 80.

32 *all the conventional things that a New England girl was supposed to do*: p. 11.

32 *boys—one brother and three cousins* Casal p. 9.

32 *To be called a "Tom Boy" never grieved me*: p. 46.

32 *great and glorious games . . . bo-bo*: p. 14.

33 *pulled and hauled*: p. 16.

33 *alike . . . crushed and broken*: p. 15.

33 *private parts*: p. 18.

34 *playing hen and rooster*: p. 21.

35 *During the earlier sessions*: p. 32.

35 *I was terrified*: p. 30.

35 *I was filled with disgust . . . I was not wholly cast down*: p. 33.

35 *An argument*: p. 31.

35 *The dislike for men as males was inherent*: p. 41.

35 *As our lives fell far apart . . . a clean and good father*: p. 94.

35 *large rambling house*: p. 98.

35 *Friend husband . . . any accidents should happen*: p. 95.

36 *pure delight . . . At night*: p. 102.

36 *pleasures*: p. 95.

36 *the thought of being a legitimized prostitute*: p. 112.

36 *I did not care to be wooed*: p. 108.

36 *I was happy mentally . . . strenuous efforts*: p. 99.

36 *that little body . . . short minute*: p. 101.

37 *anxious to become pregnant again*: p. 104.

37 *In no gentle manner . . . females had before*: p. 106.

37 *began planning a play*: p. 107.

37 *mad summer . . . grief*: p. 108.

37 *consent*: p. 109.

38 *Both the Professor and I were in a dangerous mood . . . excuse for marriage*: pp. 110–111.

38 *I simply refused*: p. 111.

38 *Mrs. B.-J. and I enjoyed our life together*: p. 112.

39 *The boat docked . . . delicious*: p. 155.

39 *could be made as holy and complete*: p. 156.

39 *We lingered and loved and rested*: p. 157.

39 *Oh, yes, there came a break*: p. 181.

40 *Juno and Mother . . . real union, of our bodies*: p. 165.

40 *When she appeared as a young man*: p. 175.

41 *best girl*: p. 176.

41 *insisted . . . more than that of good friends*: p. 177.

41 **"Ella Wesner Lies in Man's Garb"**: *The New York Times*. November 14, 1917.

41 **The "Swell," the "Dude," and the "Captain"**: These are all characters listed in Ella Wesner's entry on the Drag King History site, authored by Drag King Flare.

42 **"Girl in Male Garb Tries to See Fight"**: *The New York Times*. September 4, 1913.

42 **"Dressed as a Man to Earn Her Living"**: *The New York Times*. January 21, 1910.

44 **"The statute was based on an older law"**: For more on the Masquerade Law, see Ryan p. 86.

44 **"While they cross-dressed to gain employment"**: Ryan p. 86.

45 **"Female Husbands"**: *The New York Times*. November 4, 1883.

45 **"Murray Hall Fooled Many Shrewd Men"**: *The New York Times*. January 19, 1901.

45 **"Her "Husband" a Woman"**: *The New York Times*. September 21, 1913.

45 **"Though assigned female at birth"**: Manion. p. 1.

46 **expanding rapidly both in circulation and influence**: For more on the role of local newspapers in circulating stories about female husbands, see Manion p. 7.

46 *I looked at life through a man's eyes*: Casal p. 138.

46 *role . . . that of the male*: p. 171.

46 *all the summer girls*: p. 107.

47 *tearful . . . I knew at once that she too knew!*: p. 178.

47 *At last, and too late*: p. 180.

47 *We saw her frequently and became warm friends*: p. 179.

47 *the purest and most ideal . . . She was my child, my sister*: p. 181.

47 **her new friends**: For more on Mary Casal's circle of lesbian friends, see Ryan pp. 63–67.

48 *Even now*: Casal p. 205.

48 *An artist of note*: p. 202.

48 *I will always look upon those years*: p. 227.

48 *Courage failed me*: p. 201.

49 **unmasking Mary Casal**: Ryan p. 63.

49 **June 17, 1864**: Darling p. 22.

49 **"is a Portuguese word meaning"**: Darling p. 3.

50 **Eyncourt Press**: Details on McMurtrie, Putnam, and their motives for publishing drawn from Darling, pp. 6–11.

50 **"The 'Lesbian' manuscript I told you about has come in . . . than any I have ever [cross-out] read"**: quoted in Darling, p. 13.

51 *summer girl . . . Governor of Massachusetts*: Casal p. 53.

51 *enjoined*: p. 74.

51    **property records**: For an outline of her use of property records, see Darling pp. 1–2.

51    **Johnstone Bennett**: Darling p. 88.

51    **Vittoria Cremers, "the illegitimate daughter of a wealthy Englishman"**: Darling pp. 91–92.

51    **Emma Altman**: Darling pp. 54–55.

51    **"While Ruth Fuller Field's name does not appear anywhere"**: Darling p. 54.

51    **"How strange it is to retrace someone's life so intimately"**: Darling p. 125.

52    **"The children . . . August 7, 1902"**: Helen Miller Gould Shepard Papers, MS 1422, The New-York Historical Society.

## 2. *In the Life*

57    *On the ground floor*: Unless otherwise noted, all Mabel Hampton quotes come from the Mabel Hampton Oral History Collection, housed in person at the Lesbian Herstory Archives and digitally in partnership with Pratt. The names in these endnotes correspond with the names of the individual tapes. In this case, these words come from the table labeled "Mabel Hampton 1988."

57    *stud*: Mabel Hampton Undated, Tape 1, Side B.

57    *never felt ashamed of being a lesbian*: Mabel Hampton 1982, Side B.

58    *If you don't be just so, it'll kill you*: Mabel Hampton Talks About Lillian, Side B.

59    **"Gay Rights Advocate"**: "Mabel Hampton, Gay Rights Advocate, 87." *The New York Times*. October 31, 1989.

60    **"A white, working-class-born"**: Joan at 38, Tape 1.

60    *gray dress that buttons down the front*: Mabel Hampton's Story, July 1986.

60    *Oh, you're a kid. Come on in . . . one in the back of the room*: Mabel Hampton's Story, July 1986.

60    **Viola**: Ryan identifies Mabel's companion as Viola, p. 113.

61    **"an efficient servant, obliging, neat about her work and person and honest"**: These words, as well as the dates of her prison stay, are taken from Mabel Hampton's prison record, housed by the New York State Archives. Mrs. Howard's words are paraphrased in a letter from Amy M. Prevost at the Church Mission of Help to the prison superintendent, Dr. Amos T. Baker, concerning Mabel's case.

61    *had a belt on . . . stool pigeon*: Mabel Hampton, Tape 1.

61    **"Every black woman was a prostitute in the eyes of the law"**: Hartman p. 165.

62    **"Who didn't hate domestic work?"**: Hartman p. 47.

62    *a very striking white woman*: Mabel Hampton, Tape 1.

62    **"she prided herself on the number of women she found guilty on vice charges"**: "Removal of Judge Norris Is Demanded by Seabury." *The New York Times.* May 29, 1931.

62    *It's a damn shame that she's a judge*: Mabel Hampton, Tape 1.

62    *It's early . . . a couple girls in Jersey City*: Mabel Hampton's Story, July 1986.

63    **"very much infatuated with a middle aged colored woman"**: Mabel Hampton's Bedford Hills prison records.

63    *"Any of the girls up here you like?" . . .* **"Say the truth"**: Mabel Hampton's Story, July 1986.

64    *I can't hear so good*: Mabel Hampton 1982.

64    *I tell you, she's a bad girl*: Joan at 38, Tape 1.

65    **"I want to tell tales of a lesbian life"**: Joan at 38, Tape 1.

66    **"Bedford Cruelty Charges Against Officials Upheld:"** For more on the abuses women suffered at the hands of the state while imprisoned at Bedford Hills, see Hartman p. 263.

66    *We made whiskey . . . Me, I was havin' a ball*: Mabel Hampton, Tape 1.

67    **"And what year is this about:"** Mabel Hampton's Story, July 1986, Side B.

67    **"questions that we thought would elicit the kind of history we wanted"**: Nestle pp. 26–27.

67    **W. E. B. Du Bois**: For more on the scope of Du Bois's sociological study of Black communities, see Hartman p. 99.

67    **They can't see your hands**: Mabel Hampton Talks About Lillian, Side B.

68    **"I know what it is to be marginal"**: Joan at 38, Tape 1.

68    **"small black Christian Woman"**: Nestle p. 24.

68    **"I'm gonna kill myself"**: Interview with Joan Nestle, February 15, 2022.

68    **"Mabel I want to ask"** . . . *you gonna ask me?*: Mabel Hampton talks about Lillian and More, Side B.

69    *I forget right this minute*: Mabel Hampton's Story, July 1986, Side B.

69    *pigs, vegetables, chickens, turkeys, all kinds of things*: Joan at 38, Side B.

69    *My Younger Aunt*: Joan at 38, Side B.

70    *was tall, dark*: Joan at 38, Side B.

70    *In the back of my head, I knew he was no good*: Mabel Hampton 1982, Side B.

70    *my mouth and things swole all that . . . Grove Street!*: Joan at 38, Side B.

70    *I never had no pleasure*: Mabel Hampton 1982.

70    *Where's your people . . . That was grand*: Joan at 38, Side B.

71    *After I met Lillian*: Mabel Hampton 1982.

71    *chitlins, pig's feet, sauerkraut, cole slaw, sauces, bread*: Mabel Hampton Talks About Lillian.

71  *They danced up a breeze*: Mabel Hampton 1988.

72  *The words I heard it was*: Mabel Hampton, November 28, 1986.

72  *up on the hill . . . On the floor was nothing but pillows*: Mabel & Lillian 1976.

72  *short, short hair . . . a very good-looking girl, see*: Mabel Hampton, November 28, 1986, Tape 1.

72  *They had nice gay parties*: Mabel Hampton 1982, Side B.

73  *made love a coupla times*: Mabel Hampton's Story, July 1986.

73  *very seldom that any of them had slacks*: Mabel Hampton 1988.

73  **Ma Rainey**: For more on the story of Ma Rainey's arrest, see Faderman, p. 74.

73  *Sometimes I have narrow escapes*: Mabel Hampton, Tape 1.

74  *The dead takes care of me, and the living*: Mabel Hampton, November 28, 1986.

74  *a couple of months . . . I could dance pretty good*: Mabel Hampton's Story, July 1986.

74  *There were lots of girls there. They were lesbians*: Mabel Hampton 1982.

74  *like dancing that much*: Mabel Hampton 1982.

75  *danced very nicely . . . She was light-brown-skinned*: Mabel Hampton, November 28, 1986.

75  *DC: Dark Cloud*: Mabel Hampton, November 28, 1986.

75  **Bert Whitman**: For more on Bert Whitman, see Forschler's entry on the Drag King History site.

75  **Faderman documents**: p. 68.

76  *very seldom . . . And we got along fine*: Mabel Hampton 1988.

76  *When I met Lillian . . . I could stay in New York*: Mabel Hampton, November 28, 1986.

76  **"was granted her discharge from parole"**: New York State Archives.

77  *right up until I pass away*: Undated, Side B.

77  *suit . . . She was smaller than me, shorter than me*: Mabel Hampton Talks About Lillian.

77  *low-heeled shoes*: Mabel Hampton 1988.

77  *You want to get in that streetcar? . . . I just live from one day to the other*: Mabel Hampton 1982.,

78  *Two days passed . . . And we got together*: Mabel Speaks/Talks About Helen, Tape 1.

79  *She knew more about it than I did . . . You can have Lillian*: Mabel Hampton Talks About Lillian.

79  *Men are funny*: Mabel Hampton's Story, July 1986.

79  *had a bitchy old husband*: Joan at 38, Tape 1.

79  *Everywhere I went, some man*: Undated, Tape 1.

80 *Francis come down . . . Francis was fresh*: Mabel Hampton 1988, Side B.

80 *I never hit nobody at all*: Mabel Hampton's Story, July 1986.

80 *liked to dress like a boy*: Undated, Tape 1.

80 *Nobody know what you was*: Mabel Hampton 1988.

80 *I didn't think that much*: Undated, Tape 1.

80 *She never wore pants . . . She made more money than I did*: Mabel Hampton Talks About Lillian.

80 *That girl looked so much like*: Mabel Hampton 1988.

81 **Prison culture**: Faderman p. 72.

81 "**25 Men and A Girl**": "Drag King History of the Village and NYC."

81 *The women wore pants*: Mabel Hampton 1988.

82 *When you find one*: Mabel Hampton 1988, Side B.

83 *She was poisoned . . . so I never seen him*: Mabel Hampton's Story, July 1986, Side B.

83 *I don't have any family*: Mabel Hampton 1982.

83 *I have a spirit that walks around with me*: Mabel & Lillian 1976.

83 *I got people*: Mabel Hampton, November 28, 1986.

84 *We played and we sang*: Undated, Side B.

84 "**Letters are built of longing**": Fellman p.80.

86 "**Was Lillian passionate?**" . . . *She was running with Helen*: Mabel Hampton Talks About Lillian, Side B.

86 *mulatta . . . I'll catch you anyways*: Mabel speaks/Mabel Talks About Helen.

87 *Didn't bother me*: Mabel Hampton Talks About Lillian, Side B.

87 *I had a good time on the sly*: "Mabel Hampton's Coming Out Story" p. 32.

87 "**How many women**" . . . *That's all*: Mabel Hampton Talks About Lillian, Side B.

87 *when she kissed me I fainted dead away*: Mabel & Lillian 1976.

88 *a nasty woman*: Mabel Hampton Talks About Lillian, Side B.

89 *Don't bother with Mabel*: Mabel Hampton Talks About Lillian.

89 "**Mabel, in those years**" . . . *those type of people*: Mabel Hampton, November 28, 1986.

92 "**Telling Mabel Hampton's history**": Nestle p. 20.

92 "**I am going to buy a mountain here for us**": Lesbian Herstory Archives.

93 "**The loss to me personally is too huge**": Interview with Joan Nestle.

93 "**You have lots of stories to tell**": Mabel & Lillian 1976.

93 *Somebody should*: Breakfast at Pam's.

93 *What I wanted out of life*: Mabel Hampton, Tape 1.

93 *When you're in this life*: Mabel Hampton, November 28, 1986.

94 *I gave Joan over 300 novels*: Mabel Hampton, Side B.

94　**Marijane Meaker**: Lo p. 399.

94　**Sylvia Sharon**: Koski and Tilchen p. 263.

### 3. *A Golf League of Her Own*

95　"**half gold, half silver**": Cayleff p. 71.

95　*to be the greatest athlete that ever lived*: Didrikson Zaharias p. 40.

96　*Most things come natural to me*: quoted in Cayleff p. 118.

96　"**She never did beat me**": quoted in Cayleff p. 119. Cayleff is also the one to note that Babe was pictured with the golf team in the 1929 Beaumont High School yearbook p. 82.

97　*He was so winded*: Didrikson Zaharias p. 70.

97　"**love at first sight**": from *Coronet Magazine*, 1948, quoted in Cayleff p. 134.

97　"**the world's champion lady athlete**" . . . "**Her legs are powerful and hirsute**": "The Texas Babe" pp. 36, 71.

98　"**too well known to require any introduction**": Didrikson Zaharias, preface by Harry T. Paxton, p. 7.

98　*without whom there never would have been a life to lead*: Didrikson Zaharias, dedication.

98　**ninth-greatest athlete of all time**: as ranked by ESPN Sports Century.

98　**second-greatest female athlete of the twentieth century**: as ranked by *Sports Illustrated*.

99　*The stories about me sometimes get a little tall in the telling*: Didrikson Zaharias p. 57.

99　"**Our sport grew because of Babe**": from Johnson and Williamson's "Babe," quoted in Cayleff p. 164.

100　**eight sports that were suitable for women**: The acceptable sports for women are taken from Cayleff p. 86.

100　"**the gentlemen of course**" . . . "**(and even better, the private beach)**": "Babes in the Drink" p. 48.

101　"**derogatory term for women athletes**": Cahn p. 347.

101　"**Sapphic, Brobdingnagian woman**": from a 1970s *Austin American Statesman* column by Jim Murray, quoted in Cahn p. 343.

103　**freckled redhead**: This description of Betty Dodd comes from Cayleff p. 202.

103　"**nineteen to Babe's thirty-nine**": These ages come from Van Natta Jr. p. 270.

103　*Couldn't hit an elephant's ass with a bull fiddle today*: Cayleff p. 163.

103　*You've got to loosen your girdle and really let the ball have it*: Didrikson Zaharias p. 57.

103     **Red Cross charity exhibition**: Van Natta Jr. places the two at the exhibition game together p. 270.

103     **"magnificent specimen of athletic womanhood"**: Jack Dillo, 1939, quoted in Didrikson Zaharias p. 117.

104     *they didn't want me to beat*: Lawrence Lader, "The Unbeatable Babe," *Coronet*, January 1948, quoted in Van Natta Jr. p. 135.

104     *Momma's sugar bowl*: Didrikson Zaharias p. 40.

104     **"traveling advertising campaigns for the companies that sponsored them"**: Van Natta Jr. p. 48.

105     **women in New York City garment factories**: These wages come from Cayleff p. 107.

105     **a quarter of the workforce was unemployed**: This Depression-era unemployment rate and these ideas about women, work, and lesbianism are taken from Faderman p. 96.

105     *The Depression didn't bother me . . . I stayed on my jobs*: Mabel Hampton's Story, July 1986, Side B.

105     **the decision was made for her**: Babe's journey to becoming a pro is detailed by Van Natta Jr. pp. 132–136.

105     **she killed an old man**: Babe's car accident and the subsequent silence surrounding it are revealed by Cayleff p. 106.

106     **transformation in montage**: These invented scenes are inspired by Van Natta Jr.'s depiction of Babe's relationship with the Bowens pp. 183–185.

106     *sissy*: Gallico, "The Texas Babe," p. 71.

107     **a photo of herself**: The photo described here was originally printed alongside Gallico's short story "Honey" in the April 1933 issue of *Vanity Fair*.

107     **the Women's Texas Amateur Championship**: For a fuller description of Babe's performance at the Women's Texas Amateur Championship and the banishment from amateur competition that followed, see Van Natta Jr. pp. 167–73.

108     *Their idea is that I used to be all tomboy . . . cooking and sewing and decorating*: Didrikson Zaharias p. 106.

108     *quite a rhubarb*: Didrikson Zaharias p. 142.

108     **to take the girl back to Tampa**: For more on how Babe approached Betty's father, see Cayleff p. 203.

111     **"The Gay Olympic Games"**: This quote comes from Symons p. 318, and much of the history of the Games comes from her article.

111     **where he had grown up** closeted: This detail and the subsequent ones about Charlie's life come from my interview with him on March 11, 2022.

112     *We all had to wear*: Didrikson Zaharias p. 63.

113     **first International Ladies' Games**: The International Ladies' Games are discussed in Van Natta Jr. p. 67.

114 **ran off to join the circus**: details about Babe and Lillie's time in the circus come from Van Natta Jr. pp. 41–43.

114 **"Where are your whiskers?"** . . . *I'm sitting on 'em sister, just like you are!*: Cayleff p. 108.

114 *I just love a gallery*: Didrikson Zaharias p. 103.

114 **queen Billiard Player of the World**: According to her *New York Times* obituary, McGinnis earned this title from the Billiards Association in 1934.

115 *large feet, and large hands*: Didrikson Zaharias p. 48.

115 **"gender test"**: Van Natta Jr. p. 144.

115 *She's like a daughter to me*: Didrikson Zaharias p. 193.

115 *swimmer*: Van Natta Jr. p. 284.

115 *George and I see a lot of her*: Didrikson Zaharias p. 193.

115 *my buddy*: Didrikson Zaharias p. 186.

116 *Bertha made a lady out of me*: Johnson and Williamson p. 202.

116 ***Ed Sullivan Show***: Details on their appearance and their fees come from Van Natta Jr. p. 310.

117 **"empowered by a changing cultural climate"** . . . **"elderly scrawl"**: Interview with Cayleff, January 27, 2022.

118 **Fort Worth Women's Invitational**: The Fort Worth Women's Invitational became the Women's Texas Open, Van Natta Jr. p. 183.

118 **reinstated as an amateur**: details from this era in Babe's life are taken from Van Natta Jr. pp. 204, 208.

119 **seven pro tournaments**: This detail, and the story of the formation of the LPGA, come from Van Natta Jr. pp. 257–58.

119 **"the most successful women's sports association in the world"**: Van Natta Jr. p. 262.

119 **one thousand dollars just for showing up**: Van Natta Jr. p. 271.

119 *Well I'm the star*: Johnson and Williamson p. 190.

119 **first female athlete to bring in six figures a year**: Van Natta Jr. p. 272.

120 **Gertrude Ederle**: Facts about her life from Van Natta Jr. pp. 127–29.

120 *I am seriously considering taking up long distance swimming in a big way*: Johnson and Williamson p. 117.

120 *"I'll cut two seconds off that next year"*: Gallico, "The Texas Babe," p. 71.

120 **"The Texas Marvel"**: Eaton, "The Wonder Girl."

120 *I didn't care too much for just swimming . . . if I had concentrated on it*: Didrikson Zaharias p. 54.

121 **"versatility"** . . . **"the lack of opportunities"**: Johnson and Williamson, "Babe," quoted in Cayleff p. 110.

121 *I expect to play golf until I am 90*: Introduction to Babe Didrikson Zaharias's *Championship Golf*, 1948, quoted in Van Natta Jr. p. 254.

122   *It was good having Betty in the room with me at night*: Didrikson Zaharias p. 197.

123   *All she had to do was just touch my finger*: Didrikson Zaharias p. 200.

123   **skip the funeral**: The details of Betty's last viewing of Babe come from Cayleff p. 241.

123   **"I never wanted to be away from her"**: Cayleff p. 203.

124   **"I could even have strangled George"**: Cayleff p. 236.

## 4. *On the Island of Lesbians*

Unless otherwise noted, all translations of Sappho's poetry are my own invention, based on Edward Marion Cox's translations of the ancient Greek in *The Poems of Sappho: With Historical and Critical Notes, Translation, and a Bibliography*. 1924. New York: Charles Scribner's Sons. Translations marked "Possanza" were developed in consultation with my father, Dr. D. Mark Possanza. For our family translations, I have followed Campbell's numbering system, except where otherwise noted.

130   *violet-weaver*: fr. 26 / p. 88.

130   *soft woman*: fr. 25 in Carson / Possanza.

130   *refinement, the splendor and the beauty of the sun*: fr. 76 / p. 107.

131   *white goat*: fr. 8 / p. 81.

131   *honey*: fr. 107 / p. 119.

131   *chickpeas*: fr. 143 / Possanza.

131   *more golden than gold*: fr. 115 / p. 122.

131   *rosy-fingered*: fr. 96 / Possanza.

131   *soft beds . . . satisfy . . . longing*: fr. 94 / Possanza.

131   *rejoicing bride*: fr. 100 / p. 116.

131   *delicately woven garlands around her tender neck*: fr. 43 / p. 94.

131   *bridegroom*: fr. 100 / p. 116.

131   *Goodbye bride*: fr. 116 / Possanza.

131   *you cooled my heart*: fr. 48 / Possanza.

131   *Honestly, I wish to be*: fr. 94 / Possanza.

131   *You, who I treated so well*: fr. 12 / p. 82.

131   *immortal Aphrodite*: fr. 1 / p. 59.

131   *Oh, Aphrodite*: fr.1 / p. 59.

132   *How unhappy we have been . . . Against my will*: fr. 94 / Possanza.

132   *When you lie dead*: fr. 55 / Possanza.

132   *Go and goodbye*: fr. 94 / Possanza.

133   *shining ankles*: fr. 19 / p. 85.

133   **"Archivable meaning"**: Derrida p. 18.

134   *salt sea*: fr. 96 / Possanza.

134   **"Cats"**: Wittig and Zeig p. 28.

134   **"Companion lovers"**: Wittig and Zeig p. 35.

135   *First Notice*: Campbell pp. 5–7.

136   *floruit*: For further discussion of the Greek verb translated as "flourished" and the efforts to pinpoint when Sappho lived, see Campbell p. xi.

137   **"The case-history"**: Campbell p. xii.

137   **"Prick from the Isle of Man;"** Campbell p. 5.

137   **"Rod Johnson from Dudesville"**: Haselswerdt.

137   **"The other Sappho"**: Campbell p. 7.

138   **"A despicable public administrator"**: Schmidt p. 170.

138   *apple branches . . . quivering leaves*: fr. 5 / p. 79.

139   **"Destroyed . . . by the enemies of lesbians"**: Wittig and Zeig p. 39.

139   *A discussion of the use of garlands*: Carson p. 369, in reference to fragment 81.

139   *A discussion of chickpeas*: p. 379, in reference to fragment 143.

139   *A discussion of hyperbole*: p. 380, in reference to fragment 156.

139   *To comment on the spelling*: p. 381, in reference to fragment 166.

139   *An unusual word for "sleep"*: p. 375, in reference to fragment 126.

141   **"A corruption of** *Myrrhina*": King p. 53.

141   **"Lisbians"**: King p. 56.

141   **"She daily practiced"**: King p. 18.

143   **"If you have ever been"**: Rosenberg p. 169.

144   **"Lesbian meant she"**: Wittig and Zeig p. 97.

144   **"male Gallants"** . . . **"unsated"**: King p. 18.

146   **Respectable women of Ancient Greece**: For more on head coverings, see Carson p. 372.

146   *many-colored headband* fr. 98B / Possanza.

146   *maidens all night long*: fr. 30 / Possanza.

147   **"Masculine Sappho"**: Campbell p. 19.

147   *hetairai*: For a discussion of the translation of this word see Carson p. 378.

147   **"yoke-mate"**: For a discussion of the translation of this word see Carson p. 363.

147   **"What did Sappho of Lesbos teach her girls, except how to love?"**: Ovid's *Songs of Sadness*, quoted in Campbell p. 43.

148   *I know not what to do: I have two minds*: fr. 34 / p. 90.

148   *youth and beauty*: Pseudo-Palaephatus's *On Incredible Events*, quoted in Campbell p. 193.

149   *lonely mountain peaks*: fr. 44AA / Possanza.

149   *Death is an evil*: Aristotle's *Rhetoric*, quoted in Campbell p. 187.

149   *I shall love*: fr. 88 / Possanza.

149   *into desire I shall come*: Carson fr. 96 / p. 193.

149     *sweet-speaking desire*: fr. 73A / Possanza.

149     *streams over your lovely face*: fr. 112 / Possanza.

149     *and I will lay down my limbs*: fr. 46 / p. 97.

149     *I say someone in the future*: fr. 147 / Possanza.

149     *I don't think any girl*: fr. 66 / p. 103.

149     *no day will ever dawn that does not speak the name of Sappho, the lyric poetess*: Palatine Anthology: Tullius Laurea, *On the Same*, quoted in Campbell p. 29.

## 5. *Who Wears the Pants?*

155     *curb . . . that day to this*: Evans p. 4.

155     *58, '59 . . . depended on it*: Evans p. 19.

155     *a perfectly straight club . . . Nobody questioned*: Evans p. 18.

155     *worked with once . . . hunk of steel across the room*: Evans pp. 14–15.

158     **"We actually won our heat"**: Sowers p. 31. This history of Pink Flamingo is based on Sowers' article, Allison's article, and my own original interviews, both formal and informal, with Charlie Carson.

159     **"a Freudian delight"**: Sowers p. 30.

160     *I was raised in the country*: Evans p. 4.

160     *god damned ribbons and bows and flounces . . . got sent away*: Evans p. 5.

161     *the Society for Prevention of Cruelty to Children*: Evans p. 1.

161     *the Edwin Gould Foundation . . . Florence* **Crittenton** *Home*: Evans p. 2.

161     *the Salvation Army home*: Adelman p. 145.

161     *Bellevue . . . the people who ran the home*: Adelman p. 144.

162     *the first thing I heard them say . . . maybe I'm not crazy after all*: Evans p. 1.

162     *there I got my education . . . homosexual potential*: Evans p. 2.

163     *I tried to stay in contact with*: Adelman p. 144.

163     *corrupt . . . away again*: Evans p. 2.

163     *blew a fuse*: Adelman p. 145.

163     *I found out they were going to . . . walked out of the hospital*: Evans pp. 5–6.

164     **"Women and drag"**: Sowers p. 33.

166     *engine room . . . main corridor*: Adelman p. 146.

167     *a little foreplay . . . brass tacks*: Adelman p. 147.

167     *If word had gotten out*: Adelman p. 146.

167     **three hundred thousand**: Faderman p. 120.

167     *I was old enough*: Evans p. 6.

167     *March of 1941 . . . chicken farm in New Jersey*: Adelman p. 145.

167     *problem, getting a job without . . . World War II was coming*: Evans p. 6.

167     *one, I'd been in a home*: Adelman p. 145.

168     *I got to do . . . wherever I went*: Evans p. 6.

168  *a friend of a friend of a friend's house*: Adelman p. 146.

168  **Even Babe Didrikson**: Van Natta Jr. p. 208.

168  *Somebody squealed*: Mabel Hampton Talks About Lillian and More, Side B.

169  **"a printed series of Sex Hygiene lectures"** . . . **"in this regard will be severely reprimanded"**: Faderman p. 123.

169  *At night time*: Mabel Hampton Talks About Lillian, Side B.

170  **"I get the most phone calls about her"**: Interview with Dr. Marcy Adelman, July 21, 2021.

171  *when the Japanese signed the surrender*: Adelman p. 147.

172  *I get along better with machines*: Adelman p. 150.

172  *little problem: I was female . . . eventually I had to quit*: Adelpman p. 148.

173  *if a cop walked in*: Evans p. 16.

173  *oh, I can't remember . . . a very high-class stripper*: Evans p. 7.

173  *Then she took another look . . . Cookie Castle*: Adelman p. 149.

174  *This chick, this chick*: Evans p. 7.

174  *It was a slow seduction . . . on the road anymore*: Adelman pp. 149–150.

175  *low on work because of the way things were shut down*: Evans p. 16.

175  *Things are getting a little rough*: Adelman p. 150.

175  *The Butterfly Lovers* and **"breeches roles"**: These terms, and the biographies of the male impersonators that follow, come from Drag King History, dragking history.com/.

176  **Stormé defined the art of male impersonation**: Volcano and Halberstam p. 35.

177  **"anyone (regardless of gender)"**: Volcano and Halberstam p. 16.

177  **Marilyn Monroe** and **Whitney Houston** and **"sexist pigs"**: Volcano and Halberstam p. 114.

178  **"ladies man"**: Baur, *Venus Boyz*.

178  **"I want to be a household name"**: Baur, *Venus Boyz*.

178  **RuPaul**: Volcano and Halberstam p. 67.

178  **"When I donned a Drag King"**: Volcano and Halberstam p. 21.

181  **"personal performance"**: Interview with Joan Nestle, February 15, 2022.

181  *It was after the war*: Evans p. 3.

181  **"significant lesbian subculture"**: Faderman p. 125.

182  **camps of butches and femmes**: For more on the development of this dynamic, see Faderman p. 126.

182  **to big cities for work**: For more on lesbian migration around WWII, see Faderman p. 127.

183  **Eighty-two cents on the dollar**: As reported by the Bureau of Labor in 2020.

183  *sometimes we'd go to a gay bar*: Evans p. 14.

183     *a hotel in Brooklyn . . . I'm going to get married*: Evans p. 8.

184     *You should have seen . . . awfully nosy*: Evans p. 9.

184     *when New York started to get so bad*: Evans p. 8.

184     *to Oregon, Washington . . . rages*: Adelman p. 150.

185     **Goodbye to the Halloween Balls**": "If That's All There Is" by Del Martin, in *Lesbians Speak Out* p. 74.

185     **"'butch-femme' syndrome"** . . . **"a cheap imitation of a man"**: The original *Motive Magazine* article by Del Martin and Phyllis Lyon is reprinted in *Lesbians Speak Out*, and these quotes come from p. 6.

185     **"Butch is masculinity as an identity in a woman"**: Baur, *Venus Boyz*.

## 6. *The Lesbian-Ruled World*

189     *about ten years old*: Anzaldúa, *Interviews/Entrevistas* p. 112.

189     *extraterrestrial spirit*: p. 34.

189     *a throwback to the Eskimo*: p. 92.

189     *a vulture picking at my insides*: p. 93.

190     *the fusion of the two*: this translation from the Basque of Gloria's last name comes from p. 37.

190     *People thought I was water crazy*: p. 112.

190     *scandalized . . . through the suit*: p. 93.

190     *I had the feeling . . . paddled*: p. 112.

190     *Tex-Mex*: Anzaldúa, *Borderlands* p. 20.

191     *unforgivable romantic*: Barbara Noda, *This Bridge Called My Back* p. 136.

Up until this point, all quotes in italics have come from the lesbian at the center of each chapter. In this chapter, the quotes in italics come from a variety of sources, the lesbian feminist chorus.

191     *Black, lesbian, mother, warrior, poet*: Sehgal notes that Lorde introduced herself with some variation of this line at public appearances.

191     *The erotic functions for me in several ways*: Lorde, *Sister Outsider* p. 56.

192     *Within the celebration of the erotic in all our endeavors*: p. 55.

192     *one-grocery-store, two-service-stations town*: Anzaldúa, *Borderlands* p. 57.

192     *used books as my refuge*: Anzaldúa, *Interviews/Entrevistas* p. 27.

192     *there was so much work to do*: Anzaldúa, *Interviews/Entrevistas* p. 22.

192     *I would read in bed with a flashlight under the covers*: Anzaldúa, *Borderlands* p. 87.

192     *fantastic stories*: Anzaldúa, *Interviews/Entrevistas* p. 27.

192     *a seventh generation American*: Anzaldúa, *Borderlands* p. 274.

192     *a poor Chicanita from the sticks*: *This Bridge Called My Back* p. 161.

192  *I stooped over the tomato fields*: p. 164.

192  *no one in my family*: Anzaldúa, *Interviews/Entrevistas* p. 23.

193  *fifteen to seventeen hours in one sitting*: Anzaldúa, *Borderlands* p. 89.

193  *the peck peck of my keyboard*: p. 72.

193  *Forget the room of one's own*: Anzaldúa, *This Bridge Called My Back* p. 168.

193  **Daughters of Bilitis**: This history is taken from Faderman pp. 190–192.

194  **"Our goal was to understand how we were oppressed . . . once a week coop"**: Interview with Flavia Rando, March 22, 2022.

196  **"Right now the Media State . . . *Media Mindfuck*"**: C.L.I.T. STATE-MENT #2 p. 11.

196  **"a paper for all women"**: "Editorial." *Off Our Backs* p. 2.

196  **"We do not believe"** and **"Bi-sexuality . . ."**: p. 12.

196  *a man lover*: Anzaldúa, *Interviews/Entrevistas* p. 51.

196  **"refuse, to the best of their ability"**: Interview with Flavia Rando, March 22, 2022.

197  **even the basic country survival skills**: Faderman p. 239.

197  **"Van Dykes"**: The history of the Van Dykes is well-documented in Ariel Levy's *New Yorker* article.

197  *The lesbian separatist utopia?*: Moraga, *This Bridge Called My Back* p. xxxv.

197  *gender is not the only oppression*: Anzaldúa, *Borderlands* p. 270.

197  *for the most part all the performers*: Anzaldúa, *Interviews/Entrevistas* p. 147.

197  **"largest and best-known"** . . . **"lesbian majority"**: Morris p. 6.

198  **"women to go off in the woods and feel good"**: Morris p. 25.

198  **"Is it not possible for there to be"**: Morris p. 173.

198  **"Separatism is a dynamic strategy"**: Bunch p. 441.

199  *disembodied language of academic discourse*: Anzaldúa, *This Bridge Called My Back* p. 262.

199  *I was so horrified*: Anzaldúa, *Interviews/Entrevistas* p. 32.

199  *I always asked the professors*: p. 24.

200  *Somehow these women were great*: Anzaldúa, *Borderlands*, p. 270.

200  *Old Wives, one of my favorite bookstores*: Anzaldúa, *Interviews/Entrevistas* p. 56.

200  *After the forum*: Moraga, *This Bridge Called My Back* p. xxxix.

200  *which I wasn't supposed to do:* Anzaldúa, *Interviews/Entrevistas* p. 55.

200  *the Chicano community does not accept its queers*: p. 54.

201  *I've never been a separatist*: . . . *commune of fifteen people . . . a technical writer*: pp. 55–57.

201  *goddesses and heroines*: Moraga, *This Bridge Called My Back* p. xliii.

201  *a working class*: Anzaldúa, *This Bridge Called My Back* p. 262.

201  *scholarships for working-class or women of color . . . eat what they ate*: Anzaldúa, *Interviews/Entrevistas* p. 153.

201 *subtle and blatant forms of racism*: Anzaldúa, *This Bridge Called My Back* p. 262.

202 "THIRD WORLD WOMEN": Hull, Gloria T. et al. p. 199.

202 *about six months after I started*: Anzaldúa, *Interviews/Entrevistas* p. 153.

202 *Cherríe, this is your last chance*: p. 59.

202 *a different kind of anger*: p. 58.

202 *spot a Chicana a mile away*: p. 56.

203 *She had very recently begun to identify as third world*: p. 57.

203 *This book, if we do it*: s p. 59.

203 *got very very ill and almost died*: p. 153.

203 *called at home all the time*: p. 102.

203 *People don't deal with the body*: p. 64.

203 *My body wasn't dirty*: p. 93.

204 **"During her menses"**: Anzaldúa, "El Paisano," pp. 109–110.

204 *always want to control everything*: Anzaldúa, *Interviews/Entrevistas* p. 38.

204 *I have these Libra parties*: p. 149.

204 *drowned for a little while at Padre Island*: p. 34.

204 *bouts with death*: Anzaldúa, *Borderlands* p. 57.

204 *which is a Nahuatl word*: p. 276.

204 *spokes of the wheel . . . writing was the hub*: Anzaldúa, *Interviews/Entrevistas* p. 48.

205 **"We need political memory"**: *This Bridge Called My Back* p. xix

205 **"You are angered"**: p. 178.

205 **"It is as if we think"**: p. 235.

205 **"Our situation as Black people"**: p. 213.

206 *What drew me to politics . . . I want to know*: Moraga, *This Bridge Called My Back* p. xxxvi.

206 *We couldn't afford the costs*: Anzaldúa, *Interviews/Entrevistas* p. 153.

206 *used to feel more white*: Moraga, *This Bridge Called My Back* p. xxxvii.

208 *Any world*: Lorde, *Zami*, p. 197.

208 *three licks on the knuckles*: Anzaldúa, *Borderlands* p. 75.

209 *In academia*: Anzaldúa, *Interviews/Entrevistas* p. 143.

209 *I have yet to have a full sexual relationship*: p. 117.

209 *I just didn't have a sexuality*: p. 48.

209 *Do you think I'm a lesbian*: p. 117.

209 *made the choice to be queer . . . both male and female*: Anzaldúa, *Borderlands* p. 41.

209 *middle-class, white, heterosexual people . . . little adjective*: Anzaldúa, *Interviews/Entrevistas* pp. 130–131.

209 *One's own body is not one entity*: p. 158 I have removed Gloria's emphasis on the word *body* to make it clear that all these words are hers.

210    *the colored, the queer, the poor, the female, the physically*: Anzaldúa, *This Bridge Called My Back* p. 196.

210    *I'm married to the writing*: Anzaldúa, *Interviews/Entrevistas* p. 61.

211    *I locked the door*: Anzaldúa, *Borderlands* p. 66.

211    *told that Mexicans are lazy*: p. 71.

211    *Touching is an act of making love*: Anzaldúa, *This Bridge Called My Back* p. xxviii.

## 7. *A Lesbian's Best Friend*

213    *On summer Sunday afternoons*: Lorde, *Zami* p. 222.

217    *this fairy faggot named Randy . . . He and I became best friends*. Anzaldúa, *Interviews/Entrevistas* p. 45.

218    *I don't miss him*: Hoffman *Hospital Time* p. 9.

218    *He was such an asshole*: p. 121.

218    *Cleanliness, sanitation:* p. 11.

218    *Michael was brilliant*: p. 13.

218    *deep voice . . . desire and fury*: p. 11.

218    *furious: he never lost the energy for that*: p. 12.

219    *It was an impulse . . . healthcare proxy*: p. 15.

219    *I hated myself . . . better than all of them*: p. 9.

221    **675,000**: CDC 2016 AIDS Fact Sheet p. 2.

221    **69 percent**: CDC p. 19.

222    **"It helped keep me alive"**: interview with Charlie Carson, March 11, 2022.

222    *He surrounded himself*: Hoffman *Hospital Time* p. 16.

222    *photographs of their children*: p. 18.

222    *A brigade of lesbians*: p. 42.

222    *considerable expertise*: Hoffman. "Love One Another or Die." April 2, 2020.

222    *red and green bunting . . . amaze*: Hoffman. *Hospital Time* p. 45.

223    *I want to live*: p. 50.

223    *I'd clear off his night table*: p. 53.

223    *Still, I think I helped him*: p. 22.

225    *all of us lesbians*: p. 43.

225    *stopped writing*: p. 111.

225    *Mike would merely be*: p. 78.

225    *Oh, why couldn't I*: p. 96.

228    **"To 'be a man'"**: Quoted in McBee p. 127.

232    *Mike Riegle, gay liberationist*: *Gay Community News*, January 1992. Quoted in Hoffman *Hospital Time*. p. 81.

232   *I was either at the hospital . . . he'd love visitors!*: Hoffman. *Hospital Time* p. 71.

232   *He was full of excitement about*: p. 73.

232   *into a kind of sleep*: p. 75.

233   *intrepid gay men, ready for a tryst*: p. 87.

233   *a Mike collector. As I write*: p. 145.

233   *Every AIDS funeral . . . It's a virus*: p. 105.

233   *I hate gay people*: p. 106.

234   **"Wall Street trades on people with AIDS!"**: This quote, and the story of this action, come from the 1997 Wall Street Action Report on the ACT UP Historical Archive.

234   **Capitol to the White House**: "The ACT UP Historical Archive: Ashes Action '92."

234   *chaining themselves to the FDA*: p. 105.

234   **"Men! Use condoms"**: This quote, and the story of this action, come from Maxine Wolfe's story on the ACT UP Historical Archive, as excerpted from *Queers in Space: Communities, Public Places, Sites of Resistance* edited by Gordon Brent ingram, Anne-Marie Bouthillette, and Yolanda Retter, Bay Press, Seattle, Washington, 1997.

235   **About a fifth of new HIV patients**: These statistics come from CDC pp. 27–30.

235   **less than 5 percent of PrEP users**: Calabrese.

235   **Half of people living with HIV worldwide are women**: These statistics come from UNAIDS p. 12.

235   *suffocating*: Schulman p. 29.

235   *Passing acquaintances became friends*: Schulman p. 52.

236   **"sissies"**: quoted in Lewis.

237   **"in order for us to move to revolution"**: *Bridge* p. 242.

237   *actually Mike **was** my family*: Hoffman. *Hospital Time* p. 109.

237   **"What relationships, through homosexuality"**: Foucault p. 135.

238   **"There still has yet to be"**: quoted in Bendix.

239   *went at like a 45-degree angle*: Hoffman. *Hospital Time* p. 145.

239   *He loved me*: pp. 142–143.

### Epilogue: The Lesbian Future

245   *Roses*: Anzaldúa, *Borderlands*, p. 113.

# Select Bibliography

"The ACT UP Historical Archive: ACT UP 1997 Wall Street Action Report." Accessed May 25, 2022. actupny.org/10thanniversary/10th%20repor.html

"The ACT UP Historical Archive: ACT UP Storytellings by Maxine Wolfe." Accessed May 25, 2022. actupny.org/diva/CBstory-shea.html

"The ACT UP Historical Archive: Ashes Action '92." Accessed May 25, 2022. actupny.org/diva/synAshes.html.

Adelman, Marcy, ed. *Long Time Passing: Lives of Older Lesbians.* 1st ed. Boston: Alyson Publications, 1986.

Allison, Terry L. "The Pink Flamingo: A Gay Aquatic Spectacle." In *Routledge Handbook of Sport, Gender and Sexuality,* edited by Jennifer Hargreaves and Eric Anderson, 328–36. New York: Routledge, 2016.

Anzaldúa, Gloria. "El Paisano Is a Bird of Good Omen: From a Novel in Progress." *Conditions,* no. 16 (01 1989): 109–28. jstor.org/stable/community .28035113.

———. *Interviews/Entrevistas.* Edited by AnaLouise Keating. New York: Routledge, 2000.

Austen, Jane. *Pride and Prejudice.* New York: C. Scribner's Sons, 1918.

Baur, Gabriel. *Venus Boyz.* First Run Features, 2002.

"Beats Miss Didrikson; Miss McGinnis Wins Four-Block Pocket-Billiard Match, 400-62." *The New York Times.* Accessed January 23, 2022. timesmachine .nytimes.com/timesmachine/1933/01/16/105381782.html?pageNumber=18.

Bendix, Trish. "How 'Rent' Straightwashed Queer Lives and AIDS Activism." them, January 28, 2019. www.them.us/story/sarah-schulman-rent.

Brown, Rita Mae. *Rubyfruit Jungle.* New York: Bantam Books, 2015.

Bunch, Charlotte. "Learning from Lesbian Separatism." In *Lavender Culture,* edited by Karla Jay and Allen Young, 433–44. New York: New York University Press, 1994.

Cahn, Susan K. "From the 'Muscle Moll' to the 'Butch' Ballplayer: Mannishness, Lesbianism, and Homophobia in U.S. Women's Sport." *Feminist Studies* 19, no. 2 (1993): 343. doi.org/10.2307/3178373.

Calabrese, Sarah K. PhD et. al. "Current US Guidelines for Prescribing HIV Pre-exposure Prophylaxis (PrEP) Disqualify Many Women Who Are at Risk and Motivated to Use PrEP," *JAIDS Journal of Acquired Immune Deficiency Syndromes* 81, no. 4 (August 1, 2019): 395–405.

Campbell, D. A., trans. *Greek Lyric. 1: Sappho.* The Loeb Classical Library 142. 1982. Reprint, Cambridge, MA: Harvard University Press, 1990.

Carter, David. *Stonewall: The Riots That Sparked the Gay Revolution.* New York: St. Martin's Press, 2013.

Casal, Mary. *The Stone Wall: An Autobiography.* 1930. Reprint, New Delhi: Isha Books, 2013.

Cayleff, Susan. Interview, January 27, 2022.

Cayleff, Susan E. *Babe: The Life and Legend of Babe Didrikson Zaharias.* Women in American History. Urbana: University of Illinois Press, 1995.

Centers for Disease Control and Prevention. *HIV Surveillance Report, 2019;* vol. 32. www.cdc.gov/hiv/library/reports/hiv-surveillance.html. May 2021. Accessed May 14, 2022.

"C.L.I.T. STATEMENT # 2." *Off Our Backs* 4, no. 8 (1974): 11–12. www.jstor .org/stable/25771926.

Darling, Sherry A. "A Critical Introduction to The Stone Wall: An Autobiography." Tufts University, 2003.

Derrida, Jacques. *Archive Fever: A Freudian Impression.* Translated by Eric Prenowitz. 1996. Reprint, Chicago: University of Chicago, 2017.

Didrikson Zaharias, Babe. *This Life I've Led: My Autobiography.* 1955. Reprint, New York: Dell, 1975.

*Drag King History of the Village and NYC.* Accessed April 29, 2022. www .youtube.com/watch?v=svSOGLxT9UQ.

"Dressed As a Man to Earn Her Living; Ten Years' Masquerade of 19-Year-Old Marion Hamilton-Grey Exposed by Her Arrest," *The New York Times.* January 21, 1910, sec. Archives. www.nytimes.com/1910/01/21/archives /dressed-as-a-man-to-earn-her-living-ten-years-masquerade-of.html.

Eaton, Jack. *The Wonder Girl.* Blackhawk Films, 1933.

"Editorial." *Off Our Backs* 1, no. 1 (1970): 2–2. www.jstor.org/stable/25770944.

"Ella Wesner Lies in Man's Garb," *The New York Times,* November 14, 1917, sec. Archives. www.nytimes.com/1917/11/14/archives/ella-wesner-lies-in -mans-garb.html.

Evans, Len. "Rusty Brown Oral History Interview." GLBT Historical Society Archives Oral History Collection, July 7, 1983.

Faderman, Lillian. *Odd Girls and Twilight Lovers: A History of Lesbian Life in Twentieth-Century America*. Paperback ed. Between Men—Between Women. New York, NY: Columbia Univ. Press, 2012.

Fellman, Isaac. *Dead Collections*. New York: Penguin Books, 2022.

Hull, Gloria T. et al. "Conditions." *Conditions* 2, no. 2 (5) (September 1, 1979). jstor.org/stable/community.28035103.

"Female Husbands," *The New York Times*. November 4, 1883, sec. Archives. www.nytimes.com/1883/11/04/archives/female-husbands.html.

Flare, Drag King. "1870–1908 Ella Wesner." Drag King History. Accessed April 19, 2022. dragkinghistory.com/1870-1908-ella-wesner/.

Forschler, Andrew. "1914–1940 Bert Whitman." Drag King History. Accessed April 27, 2022. dragkinghistory.com/1914-1940-bert-whitman/.

Foucault, Michel, and Paul Rabinow. *The Essential Works of Foucault, 1954–1984: Vol. 1*. Translated by James D. Faubion. New York: New Press, 1997.

Gallico, Paul. "Babes in the Drink." *Vanity Fair*, January 1936. archive.vanity fair.com/article/1936/1/babes-in-the-drink.

———. "Honey." *Vanity Fair*, April 1933. archive.vanityfair.com/article/1933 /4/honey.

———. "The Texas Babe." *Vanity Fair*, October 1932. archive.vanityfair.com /article/1932/10/the-texas-babe.

"Girl in Male Garb Tries to See Fight; Fans at the Moran-Palzer Contest Detect Her Curls as They Peep from Under Her Cap," *The New York Times*. September 4, 1913, sec. Archives. www.nytimes.com/1913/09/04/archives /girl-in-male-garb-tries-to-see-fight-fans-at-the-moranpalzer.html.

Hartman, Saidiya V. *Wayward Lives, Beautiful Experiments: Intimate Histories of Social Upheaval*. New York: W. W. Norton, 2019.

Haselswerdt, Ella. "Re-Queering Sappho." Medium, November 13, 2017. eidolon.pub/re-queering-sappho-c6c05b6b9f0b.

"Her 'Husband' A Woman; Colorado Girl Says They Wished to Earn an Education," *The New York Times*. September 21, 1913, sec. Archives. www .nytimes.com/1913/09/21/archives/her-husband-a-woman-colorado-girl -says-they-wished-to-earn-an.html.

Hoffman, Amy. *Hospital Time*. Durham, NC: Duke University Press, 1997.

Hoffman, Amy. "Love One Another or Die." *Boston Review*. Accessed March 29, 2022. bostonreview.net/articles/amy-hoffman-love-one-another-or-die/.

Johnson, William Oscar, and Nancy P. Williamson. *Whatta-Gal: The Babe*

*Didrikson Story.* A Sports Illustrated Book. Boston: Little, Brown and Company, 1975.

King, William. *The Toast, an Epic Poem: In Four Books. Written in Latin by Frederick Scheffer, Done Into English by Peregrine O Donald, Esq; Vol. I.*, 1732. books.google.com/books?id=ICRcAAAAQAAJ.

Koski, Fran, and Maida Tilchen. "Some Pulp Sappho." In *Lavender Culture*, edited by Karla Jay and Allen Young, 262–74. New York: New York University Press, 1994.

*Lesbians Speak Out.* Women's Press Collective, 1974.

Levy, Ariel. "Lesbian Nation." *The New Yorker*, February 22, 2009. www.newyorker.com/magazine/2009/03/02/lesbian-nation.

Lewis, Daniel. "Larry Kramer, Playwright and Outspoken AIDS Activist, Dies at 84." *The New York Times*, May 27, 2020, sec. U.S. www.nytimes.com/2020/05/27/us/larry-kramer-dead.html.

Lo, Malinda. *Last Night at the Telegraph Club.* New York: Dutton Books, 2021.

Lorde, Audre. *Sister Outsider: Essays and Speeches.* 1984. Reprint, Berkeley: Crossing Press, 2007.

———. *Zami: A New Spelling of My Name.* Berkeley: Crossing Press, 1982.

"Louisa May Alcott." In *Wikipedia*, April 19, 2022. en.wikipedia.org/w/index.php?title=Louisa_May_Alcott&oldid=1083600593.

"Mabel Hampton, Gay Rights Advocate, 87," *The New York Times.* October 31, 1989, sec. Obituaries. www.nytimes.com/1989/10/31/obituaries/Mabel-hampton-gay-rights-advocate-87.html.

"Mabel Hampton Oral History Collection, 1976–1989. Lesbian Herstory Archives AudioVisual Collections." Accessed April 20, 2022. herstories.prattinfoschool.nyc/omeka/collections/show/29.

"Mabel Hampton's Coming Out Story." Our Lesbian Lives Tape Collection, taped at the Coming Out Stories Panel—Lesbian Feminist Liberation, June 21, 1981. Lesbian Herstory Archives.

Manion, Jen. *Female Husbands: A Trans History.* New York, NY: Cambridge University Press, 2020.

McBee, Thomas Page. *Amateur: A True Story About What Makes a Man.* New York: Scribner, 2018.

McGraw, Eliza. "Ruth McGinnis: The Queen of Billiards." *Smithsonian Magazine*, March 22, 2018. www.smithsonianmag.com/history/ruth-mcginnis-queen-billiards-180968563/.

McKinley, James C. Jr. "Gay Games; Athletes with AIDS Virus Conquering the

Challenges." *The New York Times.* Accessed February 5, 2022. timesmachine .nytimes.com/timesmachine/1994/06/23/476366.html?pageNumber=36.

Melville, Herman. *Moby-Dick*, edited by Hershel Parker and Harrison Hayford. 2nd Edition. Norton Critical Edition. 1967. Reprint, New York: Norton, 2002.

Moraga, Cherríe, and Gloria Anzaldúa, eds. *This Bridge Called My Back: Writings by Radical Women of Color.* 4th ed. 1981. Reprint, Albany: State University of New York (SUNY) Press, 2015.

Morris, Bonnie J. *Eden Built by Eves: The Culture of Women's Music Festivals.* 1st ed. Los Angeles: Alyson Books, 1999.

"Murray Hall Fooled Many Shrewd Men; How for Years She Masqueraded in Male Attire. Had Married Two Women Was a Prominent Tammany Politician and Always Voted — Senator Martin Astonished," *The New York Times.* January 19, 1901, sec. Archives. www.nytimes.com/1901/01/19 /archives/murray-hall-fooled-many-shrewd-men-how-for-years-she-masqueraded -in.html.

Nestle, Joan. *A Fragile Union: New & Selected Writings.* 1st ed. San Francisco: Cleis Press, 1998.

New York State Archives. Department of Correctional Services. Bedford Hills Correctional Facility inmate case files, 1915–2002. W0010-77B, Box 6, 1924, Hampton.

Norman, Marc, and Tom Stoppard. *Shakespeare in Love: A Screenplay.* 1st ed. New York: Hyperion, 1998.

"Removal of Judge Norris Is Demanded by Seabury," *The New York Times.* May 29, 1931, sec. Archives. www.nytimes.com/1931/05/29/archives/ removal-of-judge-norris-is-demanded-by-seabury-her-trial-set-for.html.

Rosenberg, Jordy. *Confessions of the Fox.* New York: One World, 2019.

"Ruth M'Ginnis, 64, Billiard Champion." *The New York Times.* Accessed January 23, 2022. timesmachine.nytimes.com/timesmachine/1974/05/17 /79659998.html?pageNumber=42.

Sappho. *If Not, Winter: Fragments of Sappho.* Translated by Anne Carson. New York: Vintage Books, 2003.

———. *The Poems of Sappho.* Translated by Edward Marion Cox. New York: Charles Scribner's Sons, 1924.

Schmidt, Michael. *The First Poets: Lives of the Ancient Greek Poets.* New York: Knopf, 2005.

Sehgal, Parul. "A Timely Collection of Vital Writing by Audre Lorde." *The*

*New York Times*, September 15, 2020, sec. Books. www.nytimes.com /2020/09/15/books/review-audre-lorde-selected-works.html.

Schulman, Sarah. *People in Trouble*. 1990. Reprint, London: Vintage, 2019.

Shapiro, Lynne D. "The Growing Business Behind Women's Music." In *Lavender Culture*, edited by Karla Jay and Allen Young, 195–200. New York: New York University Press, 1994.

Sowers, Pru. "Think Pink." *Gay Games IV Aquatics Souvenir Booklet*, June 1994. Charlie Carson Collection.

Symons, Caroline. "The Gay Games: A Beacon of Inclusion in Sport?" In *Routledge Handbook of Sport, Gender and Sexuality*, edited by Jennifer Hargreaves and Eric Anderson, 318–27. New York: Routledge, 2016.

"Third World Women on Liberation." *Off Our Backs* 4, no. 6 (1974): 11. www .jstor.org/stable/25771873.

UNAIDS. "We've Got the Power—Women, Adolescent Girls and the HIV Response." 2020. Accessed May 30, 2022. www.unaids.org/en/resources /documents/2020/2020_women-adolescent-girls-and-hiv.

Van Natta, Don. *Wonder Girl: The Magnificent Sporting Life of Babe Didrikson Zaharias*. New York: Little, Brown and Co., 2013.

Volcano, Del LaGrace, and Jack Halberstam. *The Drag King Book*. London: Serpent's Tail, 1999.

Wittig, Monique. *The Straight Mind and Other Essays*. Boston: Beacon Press, 1992.

Wittig, Monique, and Sande Zeig. *Lesbian Peoples: Material for a Dictionary*. New York, NY: Avon, 1979.

A full-time book publicist and part-time writer, **AMELIA POSSANZA** currently lives in Brooklyn with her cat. Her work has appeared in *The Washington Post*, *BuzzFeed*, *Electric Literature*, *The Millions*, and NPR's *Invisibilia*. *Lesbian Love Story* is her first book.